Find Your Freedom

Find Your Freedom

Financial Planning for a Life on Purpose

Jamie P. Hopkins

and

Ron Carson

Harriman House

HARRIMAN HOUSE LTD
3 Viceroy Court
Bedford Road
Petersfield
Hampshire
GU32 3LJ
GREAT BRITAIN
Tel: +44 (0)1730 233870
Email: enquiries@harriman-house.com
Website: harriman.house

First published in 2022.
Copyright © Jamie P. Hopkins and Ron Carson

The right of Jamie P. Hopkins and Ron Carson to be identified as the Authors has been asserted in accordance with the Copyright, Design and Patents Act 1988.

Paperback ISBN: 978-0-85719-984-3
Hardback ISBN: 978-1-80409-025-1
eBook ISBN: 978-0-85719-985-0

British Library Cataloguing in Publication Data
A CIP catalogue record for this book can be obtained from the British Library.

Whilst every effort has been made to ensure that information in this book is accurate, no liability can be accepted for any loss incurred in any way whatsoever by any person relying solely on the information contained herein.

No responsibility for loss occasioned to any person or corporate body acting or refraining to act as a result of reading material in this book can be accepted by the Publisher, by the Authors, or by the employer of the Authors.

The Publisher does not have any control over or any responsibility for any Author's or third-party websites referred to in or on this book.

The information voiced in this material is for general information only and is not intended to provide specific advice or recommendations for any individual. Hypothetical examples provided are for illustrative purposes only. To determine if an investment or strategy is appropriate for you, consult with a qualified professional prior to investing.

There is a surrender charge imposed generally during the first 5 to 7 years that you own the contract. Withdrawals prior to age 59 ½ may result in a 10% IRS tax penalty, in addition to any ordinary income tax. The guarantee of the annuity is backed by the financial strength of the underlying insurance company. Investment sub-account values will fluctuate with changes in market conditions.

An investment in a variable annuity involves investment risk, including possible loss of principal. Variable annuities are designed for long-term investing. The contract, when redeemed, may be worth more or less than the total amount invested. Variable annuities are subject to insurance related charges including mortality and expense charges, administrative fees, and the expenses associated with the underlying subaccounts. Investors should consider the investment objectives, risks and charges and expenses of the variable annuity carefully before investing. The prospectus contains this and other information about the variable annuity. Contact your financial professional to obtain a prospectus, which should be read carefully before investing or sending money.

Investing in mutual funds is subject to risk and loss of principal. There is no assurance or certainty that any investment strategy will be successful in meeting its objectives.

Exchange traded funds and Mutual Funds are sold by prospectus only. Investors should consider the investment objectives, risks and charges and expenses of the funds carefully before investing. The prospectus contains this and other information about the funds. Contact your financial professional to obtain a prospectus, which should be read carefully before investing or sending money.

Cetera does not offer any direct investments, endorsement, or advice as it relates to Bitcoin or any crypto currency. This is for information purposes only.

Generally, a donor advised fund is a separately identified fund or account that is maintained and operated by a section 501(c)(3) organization, which is called a sponsoring organization. Each account is composed of contributions made by individual donors. Once the donor makes the contribution, the organization has legal control over it. However, the donor, or the donor's representative, retains advisory privileges with respect to the distribution of funds and the investment of assets in the account. Donors take a tax deduction for all contributions at the time they are made, even though the money may not be dispersed to a charity until much later.

Please note: The charitable entities and/or fundraising opportunities described herein are not endorsed by, or affiliated with Cetera Advisor Networks LLC or its affiliates. Our philanthropic interests are personal to us and are not reviewed, sponsored, or approved by Cetera.

*Ron Carson and Erin Wood are non-registered associates of Cetera Advisor Networks LLC.

*Emily Binder, Marguerita Chong, Dr. David Rhoiney, and Dan Anspach are not affiliated with Cetera Advisor Networks LLC.

*Matt Lewis is a non-producing registered representative of Cetera Advisor Networks LLC.

Contents

Introduction

by Ron Carson, CFP®, ChFC®

Finding freedom and expanding your impact

F REEDOM MEANS SOMETHING different to each of us. Think about it. What feeling does "freedom" evoke in you when you hear the word? Uncovering that fundamental truth inside you takes time and reflection, but I promise you it is one of the most meaningful questions to ask yourself.

There is so much that goes into our relationship with money, from our first memories in childhood to our milestone moments in adulthood. I remember as a kid we once had our house broken into, only to find my cherished piggy bank smashed. It was devastating.

Several years passed and again as a teenager I saw my parents struggle with money, going broke on their farm. This implanted a deep-seeded feeling of scarcity in me, shaping the way I managed my money and eventually leading me to the profession of being a financial advisor.

Why do I tell you this story? Well, because I was running from that scarcity most of my life, only to find I could never outrun it. No matter how much I accumulated early in my career, I couldn't satiate my appetite for more. Yet, when I arrived at "more" I still wasn't satisfied.

This was the beginning of a new chapter for me. A phase in life when I realized I needed to be thoughtful about what freedom meant for me. Frankly, that manifested into the need for planning. Without a clear definition of what true wealth—which we define as all that money can't buy and death can't take away—meant to me, I would continue the endless journey of directionless wandering.

When you hear "freedom" you may think of financial freedom. Many of us do; however, I didn't truly experience the meaning of freedom for myself until I spent time really getting to know who I was, what motivated me, and how scarcity and worry drove so much of my direction. For me, ultimate freedom is living an untethered life and being able to have maximum impact on the lives of others.

So how would I get there? The short answer: by having a financial plan. The longer story: by better understanding my worry, where it originated from as that resilient boy on the farm trying to make each day count. Then, I found purpose in wanting to provide that sort of planning for others, to let them know they would be okay so they could free up that mental space for the work they were meant to do. This process of finding my freedom led to helping others find theirs.

Encountering the unexpected on Mount Everest

In the spring of 2022, I embarked on a once-in-a-lifetime trek to Mount Everest's South Base Camp. Around 40,000 people per year make their way to the camp, while only 4,000 climbers have ever successfully summited Everest.

Preparation for the climb is extensive, not only in terms of physical exertion but also in terms of mental sharpness. However, over the course of our weeklong journey to base camp's elevation of 17,598 feet, I was not surprised as much by the individual challenge of traversing glaciers and rough terrain as I was by the living conditions of those who called Nepal home. From Kathmandu to base camp, we witnessed a degree of poverty and pollution I'd never seen before.

With so many tourists and climbers making the expedition each year, and so few ways to properly dispose of everything from human waste to debris and trash, the mountain has been called "the world's highest garbage dump". National Geographic wrote a piece claiming that as much as eighteen pounds of trash is generated by each person climbing the slopes. With all this waste littering the tallest peak on

Earth, locals are the ones suffering. The Sagarmatha National Park watershed, an important water source for thousands of local people, has been so affected that many Nepalis have no easy way to get access to clean water.

As you can imagine, this experience shook me. Instead of celebrating an individual accomplishment—reaching one of the highest base camps in the world—my heart turned to the masses living and suffering in such extreme poverty. It changed my perspective on giving back and helped me redefine what it means to truly leave an immeasurable impact while I am here.

Every human should have access to the basic rights of clean water and food, and yet not enough is being done to ensure that they do. Too many people are fighting just to make it to tomorrow. On one occasion, I crossed a few children during our ascent. I handed them some chocolate and they smiled, but those were the only smiles I encountered during the entirety of my trip. Deep down I knew that even those smiles wouldn't last long.

I share this experience with you for a number of reasons, the most important of which lies at the heart of why we are writing this book: to inspire a spirit of generosity, resolve, resolution to gain clarity on how to meet your base level of needs so you can move up the hierarchy and focus your energy on self-actualization, and helping others. And, while we can all agree that our challenges are not as dire as those who fight for food and water every day in less-developed countries, we can take steps to pursue a life of greater purpose. So much of this process you are about to embark upon starts with attaining financial freedom.

I started my trip in Nepal with a self-centric perspective on what I was going to get from the adventure.

Instead, the experience taught me what I could learn from those around me. Those who don't even have some of their most fundamental needs met.

The butterfly effect

I have always believed in the power of small actions leading to substantial change. Reading this book is a very simple decision you've made that could have life-altering ripple effects across the rest of your life. You may have heard the term "the butterfly effect", a tenet of chaos theory that states small, seemingly random events in a system or environment can lead to large-scale change and unpredictable results.

I have witnessed this cosmic connection tying all things together countless times in my life. My parents went broke when I was 17 years old. This period in the early 1980s humbled me. It imprisoned me in the state of fear and scarcity that drove so much of our family's decisions, particularly our financial ones. But it also lit the path that showed me how I could break free. Watching my parents struggle was eye-opening. I watched my dad cry for the first time in my life. It bred so much fear in me that I vowed never to let it happen to me again, never to be in a position where I could not provide for my future family.

I don't believe in accidents when they happen at such a crucial stage in life, and this time as a teenager was no different. I went to the library, picked up an issue of *Money Magazine* and saw a top ten list of best careers. There, ranking at #1 as the top profession of the future, was "a financial advisor with a CERTIFIED FINANCIAL PLANNER™ designation". I said to myself, "That's it! That's what I'm gonna do."

I took this as the universe speaking to me and went off to college to pursue my degree. My career was born in that college dorm room at the University of Nebraska back in 1983, and I never looked back.

More than three decades had passed when I found myself in Napa, California, at the Napa Valley wine auctions. I was chatting with an executive who had connections of her own in financial services, and she suggested I talk to a contact of hers who was also attending the wine auction. I approached this contact and we introduced ourselves. She asked, "Oh, where are you from, Ron?"

I answered that I was from Nebraska.

She then asked, "What do you do?" To which I responded that I was a financial advisor and entrepreneur. She continued with, "How'd you get into that?"

I told her my story, and total shock washed over her face.

She exclaimed, "I was at *Money Magazine* in the early eighties, and I wrote that article!"

We both sat back in utter disbelief. Here in front of me was the very woman who had single-handedly influenced the trajectory of my entire career, more than 30 years later. If that isn't proof of how connected we all are, I don't know what is.

For years, unknowingly to me, she lived her life and I lived mine, not having realized the large-scale change we had made in each other's lives. Then, to meet each other, by chance, at an event 1500 miles away from my home—this tapped something close to my soul about what it means to impact others. To influence so many lives at scale around us, by one person taking a simple action.

Recently, I ran into a former colleague who told me that he had been watching my "Ronsense" videos for the past couple of years. He walked up and said, "Thank you, Ron. I've watched some of the content you're putting out there and really took to heart the things you said. I quit my job as a compliance officer, started my own firm, have six people working for me now, and have built this business I love because of how much your message stirred me to make a change. I found my version of freedom. I started my journey four years ago, I lost eighty pounds and took the three things you mentioned in an episode about personal health to heart: my exercise, my diet, and my sleep. I got serious about all three. I don't drink anymore, I lost a lot of weight, I'm doing a triathlon, and I've never felt better."

I stood there in surprise, not having known the impact I had on his life from sharing a three-minute video on social media three years prior.

The butterfly effect in full force.

There's something I want you to think about after hearing these stories. What does it mean for you to find this plane of existence where you are impacting the lives of so many people—minutes, months, or years into the future? This is where you will find the answer to your own personal version of freedom.

In my life, I'm trying to explore the outer reaches of my influence. How can I have so much impact on the world, in helping others find their freedom, that there is no way to measure it? No way to know everyone I touched. No concern for how to get credit. Completely boundless. That is what I want my legacy to be. And it all starts with an unsuspecting seed that can quickly germinate into trees and forest.

Living up to your infinite potential

Chances are, you are reading this book because you have had a realization that something in your life needs to change. That realization may have come as a sudden epiphany or a slow burn over months or years. It may be born from a mistake or a resolution. You may be entering the workforce for the first time as a 20-something, energized by the endless possibilities to set healthy habits in your financial life. You may be going through a milestone moment in your 30s or 40s—marriage, your first home purchase, a growing family, an unexpected divorce, a career change—and awaken to the need for a clear path for your next chapter. Or, you may be quickly approaching retirement, still baffled by what life has in store for you as you care for aging parents, exploring the idea of freedom beyond your working years, and find yourself rattled by the meaning of leaving your own legacy.

No matter your life stage or situation, we all come to those crossroads in our life where we know that what got us here today will not get us to where we want to go tomorrow. We see the path ahead of us split, and we must choose. Is this a shift in my core values and priorities? Are the priorities that were important to me years ago still as important today? Are the goals I set for myself still aligned with those values and what I want to accomplish in life? These are the questions that lead to clarity and choosing the path that makes the most sense for you.

Spending the last 40 years as a financial advisor has opened my eyes to a stark reality. Most of us avoid exercising enough of this self-reflection when examining our financial lives, and even when we do, we tend to do it alone. We require a set of tools and a framework to help us act when motivation isn't present. That's what this book can help provide.

One of my favorite reflections to ask clients when exploring life's goals and wishes is from our Blueprinting Guide, which Jamie will talk more about in the chapters ahead. I pose a simple statement to the client, "If I wasn't so afraid, I would…"

Giving our clients the space to sit with this statement and finish it on their own is crucial to helping them find their freedom.

What emotions spill out of you when you think about how you would finish that statement?

Every day we wake up competing against our own potential, and most days we come up short. Fear, guilt, shame, envy—these emotions drive so many of our financial decisions. And they keep us from living our full potential. We are so fortunate as Americans to have an economic system that gives people the ability to define success for themselves and go after it. Unfortunately, this definition of success normally comes in the form of financial gain even though success can mean so many different things to different people.

As my career advanced and my company grew, I became consumed with acquiring. I zoned in on acquiring more wealth, building a bigger business, chasing new capabilities, seeking further investment capital, and the list goes on. I was so busy with the pursuit of "more" that I never took the time to understand what I was chasing. More importantly, I wasn't aware of how this desire to accomplish and achieve more was driven by a childhood need to avoid scarcity and loss. Think of the time, energy and resources wasted when living a life this way—by default, not by design. Much can be learned when these core emotions are identified.

The foundational concepts outlined in *Find Your Freedom* were developed not only to clearly articulate a mental framework for how to take ownership over your financial life but also to help you gain a better understanding of your core emotional ties to money. Without this foundational level of awareness, your infinite potential is limited, and your financial future is directionless.

My wish for you is that the stories and best practices included here allow you to take personal inventory of your life. That this process awakens you to get to that next level of realizing your infinite potential. When you commit yourself to continual improvement, you also acknowledge that the journey never ends. There is no finish line to living in financial freedom. It's a process of redefining what is most important to you and pursuing those ideals, knowing they will shuffle and change with time. If you can find joy in this state of continuous improvement, you will be more prepared for the future, and best of all, you can live more fully in the present.

There is no better gift than that.

Why you need this book

I've known my co-author Jamie Hopkins for a long time. I first met him when I was on the board at the American College, an educational institution with a longstanding heritage of advancing financial advisors with designations and degrees, and very quickly realized he was an intelligent young man; but more impressively, he was someone who got stuff done. A few years ago, Jamie joined Carson Group and he is now a member of our Executive Board. I wanted his perspective and expertise on how we could continue to build a firm of advisors that put financial planning first. I now understand why he is so good at decoding the financial planning process. His backstory is similar to mine, in that his first money memory shaped the very fabric of who he is and how he had to provide leadership for his family at such an early age. He's one of the most brilliant, well-read individuals I've crossed in my 40-year career. There isn't another person I would trust more with clarifying and simplifying the sometimes perplexing concepts of financial planning.

I've experienced firsthand the power of financial planning, both in my life and in the lives of thousands of families we serve across the country today. It's perhaps one of the most influential exercises a person could undertake in their adult life. So many of the decisions we make every day boil down to our conscious and subconscious worries of whether we are going to be okay.

Can I support my family?

Will I have enough money in retirement?

Who around me is impacted if something unexpected happens to me? Do I have enough money, time, resources, energy?

These questions are all normal, and they are being wrestled with every second of every day in the minds of millions of Americans. But they all can be addressed with the power of planning. When you have a team you can rely on, running the numbers, anticipating scenarios, and keeping their eyes on the things you can't see, you have the freedom to focus on the truly important aspects of life. This is something we call operating in the Third Level of Trust—anticipating our clients' needs and delivering solutions before they know they have a problem. When this confidence isn't present, we start to sense instability—financially, emotionally, or otherwise. These feelings of scarcity and fear easily seep into our subconscious mind and steer our actions in ways that keep us chasing things we shouldn't expend our energy on, much like I did as a young man.

Planting your root system with a plan starts now

Ideally, the time to plan for the challenges ahead is when things are going well, not once the storm clouds have rolled in. While many of us cringe at the thought of spending our days worrying about things that could possibly happen in the future, it is important to evaluate the strength of your root system. That's because—whether we're talking trees or humans—the things we see on the surface are not necessarily indicative of what lies below. Sometimes, a tree that looks beautiful above ground can have a weak or unhealthy root system hidden deep below ground. Similarly, outward appearances don't always tell the full story when it comes to our own physical, emotional, or financial health.

I spend a fair amount of time taking in nature throughout the American West, and the whole idea of building a financial plan often reminds me of the forests in the Sierra Nevada mountains. Take the majestic redwood, for example. The giant sequoia, one of three species of coniferous trees known as redwoods, is native to Northern California. They are among the planet's oldest and largest trees and can grow to up to 350 feet tall and 20 to 30 feet or more in circumference. These giants are known to live up to 3,400 years and hold the distinction of being the largest trees on earth in terms of total wood volume. So, you might think their root systems reach deep into the earth to support all that weight and height, but you'd be wrong. These enormous trees have a uniquely shallow root system of six to twelve feet. Yet, they rarely fall. Why? Their root system is intertwined with the other redwood trees, literally holding each other up. The trees, which grow very close together, are also dependent on each other for nutrients. For more than seventy million years they have thrived by intertwining their root systems to create the foundation required to maintain their equilibrium and access the resources they depend upon to flourish—individually and collectively.

I share this little fact because a healthy root system not only creates a stable foundation for nurturing growth but also provides the resilience required to thrive under challenging and stressful conditions.

Like the roots of a giant sequoia, your finances are interconnected. Each financial decision you make impacts other decisions, which—in turn—influence your ability to accomplish your life goals.For example, choosing whether to contribute to a traditional or Roth IRA determines whether you pay taxes now or later on that income. Doubling monthly payments on credit card debt now means less money lost to high interest debt maintenance later. And how much you choose to save now will influence when you can retire with the confidence that you can pursue all the goals you have set for the next great chapter of your life.

However, when financial decisions—and your financial plan—are made in a vacuum and not tied to a bigger purpose, your ability to accomplish your goals is drastically diminished.

That's the inherent power of a financial plan. Planning helps to build a strong foundation while anticipating the unexpected, so that you're in a better position to weather changing circumstances. It provides a framework for evaluating important decisions—from career changes to buying a new house, or how you will pay for a child's education costs—in a way that's aligned with your goals and timeline.

If you have alignment, you have freedom. And, if that alignment is strengthened by the root system of a sound financial plan, your definition of freedom will extend far beyond anything you can imagine. That is a realization I hope you glean from reading this book, and a truth I hope you find for yourself after hearing the practical approach Jamie outlines in the chapters ahead.

Here's to helping you find your freedom.

Part 1

Foundations of Financial Freedom

1

Financial Planning is Deeply Personal: Jamie's Money Story

❝ Financial planning is about moving along your path in life, finding the things that you want to accomplish, finding the freedom that you want to have, being able to define those things, prioritize, and execute on them. ❞

—*Jamie P. Hopkins*

Financial Freedom Framework

The events in our lives shape the way we feel about money. What happened to us when we were younger could make us feel fear and scarcity around money. And while people have historically mistrusted the financial services industry, progress has been made in recent years to change the industry for the better. Finding a trusted partner to guide you is critical to overcoming negative emotions around money and helping you find your financial freedom.

L IKE MANY PEOPLE, I didn't grow up understanding everything about financial planning, money, finances, or business. I grew up in a household where neither one of my parents graduated from college. My dad did construction—he hung gutters, and did roofing, fascias, and siding—and my mom helped him run that business.

My parents were business owners and entrepreneurs, but were not entrenched in financial planning and did not have a financial plan. My parents did not have a pension plan or a 401(k). Much of my story starts off with trauma around finances, not abundance.

My dad passed away coming down a ladder from a job site up on a roof; he slipped and fell and was gone. All of a sudden my mom was caring for me and my sister without the person who was really the breadwinner—the one doing the work up on roofs and earning.

My mom had a moment where she realized she just had to find a way to keep going because her kids relied upon her to survive. Even to this day, she's still working, running the gutter company, and looks like many other Americans—she's almost got her mortgage paid off, she's in retirement, and she'll likely be very reliant on Social Security and Medicare.

I remember being young and seeing my mom cry about where the money was going to come from to pay the mortgage, where we were going to get our food from next, and how to pay for the extra unexpected things that made it feel like the world was collapsing— like an unexpected $20 expense, or money for gas.

My mom pulled things together, kept working and pushed us forward. She created opportunities for my sister and me—and our future sisters, too—to be able to go to college and build careers, invest back into ourselves, develop our own financial knowledge and understanding of the world, and provide for our families later on.

When people ask me why I care so much about financial planning, it's because it's deeply personal. It's rooted in my upbringing, in loss and tragedy, and not rooted in abundance. I know what it's like not to have the things that I want to have. I know what it's like not to have the things that I need.

My life philosophy has been to ask myself how I can have an impact on the world. How do I change the future and financial security for millions of people like my mom—who didn't have financial planning and life insurance? We were the perfect example of a family that should have had both—parents with young children, one working a dangerous job whose income we were reliant on. But this advice never got to my parents—not about insurance, not about retirement planning, not about IRAs, and not about 401(k)s.

So many Americans fall outside of the demographics served by the financial planning advice world, and my goal was to help change that. To help more people find financial stability and eventually get to financial freedom, so they don't have to live with the pain, tragedy and fear around money that so many people grow up with because they don't have enough and they worry about it. It's not always happy when you think of your first money memory—instead it can be traumatic. That's really where it was for me.

Every day that I go to work, I think, "How do I make somebody like my mom more secure for retirement?" That's what gives me a drive for this industry.

My journey into the industry

I also liked deals. I always liked conversing with people and coming up with solutions. I was really interested in the deal side of the legal world and I wanted to put those together. I ended up going to Davidson College outside Charlotte, N.C. I got to see amazing things, like Steph Curry playing basketball, and got to spend some time with and learn from Coach Bob McKillop, who's one of the all-time winningest college basketball coaches. I got to be captain of a Division I swimming and diving team at Davidson. And I got to take those skills and go to law school. All those things helped shape me.

In law school, you really learn how to think, evaluate the world, question things, and stand on both sides of an argument. That was a useful skill that I was later able to bring into the financial planning world. But at this time, I didn't know much about money. Money wasn't talked about much in my family, I hadn't met money; hadn't dated it; hadn't developed a relationship with it. The reality is that we were strangers.

When I decided to go to law school, I knew that attorneys could have good careers and impact many people. However, I knew nothing about how to pay for law school. As such, I picked the best school I got into—also the most expensive—and took out a tremendous amount of debt over three years to fund the education. All in all, I was nearing $200,000 of debt by the time I graduated. I now had a very real relationshiop with money, but it wasn't the one that I probably wanted.

After graduating school, I started off my career in private equity, where I was with a firm for a short time and got the opportunity to clerk in the Appellate Division under Judge Marie E. Lohtz. She was an amazing individual and a great mentor for me. During my time there, we got to work on one of the Bernie Madoff cases.

Bernie Madoff really stood at the pinnacle of what I didn't want to see in the world—the abuse of trust, the abuse of financial advisory clients, the abuse of money, the abuse of power, lying to people, stealing, and fraud. Terrible things that hurt the financial services industry, but also millions of Americans who lost faith in the people who should be there to help them.

The positive side of things like the Bernie Madoff scandal is that all of a sudden we get people who want to change the industry for the better; who want to be more transparent; who want to be at the pinnacle of trust; who want to not just *say*, "Hey, trust me, we're putting your money in good investment," but who *show* you the investments so you can log in, see them, and know that they're there and that they're real.

Mistrust is something we have to overcome. Overcoming obstacles can be done alone, but it is a lot harder. For some people, they hold on to their financial planning tight because of this mistrust; and for others, they need to go out and find the right trusted professional to walk alongside them—to be their guide, their sherpa—on this lifelong journey of trying to reach both financial security and eventually financial freedom.

I've had amazing teachers and coaches over the years. For instance, my gradeschool math teacher, Miss Prendergast. She embodied and lived the sherpa and caring guide. She took the route of guiding young minds. What always stuck out to me about her was how she was able to teach so many students and reach them because she cared.

You trusted her. She would follow up with my mom decades later to ask how I was doing. The best interest of her students was always present. She made me love math—not just learn it, but love it. If you were struggling with a concept, she would find new ways to explain it, to visualize it, to help you find your path to understanding. Her impact on me, and thousands of others, cannot be measured; but I know she changed our worlds through her approach, which was founded in caring and love.

So as my career progressed, I decided to go down that route—to be a teacher, an educator—to follow the sherpa and trusted guide path. I was fortunate enough to get an opportunity to go teach and build a brand new retirement education program at The American College of Finanical Services. I spent almost seven years teaching financial advisors about retirement planning and behavioral finance in the Certified Financial Planning Professional program. This really helped create the next generation of knowledgeable, trusted financial professionals. What I learned during that time was that just teaching people wasn't enough. I could educate, educate, educate; but if I couldn't help people execute, if I couldn't help people change their systems and processes for the better, a lot of people were still left out in the cold, not getting the help they needed.

So I made a decision to leave my full-time role in academia—though I keep a part-time role at Creighton University Heider College of Business—and joined a company out of Omaha, Nebraska, called Carson Group.

Carson is solely focused on becoming the most trusted in financial advice, leading with transparency and financial planning, not products and sales, and helping people along their life journey. To help people go from struggle to a place of excitement and abundance. To help them get where they want to end up by looking at their financial planning through a goals-based lens.

That's really what financial planning is to me—it's about moving along your path in life; finding the things that you want to accomplish; finding the freedom that you want to have; being able to define those things, prioritize, and execute on them. It's about creating your life journey and your life's meaning and having the financial knowledge and ability to reach those goals.

Helping you find your planning promise

Financial planners are very different from many other professionals. Financial planners sit at this pinnacle of trust because a lot of the things they do for you are outside your vision—they're managing your investments, helping with your financial planning and tax efficiency, and in some cases they're going to be involved with your estate after you pass away. You're not going to be there at that time, so you really have to innately trust the person that you're working with and understand that they're not going to abuse that trust or deviate from your goals and objectives. Trust becomes so important. With financial planners, it's just such a different relationship on so many levels because of this trust factor.

Many of the most challenging aspects of financial planning occur when you're incapacitated, when you're aging, when you're in retirement, or when you pass away and you're not physically there to alter the outcome if something were to go wrong.

I heard this analogy once: to a large extent, financial planners are like a caddy to a golfer. Their job is to help other people achieve their dreams. That's the sole role of a financial planner. They're really there to educate; to design structure and process; to help if you need to delegate certain decisions, like investment management; to help find the rest of the team—the estate planners, the trust services, the tax professionals—and to put that all together so you can go to where you want to be.

You also have to answer the questions of: who do you want to take care of your loved ones when you are gone? Do you trust the plan you have today? Who will help them make decisions when you cannot? Have you shared your desires with your family and trusted advisor? The financial planner can help design and execute the plan in accordance with your wishes, in the best interests of your loved ones, creating a bridge from where you are today to the best decisions, strategies, solutions, and execution for your spouse, children, or grandchildren. A lot of planning is not selfish, it's not about us; it's selfless and truly about our loved ones. Most of my own planning is about my family, my kids and my spouse.

So in this book, that's what we're going to focus on first: how do you even start that process, beginning with learning who you are today? What was your financial memory story? What was your journey to today like? How do you feel about money? How do you feel about your path? Who can you help along the way?

Feelings and emotions are so important; we can't disregard them. Our brain craves emotional information to make good decisions. If we try to remove emotions from our decision-making, we get terrible outcomes. But at the same time we don't want to let our emotions overrun our decision-making, so we want to create balance between the two.

Next, we're going to look at financial freedom and what this means to you. The reality is that financial planning is about you—what you want to achieve; your aspirations, goals, desires, wants and wishes. It's not about the dollars and cents. It's not a high-score game where you want to die with the most money humanly possible left in your bank account; it's about your destination and financial freedom. So we'll spend some time dissecting that term, understanding what it means, and walking you through how to figure it out yourself.

Then we'll talk about how to build a financial plan. What are the pieces and how do they change at different points in time for different people with different objectives? Financial planning isn't static, and as soon as we create a plan, the world is changing around us. Our plan needs to have the flexibility to adapt as the world changes.

We also need to know what different stages of life might look like and how planning can adapt to those stages in life. Our financial planning solutions at age 22 when we have zero kids and are in our first job will not be the same solutions that will be good for us when we're 35, 50, 75, or 90.

The reality is our planning is across a spectrum, and the solutions and tactics will change. The markets and public policy will change, and our plan needs to adopt those changes and move with us, while at the same time providing guidance throughout these changes. We don't need plans that change daily—they should be bold enough and big enough that they can withstand some of the winds of change over time, and still keep us on our path.

Lastly, we'll talk about how to find the right partner to get you there. Are you going to guide yourself? Are you going to find a financial coach or financial advisor to help you along this journey? Think about it: the best athletes in the world—Tiger Woods, Serena Williams, Michael Phelps—all had fantastic coaches and mentors along their journeys who helped them get better and better at their craft. The single best person in the world at golf, the single best person in the world at tennis—they have coaches. They have hired people to help them get better at something *they're already the best at doing.*

A lot of people say: "I need to focus on my weaknesses." I often tell people they should actually outsource their weaknesses. If you're not good at investment management, go find somebody who is good at investment management and delegate that out. You should focus on the things that you're strong at. I talk about this later in the book, but Tom Brady, perhaps the most successful football player of all time, would not work on tackling during the off season. While that might come up a few times during the year after he threw an interception, in training he was better off focusing on what he was good at— throwing the ball, understanding the offensive plays, working with coaches who helped him get better at those things, and outsourcing the other things. Again, he looked for teams to surround himself with to achieve his ultimate outcomes. He didn't go at it alone. When you look at the best of the best in different fields—whether it's medicine, law, or sports—they surround themselves with great talent and bring in people they can delegate to, to help them along their journey.

If you really want to reach that end goal of financial freedom and have the plans and tactics in place to do so, you're going to need that partner. Finding the right one that fits you is incredibly important to reach your ultimate aspirations.

Five key takeaways

1 Feelings about finances are deeply personal and impact how we feel about planning for our futures.
2 Working toward achieving financial freedom can potentially help you avoid fear around money.

3 While the Bernie Madoff scandal was tragic, it led to people wanting to change the financial services industry for the better.

4 Emotions play a critical role in your finances, and you need to create balance between your emotions and your decision-making.

5 While financial planning is primarily about you, it's also about your loved ones and the legacy you want to leave.

Five reflection questions

1 What events have happened in your life that impacted the way you feel about money?

2 Are there people in your life who rely on your income?

3 Do you have a financial plan today? If so, do you feel it does what you want it to do?

4 Does your financial plan have the flexibility to change as your circumstances change?

5 Have you found a partner to help you in your journey to financial freedom?

Notes

2

Your Money Story

&& I have great respect for the past. If you don't know where you've come from, you don't know where you're going. &&

—Maya Angelou, poet and activist

Financial Freedom Framework

Your financial freedom isn't about your financial advisor or your money, it's about you. Understanding your money story and the emotions you associate with it is a critical step on the journey to financial freedom.

MOST BOOKS LIKE this start with at least one of the following elements: an introduction of the authors designed to establish their credibility on the subject, or a background story to foreshadow what will come later. These techniques are both about making you feel connected to the authors or to the protagonist of the story.

But since we've shared enough for you to be familiar with us, let's also cover that second element: a good story about this book's protagonist—you. Fill in the blanks:

_____ was born in _____ on
(Name)   (City)

_____ . But this isn't really where my money
(Date)

story begins. Instead, my first money memory was when I was

_____ years old and I remember _____
(age)

_____

_____

_____ .

With this book, the goal is different, so the beginning is different. While I started with a story about myself to establish my credibility on this topic, know that this book isn't about me. And I can't tell you a story about the protagonist because I don't know them yet and, perhaps, until the next sentence, you didn't either. The hero of this story is you. Your financial freedom isn't about your financial advisor or your money, it's about you—the person who gets to live his or her best life.

Look at what you wrote down. It's crucial that we reflect on our first money memories because they're like our own personal money fingerprints—unique and special to each of us. But really, these memories and early childhood experiences are even more fundamental to our stories than our fingerprints—they're actually more like part of our DNA. They don't fully define us, but they do help shape us over time.

In the first part of the exercise, I asked you to write down the "facts" about your first money memory. **But now, let's expand this a little further and consider how you felt about this experience at the time.**

Where did your first money memory come from? Was it from a place of abundance and joy? Or was it from a place of scarcity and fear?

In the last chapter, I confided in you how my first money memory is rooted in trauma and scarcity. What's your first money memory associated with? With feelings of abundance, joy, or self-confidence? Or with feelings of scarcity, anxiety, or lack of control? We remember most of our memories—especially those from our childhood—in part because they are associated with powerful emotional responses. But it's certainly okay if your money memory is not. It's important to better understand our past and to recognize the emotions we attach to our memories, as those emotions might color in our relationship with money.

Finally, see if you can identify ways in which those attitudes and beliefs are informing your behaviors toward, relationship with, and decisions around money. You may be surprised by what you find. Let's walk through an anecdote that shows this process in action.

A tale of two gifters

Gifting in this country is such a big part of so many holidays. Your birthday, for one, is so centered around getting everybody together to eat cake and give you gifts. Christmas, too. Gifts play an important role in our economy—even in religious history, going back to the Three Wise Men bringing Baby Jesus three gifts.

For many people, gifting is part of their love language, and that's true of my mom. She loves giving gifts. You can even go back another generation to my grandmother, who also loved giving gifts. For both of them, giving was a sign of their love for their family members. It's one of the ways they showed they cared. They loved seeing the smile on their kids' or grandkids' faces when they gave something of value to them.

I'm not saying people are wrong when they give gifts or telling you not to give, but many people don't budget to give gifts and give beyond their means because they want to positively impact those around them.

I've seen that when people buy too many presents for others and max out credit cards, it can put a financial burden on the family. You see this every year—from Black Friday through the holidays—where people's credit card balances go up because they're spending beyond their means. They're not necessarily being irrational; they do this because they care, but I've been through the burden this causes.

My father passed away at a young age, so we didn't always have money in our single-working-parent household. As holidays and birthdays rolled around, it was obvious to me that buying and giving presents put a financial strain on our family. I saw how carrying credit card debt and trying to meet those payments month after month, long after the holiday season, impacted our family. It forced us to make decisions about food at the grocery store three months later because we went past our budget during the holidays. I grew up with a sense of trauma that if you gave too much, if you were too generous, if you took care of others before you took care of yourself, that would weigh on you, hinder your ability to meet your basic needs and potentially impact your happiness long term. I don't like giving or receiving gifts since it can bring up those feelings of trauma and scarcity.

Again, I'm not saying that gifting is wrong, but this money story was important to show you how one very powerful and emotional financial experience—giving gifts—for one person can be such a positive, but another person can look at that same powerful and emotional experience and say, "You know what? That's painful for me because I remember when we had to make decisions around what to eat and not eat and how to pay bills because we over-gifted."

My mom still loves gifting, but for me, it's never felt exciting. It's never felt like a way for me to express myself to other people. It's actually felt painful. I don't like giving or receiving gifts anymore because I know that somebody had to make a decision to spend and not invest and not do something else, because they gave me this gift. Then I have to make that same decision any time I want to give something. I grew up seeing the dynamics and trade-offs of giving, so I took a different approach.

The interesting thing is my mom also grew up in a situation of relative scarcity, and then experienced it again when she led our household and managed the family finances after my father's death.

My mom also took her own approach. As I said, giving is part of her love language. Whether it's for birthdays, Christmas, Halloween, St. Patrick's Day—she loves to find ways to give to her children and grandchildren. It brings her joy. Her gift-giving doesn't just stop at the household and family level—she also gets a sense of joy giving back to those in the community, the church, and around the world.

But there is one way my mom and I are similar in our giving: giving to the community to make an impact. As I've developed more financial freedom and stability, one of my favorite things to do is give back to charity, because I know I'm putting my dollars toward a need. I'm not trading off my needs for the wants and wishes of other people for toys and fun things, I'm trading potentially having things that I can live without to provide for the basic needs of others.

Attitudes and beliefs impacting our relationships and behaviors around money will be different for different people. My mom and I are two people, similar in many ways, whose feelings around our money memories led us to two different behaviors around gift-giving. Neither reaction is wrong. Both are reasonable considering our histories. This shows that our responses to our money histories are not determined or predictable—they are unique and dependent on a variety of factors and influences. Both my mother's predilection for and my aversion to gifting are informed by more than our childhood experiences of scarcity.

Figuring out what might inform your attitudes and beliefs around different aspects of money is critical to understanding your money memories and responses. If you can't identify important aspects of your family's orientation around money, it can be helpful to talk to other family members about their experiences and see how they resonate with your own and how they are different.

And keep in mind that while it might be important for you to give to others, to charity, and back to society, you must understand your capabilities and long-term goals. If you don't take care of yourself, nobody else is going to do it for you. You have to take care of yourself, you can't go beyond your means—even if gifting is very important to you. That balance in life is so hard to find. Later in the book, we'll dive into goal setting and how to identify and craft goals that will help you find your financial freedom.

Looking back to look forward

We shouldn't look back on the past merely to reflect, like a pond reflects the sun on a hot summer day. Instead, we should reflect on our past with purpose. This can be challenging, as the past might be painful and emotional, and thinking about it might evoke stress or anxiety. Ignoring the lessons of the past—especially if they're painful—might appear easier in the moment. However, as the philosopher George Santayana famously said, "Those who do not remember the past are condemned to repeat it."

We should start with exploring our own money memories and then dive into our family legacy money memories, because both of those help shape our path forward. Our family's legacy money memories could have shaped our lives without us even knowing. We need to know where we've come from to forge paths toward achieving our dreams and reaching a level of financial security that eventually leads to true wealth and financial freedom. This is core to the planning promise. If we ignore the past and the blocks that built us, we can't truly and genuinely move forward.

Remember, finances are just a means to our end, not the end itself. Money isn't valuable in and of itself; it's valuable for what it enables us to do and not do, to feel or not feel. It's a tool to help us live our best lives by design, not by default.

Societal norms might also hold us back from being honest about our money history. In our society, we tend to honor and idealize those who've amassed great amounts of wealth as the beacons of financial success. If you feel you aren't one of these people, you might feel embarrassed or ashamed of your own financial success. Some people feel that finances are private. If that's you, you likely feel you don't need to tell anyone about your finances because it's your story.

By putting aside our fears, pain, and societal pressures, we can examine and learn from our past. By taking a deep dive into our money history, as I did in the beginning of the book, we can understand why we care about the things we care about and why we fear certain things. This can make the journey to financial freedom a little smoother. Our money history also provides a roadmap of mistakes we've made. It's helpful to learn from these mistakes so our future selves can avoid them. We aren't condemned to relive past money mistakes—ours or our families'—like some sort of financial Groundhog Day. Plus, understanding our past behaviors will help us to better anticipate what might happen in our future. While past behavior doesn't guarantee future behavior, it can be revealing.

Reflecting on negative memories is important because while scars often fade, they never truly go away. And looking to the past isn't all negative. Also recall a money memory you're proud of, so you can replicate it and build on that success. Did you delegate a decision? Did you buy something meaningful? Did you invest in yourself? Did you pay off debt or leverage debt in a meaningful way?

We all inherit something

As I like to say, we all inherit something—whether it's wealth or behaviors—and we evolve and grow from our past experiences. Your money memories aren't just yours—they've been passed down through other experiences, biases, beliefs, and decisions that continue to impact you.

Our attitudes and beliefs about money are never formed in a vacuum. They're shaped by experiences in our own family, the community around us, and the wider world that's grown closer through social media. Communities can inform our money experience/orientation because the people we know within those communities can provide examples that are impactful and shape our opinions. For example: "People who save like this are smart and virtuous," and "People who spend like this are foolish and selfish." Communities give us an idea what a good life looks like—and the things that money can (and should) be used to consume. Communities can be cooperative or competitive around money, and this can inform how we think about our goals and aspirations around building and maintaining wealth.

Often community forms when someone has been able to do something that others want to do. Community creates a sense of belonging and belief in yourself. Think about communities that develop around overcoming and surviving an illness. You look to the community of survivors because you know they did it and you can too! Ultimately, it shows us we matter and can achieve something we might have otherwise thought impossible.

Now think about how communities impact your beliefs around money. Do your communities have a positive or negative impact on your money beliefs? Do they make you competitive in a way that you want to "keep up with the Joneses?" Are there people in your community who you aspire to be like when it comes to money? Do the people in your communities think about money the same way you do? Have you ever asked?

As we build our positive path forward, look to your communities to see how they raise you up toward your financial freedom or how they pull you down. Like in any area of life, we want to surround ourselves with a community that helps us move forward toward our life's purpose.

Tying it all together

The benefits of thinking purposefully about our history with money expand beyond creating financial freedom for ourselves—it's essential to building and maintaining good communication about financial matters with those around us. Unless we understand our money memories—and the feelings associated with those memories—our behavior can seem inexplicable to ourselves and those around us. It can lead to tensions when we aren't aware of the implicit emotions and motivations that are driving our actions. Getting clear on how your family history impacted your money lessons, behaviors, and experiences makes it easier to identify areas of alignment as well as possible areas of conflict. Interestingly, we often avoid these conversations even though our patterns of spending and saving are typically readily apparent to people around us.

There are multiple resources available to help guide these conversations, but here are a couple of helpful questions and takeaways that you can use to identify how your history has impacted your behaviors around money.

Five key takeaways

1 Our first money memories can be transformational to our life experiences.
2 Our relationship with money is determined at an early age.
3 Our relationship with money is not just financial and rational, but emotional and transformative.
4 Money can come from a place of joy or pain.
5 Money is about ability—what it can enable us to achieve.

Five reflection questions

1 How would you describe your parents' approach to money?
2 What is one thing you would like to emulate about your parents' attitudes, beliefs, and behaviors around money?
3 What is one thing you do not want to emulate about your parents' attitudes, beliefs, and behaviors around money?
4 What is a financial accomplishment you are proud of?
5 What financial situation has caused you to feel disappointment or embarrassment?

Notes

3

A Blueprint for Your Financial Plan

—Ma Jian, author and activist

Financial Freedom Framework

Regardless of your past relationship with money, you deserve financial freedom and are worthy of quality financial guidance. If you are alive, and you have goals and aspirations, financial planning is for you.

I RECENTLY SAT down with a stakeholder who works with me to map out her goals for the year. I kicked off the conversation by asking her what she considers her massive, transformative purpose—or her MTP.

After we identified her MTP, we figured out which top five elements of her job description tied into her MTP. While we concluded that not everything she did day to day would tie into her MTP, at least she had the big five areas of focus to work on toward it.

What is your MTP? At Carson Group, we understand that there's no point to a financial plan unless it's working toward your unique vision of freedom. To help you define that vision, we use a process called Blueprinting. Blueprinting helps you paint a clear picture of what you want your life to look like based on your values and priorities, then set the goals to help you get there.

You can find your financial freedom by creating a blueprint for your financial plan.

You deserve financial freedom

As the quote at the beginning of this chapter suggests, we carry our past experiences with us. Unfortunately for some people, the past experiences that they carry with them give them "limiting beliefs" which, if left unchecked, can create obstacles to their success. Limiting beliefs around money, like "I can't stick to a budget," or "I just can't get my head around all I need to do for retirement," or "Financial planning is for rich people, not for someone like me," can make us feel shame and self-doubt that prevent us from taking action. Perhaps even more insidious—because they're unexpected—are beliefs that can create feelings of guilt or inadequacy around financial *success*. These sorts of beliefs can lead people to unconsciously undermine the success they're working so hard to achieve.

Before we move on to thinking about our financial future, it's vital that we stop for a moment and try to identify any of these limiting beliefs that may get in our way.

One of the most common limiting beliefs when it comes to money is that you don't need—or aren't worthy of—financial planning. So many people have told me that the reason they don't work with a financial professional or have a more complete financial plan is because their situation isn't complex enough. But in reality, everyone's situation is complex. Our wants, needs, desires, fears, and goals are unique, which makes our situations naturally complex. This is, at its core, why the field is called personal finance—because it's deeply personal.

Exposing our limiting beliefs—along with our money memories and how they've impacted our current behavior—can be incredibly freeing. It can be a cleansing of sorts. It's like dropping the emotional and financial baggage that's weighing us down and keeping us from making it down the road to our financial freedom.

We often spend more time than we realize worrying about money. Our thinking is clouded and confused by the baggage we carry— baggage we've likely carried unaware since our childhood. Take a moment to think about how it would feel to believe that you had a financial plan you could count on.

Now take that one step further. What would happen to your life if you could shift all your focus on—and worries about—money to something that makes you happy? How would this change your life? Would you live differently? Would you sleep better? Would you smile more? Getting control of our financial situation can cause this type of transformative experience. I've seen people cry with joy and relief when they delegate their financial planning to others and hug loved ones when they realize they're financially secure. Financial planning for financial freedom isn't easy, but it's a journey well worth taking. To move forward we have to be willing to drop our limiting beliefs and financial baggage.

No matter where your money history and memories start, you're worthy of achieving financial freedom and independence. But you can't get there unless you examine your past relationships with money, understand how they developed, and then look into the future to see whether this relationship with money will lead you toward or away from your aspirations. We're often more successful in achieving a specific outcome when we start with the end goal in mind and work backward from there.

What keeps people from financial planning?

Almost everybody knows that financial planning is a good thing. I rarely have to convince anybody that looking at their finances and planning around them is good for them. However, even though almost everyone *knows* it's good for them, most don't engage a planner or go through the process. There's a natural avoidance that occurs around financial planning. If this sounds like you, that avoidance comes from a unique combination of up to six sources:

- **Trauma**
  You grew up with trauma around money and financial planning. Your experiences with money were negative—perhaps you struggled to pay bills, amassed credit card debt, had a house foreclosed on, your parents went bankrupt, or you incurred huge medical expenses. These negative experiences early in life caused you to avoid money and planning because it's painful. That's a natural thing that happens in our brains—we want to avoid painful things.

- **Not seeing the impact**
  Maybe you grew up in a scenario where you weren't super wealthy, but you didn't see the struggle or the pain behind earning, spending, and balancing money. So you didn't fully grasp the impact—not just the importance—but the *impact* of planning. You had enough to get by so you didn't grow up thinking about how things were paid for or how you were going to invest. Money stayed out of sight enough that it didn't become a core memory or a core part of your functionality. Now you have to learn that there's a huge impact here and money can be positive and additive to your life. But you have to actually *understand* the impact and bring it into your life.

- **Lack of balance**
  Like many people, you don't have balance in your life. You've got too much work, or you have kids, health issues, addiction problems, travel, study, and so on. You can't have everything. You get out of balance with your finances and don't do financial planning because other things have taken priority. To get back to doing financial planning, you have to find balance in these areas so you can prioritize.

- **Lack of planning literacy**
  It might be that you avoid financial planning because you lack literacy around it. This one is a little bit different because you

don't know what you don't know. You're avoiding financial planning because you don't know exactly what it is, though you know it's probably good for you. You aren't worried that it's harmful to engage in financial planning, but you wonder, what type of financial planning? What does that mean? How do you define it? What services are required? Is it just investments? Is it tax planning? Is it estate planning? Is it incorporating insurance? Where does it fall? Because you don't have a great understanding of the scope and depth of financial planning, you avoid it.

Think about driving through a windy mountain pass in the darkness. What happens when there's fog and you can't see? You slow down and get a little more cautious, not because you're afraid of the dark, but because you're afraid of what you can't see—what might be around the bend. It's the fear of the unknown that keeps you from financial planning.

- **Lack of trust**
  Are you the kind of person who knows financial planning is good, but doesn't have the knowledge or balance in your life needed to grasp the full impact of planning? Do you have painful money memories? If you have all or some of these hurdles, and are also distrustful of financial professionals, you won't engage in financial planning. Because you need help, you need a guide and a planner to walk alongside you, and you can't have people walking alongside you who you don't trust. That's the right decision, because if you can't trust a person, you shouldn't let them handle your money, and if you start to doubt them, you should fire them.

- **Not feeling worthy of planning**
  You think financial planning is only for multimillionaires or people with lots of money and complex situations. In reality, financial planning is as important for people like my mom—who didn't graduate from college, never had an IRA or a pension, and didn't have life insurance when my father passed away—as it is for the millionaire next door, the athlete who make millions in a year, the local business owner, and the farmer.

Remember: financial planning is personal. We call it personal financial planning because it's about the individual. There's no dollar amount that makes you more or less worthy of financial planning. If you're human; if you have goals, desires, wishes, aspirations in life; and if you want to be financially free, then you are entitled to financial planning. Yes, tactics and investment strategies will differ for different people during different time periods and situations in their life; but everybody is worthy of financial planning.

The blueprint to financial freedom

Once we can understand our relationship with money, review our limiting beliefs, and find our community, we must figure out where we're going. What is it that you see through life's window on your road toward financial freedom?

Let's go back to the Blueprinting process we discussed at the beginning of the chapter: find your meaningful purpose, identify your compelling vision, and set goals that tie into your compelling vision. This process can help you identify what financial freedom might mean and help you create a blueprint to get there.

Much like the stakeholder I talked about at the beginning of the chapter, you first need to define your MTP. What is it that you live for and are most passionate about? Identify the compelling vision of your life and your financial freedom. Start with that end in mind. Then set financial goals to get you one step closer to making that vision a reality.

Want to dive deeper into the Blueprinting process? You can download the complete Blueprinting Guide at carsonwealth.com/blueprinting-guide.

What does financial freedom mean to you?

What is financial freedom for you? While the words have some base level of meaning to most people, they also fundamentally mean different things to everyone. I recommend this powerful exercise:

First, write down what financial freedom means to you:

_____.

Second, on a scale of 1–10, how close are you today to achieving financial freedom: _____.

Third, what is the biggest obstacle to reaching financial freedom?

_____.

Fourth, what can you do about that obstacle today to get closer to financial freedom? (*Nothing* is not an acceptable answer—challenge yourself):

_____.

How did you describe your financial freedom? Did you describe it as freedom *from* something or freedom *to do* something? Is your freedom defined by trying to get out of debt, work, or pressure? Or is your freedom defined by your ability to travel, spend time with family, or do other things? This is a pivotal point for many. Freedom can be described as both removing restrictions and creating opportunities.

After seeing how you defined financial freedom and reflecting on whether it was freedom toward or freedom from something, would you change your answer?

It's helpful to define financial freedom, because you'll use that definition throughout this book. Financial freedom can be described as a place of financial independence to pursue the things in life that truly make you happy. Remember that finances are not the end, but rather a means to the end. The goal isn't to accumulate the most money possible just for the sake of accumulating money. It's about gaining access to the possibilities and freedom that money can create. Money can create the ability to change lives, build businesses, educate people, feed millions, and create a lasting legacy.

Financial freedom is deeply personal. Spouses, family members, loved ones, communities, and partners will all see financial freedom differently. Very few people are born into true financial freedom. For the vast majority, it's a continuum that starts and ends at points unique to them. But it is a journey for everyone.

There are multiple resources available to help guide conversations around financial freedom, but here are a couple of questions and takeaways you can explore to begin with:

Five key takeaways

1 Financial freedom is deeply personal and unique to each person.
2 Limiting beliefs can make us feel unworthy of financial freedom.
3 To achieve our desired level of financial freedom, we need to look inside and see what's holding us back before we can move forward.
4 Money is a means to an end; it is not an end by itself.
5 Community can give us a sense of belonging and show us the way.

Five reflection questions

1 What does financial freedom mean to you?
2 Would your spouse, partner, or family describe financial freedom in the same way?
3 What is one thing you are proud of achieving on your way to financial freedom?
4 How far away from financial freedom are you today, on a scale of 1–10?
5 Which community in your life today best reflects your goals for financial freedom?

Notes

4

Goals-Based Planning—The Mile Markers on Our Road to Financial Freedom

❝ If you set goals and go after them with all the
   determination you can muster, your gifts will take
   you places that will amaze you. ❞

—Les Brown, speaker

Financial Freedom Framework

Goals-based planning is about setting and prioritizing goals
that align with your big picture and life aspirations. It's helpful
to start with your end goals in mind, and work backward to
achieve them.

I'M A BIG believer in the power of goals-based planning to achieve
financial freedom. This is where the goals you identified during the
Blueprinting process come in. While our goals alone don't equate to
financial freedom, they are really milestones along our path.

In order for you to identify the right set of goals, it's necessary to answer the larger question: what is your conception of a "life well lived?" One way to get at your answer is to think about writing the eulogy you'd like someone to give at your funeral. This is a helpful—if daunting—exercise, because a good eulogist creates a narrative of your life that should capture who you were. As you write, it may be helpful to think through the following questions:

- What principle guided your life and decisions? How did your life choices reflect or communicate this principle?
- What is one principle that you'd like to pass on as part of your legacy to family or friends?
- Who was important to you during your life? How did you show that you valued them?
- What did you accomplish during your life? Why was it important to you and others?
- Where did you fail or fall short in your life? How did you learn from these experiences?
- What did you admire? What did you detest? How did your life reflect these beliefs?
- Would your family and friends write the same eulogy as you would write for yourself?

Perhaps not all of these questions will be helpful to you, but the process of writing down answers to a few will give you an outline of your notion of a "good life."

Once you have done so, you may be surprised at what this story of your life reveals about your values, beliefs, and priorities. I interviewed NFL star Darrell Green—an incredibly humble and amazing person—and he spoke to me about how important legacy was to him. He said he wanted to be remembered as Darrell Green—the person—first, before he was remembered for his business, career, and football. Darrell Green—the person—is a devoted father, husband, and caring member of society who constantly gives back to others. Then Darrell Green—the athlete—is a Hall of Fame football player and one of the NFL's top 100 players of all time. I thought this was so powerful—be known for who you actually are first, and let what you do and your accomplishments come second.

The takeaway here isn't that personal and professional accomplishments aren't important—but that they're mostly important because of the impact they've had on those around you. We often get bogged down by the details of daily goals or achievements and forget that progress toward our aspirations is continuous, not intermittent. Life is lived on a spectrum, not in a silo. Breaking out of that silo and shedding those limiting beliefs is about the big picture; it's the reaching for the stars and realizing and living the dream. Think about how many great journeys and stories start with the hero yearning for something more—a better life; an aspiration!

Goals versus aspirations

Aspirations are typically the vision of your future and long-term impact. These are what you hope to achieve or accomplish in the years to come. Goals, on the other hand, are typically time-bound, specific, and measurable objectives you can achieve on your way to your aspirations. In many ways, goals help you assess how far you have traveled on your journey, and how far you have to go.

As you set out to define your life's aspirations, think about how you'll be remembered. When asked about their greatest accomplishment, most people probably wouldn't bring up the process improvement they implemented or the sale they closed. But they might talk about the impact they made on the lives of the people they worked with or the clients they served.

Goals remain an important part of the process—a way to measure progress toward your ultimate aspirations. For instance, a goal might be to fund your children's college expenses. But that goal isn't really your true aspiration. Your true aspiration might be much bigger—like leaving your children with a legacy to design their own futures free of financial worry. Or maybe you have a goal to give back to a local charity this year by making a large donation. But your true aspiration might be to become a philanthropist who changes the world. The individual impact you want to have on the world—the "key takeaway" of your eulogy—is up to you, but the point to keep in mind is that your key takeaway should structure how you approach your goal setting and the ways in which your wealth can help you to achieve those goals.

While we started this book reflecting on where you came from and then took a look out of life's window into your future, we now need to look at the milestones along the way. Who do you want your future self to be? What are your ultimate aspirations guiding your journey? If you can't answer these questions today, don't fret—that's normal—but you've already made a good start by getting this far.

Many people struggle to think more than a few years down the road at any given time. But examining and reexamining your long-term aspirations over time will help you refine your plan, your path, your goals, and the actions you need to take to achieve them. Any step toward financial freedom starts with introspection. Most people want to skip this part of the process and jump right into what stocks to buy, how much to save, how to pay less in taxes, or what type of retirement account is best for them. However, as I said, most books start with a story to set the stage for what's to come; your financial journey also needs to start with your story. But unlike most stories, we wrote the ending first. Now it's time to chart how we're going to get there.

As you set out to define your life's aspirations, think about how you'll be remembered. Will you be remembered as a father, mother, brother, sister, or friend first, or as this amazing employee who did so many things at work?

Now take that one step further. Earlier we asked you, what would happen to your life if you could shift all your worries about money to doing things that make you happy? We explored how this would impact the way you lived, slept, and whether you smiled more. Gaining greater control over your financial situation is a transformative experience, and it's not easy. It doesn't matter where you started, what matters is that you know that everybody—including you—is worthy of financial freedom and independence.

But like Maya Angelou said, you can't get to that future without knowing where you came from. You can't get to that future financial freedom and independence unless you understand and know about your past relationships with money. You can't move toward your aspirations unless you understand how those past relationships with money are still impacting you. So now that you've identified what the end goal is, we can work backward from there.

What is goals-based planning?

There are many ways to engage in planning of any sort, including financial planning. We will dive into the process of financial planning in the next chapter, but for now let's focus on goals-based planning and goal setting.

Goals-based planning can be compared to cash-flow planning, both of which are part of the financial planning process. Cash-flow planning is usually a look at income and expenses over time. A successful outcome is to balance these two elements so that the planner can meet their cash flow needs. Goals-based planning starts at a different place—with values and goals.

However, the common critique of goals-based planning is that many people don't know how to answer the question: what are your financial goals? They tend to respond with, "I don't really know, maybe retire in my 60s and not run out of money." Responses to this question, if not given the proper time and guidance, are weak and don't support a foundation for planning. This is why we start with the bigger dream and bigger aspirational aspects first. Goals are then used to determine whether we are on the right path.

Goals are the way you can tell you're making progress toward your aspirations.

Goals-based planning is financial planning that starts with the aspirational big picture, then sets time-bound goals to achieve along the way. Like any good planning, goals-based planning should be continuous. There's no financial plan that is complete the first time it is created. Instead, you need consistent monitoring, adjustment, and improvement along the way. Goals and aspirations will shift and change, and the planning needs to account for these shifts.

Goals-based planning is value- and aspirational-based with the goals being the markers—nothing more, nothing less. In essence, we start with the big dream, then we set goals, then we do the planning!

Ultimately, the process of financial planning must include helping you prioritize goals, set funding parameters, review cash flow and develop time horizons.

Goal setting: an exercise of self-review

So far in this book, we've looked back at our past and reviewed our vision for the future. Now, let's look at how and why we should consider setting goals.

Goal setting can be a powerful technique to engage action. Research from Dominican University, conducted by Dr Gail Matthews, found that people who wrote down their goals, put down written actions, and committed to progress reports were more likely to achieve their goals than those who did not write down their goals.[1]

Let's start by looking at two concepts that come from the well-researched field of positive psychology:

- Well-being theory and the PERMA model outline five key building blocks for flourishing (from Dr Martin Seligman and colleagues at University of Pennsylvania). Those five key building blocks are: positive emotion, engagement, relationships, meaning, and accomplishment.[2] To increase our well-being, we must intentionally focus on how to bring more of each of the five elements of the PERMA model into our lives.
- Prospective psychology theorizes that who we are today is not simply a result of our past experiences, but is more influenced by who we believe we will be in the future.[3] Creating a vibrant vision of what we want in the future influences our lives today. What do you want your life to look like in the future? If you haven't given it much thought, you're missing out on an incredible opportunity to improve your life. Prospective psychology tells us we act in accordance with who we *think* we'll be in the future, not who we've been in the past. Let's say you have a strong picture in your minds of spending your first year of retirement on a round-the-world

cruise. That picture—when you really believe it—will change you behavior today. You'll start living as the person who's going on a round-the-world cruise. Not only might that vision help you make wiser financial decisions today, it will also give you the excitement you need to keep going and overcome challenges and roadblocks along the way.

We can use these ideas to become more intentional and thoughtful in designing and living our lives so that we can flourish as human beings—both now and in the future.

Preparation

One of the critiques of goals-based planning is the common, "I don't know" response. To overcome this, we need to prioritize and give space for reflection. Block time off on your calendar for reflection, envisioning, and goal setting. You'll need one or two days per year at a minimum, depending on whether you've ever done this work before. This might seem like a lot, but it's your future we're talking about. You've likely spent two days planning a vacation before, and companies will do weeklong retreats to plan for the next year; when you put that into perspective, your future is likely worth one or two days!

You want to give yourself plenty of time to think. Feel free to break it into smaller chunks, but give yourself at least two hours each time you sit down to work on it.

Choose a location that inspires you and gets you away from the day-to-day grind. This means you probably shouldn't be at the office or the kitchen table. Some people go to coffee shops, retreat centers, vacation cabins, or small cafés. Make sure you're well rested, fed, and hydrated before you get started. All of these impact your mindset, which is critical for envisioning and goal setting. Turn off distractions like your phone, your laptop, and your smartwatch. Most people find it's easier to stay focused by using a pen and paper instead of technology, but if you must use tech, make sure to turn off all notifications.

Reflection

I've found meditation to be very helpful throughout my sports career and life to help me get clearer on my goals. Meditation is not for everyone, nor is it the same for everyone. For me, I've found that reflection and meditation time can occur in many different places: on airplanes, on a long run, or while sitting quietly and looking inward. It's important to start with the reflection. How satisfied are you with important areas of your life right now? What would make it better? What goals can you set to get from where you are to where you want to be?

Now it's time for a reflection exercise called the "balance wheel."

Take a blank piece of paper and draw a big "plus" sign and then an "X" through it. That will give you an image that represents the spokes of a wheel. Label each spoke with an area of your life that is important to you. Examples might be:

- Finances
- Career/professional
- Education
- Relationships
- Marriage
- Family
- Community
- Spirituality
- Physical health
- Mental health
- Leisure/recreation
- Lifestyle
- Environment

You can have more or fewer spokes on your wheel—it's up to you!

Next, make a note of which of the PERMA components each spoke impacts (positive emotion, engagement, relationships, meaning, and accomplishment). Then, record your current satisfaction level with each area at the end of the corresponding spoke of the balance wheel, using a scale of 1 to 10—"Incredibly unsatisfied" would be a 1, and

"Incredibly satisfied" would be a 10. Finally, for each spoke, answer the question, "What would make this a '10' in my life?"

Great job! You have made a fantastic start to your vision and goals.

When it comes to more specific goals, I tend to use a modified version of a popular technique called SMART goal setting. But I add an additional A, so SMART-A goal setting. SMART stands for specific, measurable, attainable, relevant, and time bound. Add in actionable, and you've got SMART-A goal setting.

So, let's write down your aspirations. Then try to write one goal that will help you to achieve each one. From there, you can go through the following exercise to determine whether each of those goals is "SMART."

Is it a specific goal or is it too general?

For example, say you have the goal: "I want to be successful." This goal is too general. It isn't clear what it even is in relation to your life. Now the goal, "I want to be a successful runner," might be specific enough to work with, though it is likely more of an aspiration. A more specific goal would be: "I want to run a marathon on April 1."

Can you measure the goal?

Say you chose the goal, "I want to be a successful runner." This can't be measured as written. But you can revise it to be measurable by rewriting it as: "I want to be a successful runner by completing five marathons." This goal is now both specific and measurable.

Is the goal achievable?

This is up to you. If you've never run a single mile in your life, running five marathons might not be achievable. However, if you're a regular runner, it might be achievable.

Is it relevant?

This really goes back to your aspirations and vision for your future.

If your aspirations are to be a successful and inspiring athlete, then yes, being a successful runner by running five marathons would be relevant to that pursuit.

Is the goal time bound?

Running five marathons to be a successful runner is not a time-bound goal. But you could make it a time-bound goal by revising it to: "I want to be a successful runner by completing five marathons in the next ten years."

Is the goal actionable?

To make this goal actionable, start by identifying what you can do today to start working towards achieving this goal. I always feel if you have no immediate action item to start on towards a goal, it's not a good goal to set yet.

Back to our goal of wanting to be a successful runner—the immediate action item here could be to go for a run today, set your running schedule, or pick the races you want to do. All of these would set you in motion toward reaching your goal.

A final point: some people really dislike the idea of goal setting. They just don't like the term, and if that's you, no problem! One helpful way to reframe goal setting is to simply ask: "What would make this a really awesome year?" Think about it as you being intentional about living an incredible and meaningful life. Setting your aspirations, your vision for the future, and your goals is about living your life by design, not by default. This then allows you to ignite your passion and lead you on your journey to financial freedom.

There are multiple exercises available in this chapter to help guide these conversations, but here are a couple of questions and takeaways that I've found useful as they relate to goal setting:

Five key takeaways

1 Goals-based planning is about setting and prioritizing goals that align with your big picture and life aspirations.
2 Writing down your goals can increase the possibility of achieving them.
3 Give time for proper reflection and goal setting.
4 Aspirations are different from goals. Too many people lose sight of their long-term aspirations by focusing only on goals.
5 To be more successful, start with the end in mind and work backward from there.

Five reflection questions

1 How much time have you really spent thinking about your life's aspirations and goals?
2 What is one goal you have today that might not pass the SMART-A goal-setting process?
3 What is one financial goal you have set in the past and achieved?
4 What can you learn from this past goal-setting experience that can be replicated?
5 Who do you feel most comfortable discussing your financial goals with and why?

Notes

5

The Power of a Proven Process and Trusted Partner

GG Process provides a blueprint for success. *DD*

—*Jamie Hopkins*

Financial Freedom Framework

Process alone won't guarantee success. You need to set goals, plan, and execute on the plan. This is as true with your finances as it is in life and sports.

I GREW UP playing multiple sports. I played basketball, tennis, some football, and I swam. My mom and my sister were both swimmers. I fell in love with swimming, because it was a daily challenge just to do it. I hated getting to 6 a.m. practices and diving into the cold water, but I did it. I pushed myself. It's a team sport and it is not at the same time. When training you're often alone with the black line at the bottom of the pool, counting your laps, thinking about what you're going to eat when you're done. It's a mental and physical challenge just to train. I didn't have the same experience with other sports that I played. I loved basketball practice and tennis practice and I loved the games—they were always enjoyable—but I didn't feel as challenged as I did with swimming. Swimming was just different. It challenged me to be in isolation with my own thoughts and really work. I raced against other people, but in a way I was really racing against myself. How fast was my time? How much did I improve by? These questions are core to swimming.

I swam for famed Olympic head coach Bob Bowman—who coached Michael Phelps, one of the most decorated Olympians of all time. Coach Bowman would often preach to us the importance of process, while also stressing that process alone wasn't good enough. He'd say that all the planning and process in the world still didn't guarantee success. In between process, planning, setting goals, and success, there was *execution*. Process isn't everything, but it provides the blueprint for success.

Swimming takes a training process that's different from almost every other sport. Swimmers often train six days a week—maybe nine to ten practices. Because of the lack of impact on the body— we're floating in water, almost weightless—we're able to train longer and put in more time. There are positives and negatives to this. It's very challenging to be a swimmer. You've really got to make a time commitment.

Swimming has taught me a lot about money. One tough part of swimming is that you usually can't take much time off if you want to compete at the highest levels. You need to do your research, commit, have a process, have a great coach, and execute over and over again. This is a lot like budgeting and investing. If you take too much time off, you will fall behind. If you don't follow the process you can end up lost.

Like with financial planning, in swimming, the details matter: you have to take care of your body to train that much, and you have to figure out how to eat. You have to eat a lot of calories. You also can't gain too much weight. If you know swimmers, they're incredibly fit. You also have to take care of your mind, because you're going to be isolated a lot. You're going to be looking at the bottom of the pool and you can't talk to people, you're thinking about your breathing. You're thinking about your time, how to pace yourself, how to keep your body and mind healthy. It's a very holistic sport, when you think about the training for body and mind, the distance, and the daily grind it requires. It's not an easy sport, by any means.

I also learned that in swimming we had a process that Coach Bowman instilled in us. We knew we had to train extensively. We knew we had to swim long distances. But we also knew we had to mix up the strokes that we did—backstroke, butterfly, breaststroke. And we had to train differently for each one. Coach Bowman paid attention to research being conducted on cross training and the ability to train seven days a week. While you shouldn't do the exact same thing seven days a week—you shouldn't bench press, box jump, or do sprint workouts seven days a week—you could be smart and train with different things in different ways.

The research at that time found that you could reduce injuries by being smart about the way you trained. It also found that movement—not resting—without pain could actually increase recovery time. That has come to be recognized in all sports now, but we adopted this back in the 1990s. We were able to train at a different level because we had such an amazing process and people who were excited to be around each other. We had a community. That we had swimmers like Michael Phelps, Beth Botsford, Katie Hoff, and Anita Nall who swam on this team and went to the Olympics and achieved things at the highest level of the sport showed other people who came behind them at North Baltimore Aquatic Club what was possible. It showed them there was a path and a process and that if you dedicated yourself to it, believed in yourself, and stuck with it, you could achieve greatness.

Part of that was us setting goals. Michael Phelps used to say that when he was very young, he wrote down swimming goals—like going to the Olympics and becoming the most decorated Olympic swimmer of all time. We didn't just set goals by writing them on pieces of paper and wishing they'd come true. We sat down as a group, talked about them, and set them together. As a community, we explored our individual and collective beliefs about what we could achieve. Our coach would work with us on those goals because he'd coached hundreds of people and many Olympians, and he could say, "Here's your skillset, here's what you want to accomplish, and not everybody is the same."

We'd talk about wanting to go to college, wanting to go to Olympic trials, wanting to be Olympians, and wanting to swim on scholarship. We'd explore what types of schools we wanted to swim at and whether we even wanted to swim in college—because not everybody wanted to. We had great swimmers on our team who chose to follow different paths once they got to college.

We'd build our goals and our training would develop based on those goals. The tactics that we'd use to get to those goals would vary based on what the group wanted to accomplish and what our coach helped us believe was possible—which was always more than we ever imagined. This is the role your advisor can play for you. They can help you believe more things are possible. This is helpful if you're like me. I always put self-imposed limitations on myself. I didn't believe enough in my own capabilities and it took a great coach to free me from my limiting beliefs and allow me to believe that I could accomplish more. And I was able to—I was the captain of my high school team with All-American consideration for some of the relays that I was on. I got to swim and dive at Davidson College, which had a Division I swimming and diving program, where I became team captain and won an Unsung Hero Award.

For me, the most important thing about sports is not what I accomplished during them, but how they helped form my drive and character: the goal setting and processes that I was able to apply in school and law, in financial planning, as an educator, and as a father and husband, to create a better life for those around me.

In the last chapter, we explored the importance of setting goals to ensure that your life is successful by your own standards. Maybe you don't have my athletic background, but you can learn from my story and goal-setting process. And if you look back at the eulogy you wrote in the previous chapter, it should constitute the ultimate outcome you want (at least at this moment in time!) when you reflect on your life. If we start with this as the ideal outcome, we can work backwards to design the goals that can help you get there.

As I've mentioned, goals are the mile-markers to ensure you're on track to achieve the outcome you want. You take an approach like the one Coach Bowman did with us—sit down and identify your goals, then work with your financial professional to map out the process to get there. We all know goal setting isn't enough—it's essential to have a well-designed process to help you achieve and prioritize those goals.

You need two things: a process and a partner. You wouldn't do surgery on yourself or build your own house. You wouldn't train yourself for the Olympics. As I've noted before, the best of the best in sports hire multiple professionals to help them improve at something they're already the best at. Maybe you're good with your money and investments, but you can get the optimal outcome with help. Financial planning is just as important as training to be a professional athlete. A solid plan put together by a professional can help you feel more financially secure, prioritize goals, and make more thoughtful decisions, according to Charles Schwab's 2021 Modern Wealth Survey.[4] Execution and motivation are crucial components as well.

Training under such an incredible coach and getting to see Olympians day in and day out in practice was an amazing experience—one I didn't appreciate for what it was at the time. I thought that everyone got to see this type of dedication, process, and execution. It wasn't until much later in life that I realized all the life lessons I learned from that experience. It taught me not just the importance of process, but how the little things—like eating healthy, getting sleep, warming up correctly—are what separate the good from the great.

One of the things I learned was that focusing on the details—or being painstaking in execution—is really what distinguishes the truly great competitors. And here is the thing, everyone starts at their own starting point. Everyone can set goals, learn, and execute on a process in life. Success does not have to be daunting in swimming or with financial planning. The great thing about personal sports like swimming, and with your own money story, is that you get to define what success means.

I've learned you should focus more on your strengths than your weaknesses. Think about it: we often believe there's room to improve our weaknesses, so we should make time to focus on improving them. This is the wrong approach. Instead, we should focus on improving and steering into our strengths. I want to reiterate the example of Tom Brady, arguably the most successful NFL quarterback ever. Tom Brady made a living by throwing the football. Do you think Tom Brady spent time practicing tackling in the offseason? No, he practiced what he was already the best in the world at—throwing the football. He *could* have worked on his weaknesses, like tackling other players after a turnover, kicking a football, or blocking, but these wouldn't have helped him or his team achieve their goals. He knew what he was good at and focused on that. For the other areas, he relied on his team.

This same approach should be put into play with your financial planning process. Focus on what you're good at and don't practice what you are not good at. Almost everyone will need to outsource some aspects of their financial planning to others, be it an attorney, investment specialist, tax professional, or financial planner.

If we want to take our financial situation from good to great, we need a great process. Something that can stand the test of time, help us along our journey, guide us, and evolve as our journey evolves.

Everybody has a financial planning process today—it just might not be one that's getting you where you need to be. Maybe your process is in its infancy, or maybe it's one that's 80% complete. We know a process is a series of steps or actions that can be repeated to help achieve a particular end goal. Processes can also be improved upon and refined over time. So no matter where you are today, you can improve, develop, or change your process for the better.

One of the best-known processes for creating a comprehensive financial plan has been codified by the Certified Financial Planner Board of Standards, which regulates Certified Financial Planner® (CFP®) designation. The seven-step financial planning process that a CFP® advisor will use with you is as follows:

- Understanding your personal and financial circumstances.
- Identifying and selecting goals.
- Analyzing your current course of action and potential alternative courses of action.
- Developing financial planning recommendation(s).
- Presenting financial planning recommendation(s).
- Implementing financial planning recommendation(s).
- Monitoring progress and updating.

This is a good example of a comprehensive financial planning process. It recognizes the importance of getting to know you and your goals, creating alternative sets of recommendations, and the need to monitor and revise your selected and implemented goals. There are a variety of missteps that will be avoided by a financial professional simply following the checklist provided by the process. However, while it provides a broad framework for financial planning, it leaves many of the details of the process up to the financial planner or team.

For example, questions regarding the use and type of technology, as well as how clients should be served differently as they move through different phases of their lives, are left unanswered by the CFP Board steps. These gaps create the opportunity for financial professionals to think through the additional layers of the process needed to fill in the details, and it's the quality of these processes, as well as the disciplined execution and the motivation for continuous improvement, that transforms good financial planners into great financial planners.

At Carson Group, we talk about our financial planning process as the "proven process." Our founder and CEO, Ron Carson, started this process back in the 1980s, and it's been continually improved upon by the thousands of minds who use it in the myriad client situations and scenarios they've seen over the years. The financial planning process must constantly evolve and improve to solve clients' ever-changing needs.

Visioning & Discovery	Document Deep Dive	Personalized Financial Planning Proposal	Plan Implementa-tion	Regular Check-Ins	Annual Review

Visioning & Discovery

First and foremost, the financial planning process is all about *you*. Investment choices don't mean anything if they're not working toward your unique vision of the future. In Visioning & Discovery, your financial planner will help you determine what you want your future to look like, and to understand what drives your happiness and fulfillment.

Document Deep Dive

This is where the planner gets into the numbers and develops a clear, comprehensive view of your current situation. You provide the documents, and the planner and team set about painting an accurate picture of your current financial life.

Personalized Financial Planning Proposal

Your Financial Planning Proposal is the path to get you from point A (which we established in the Document Deep Dive) to point B (what we laid out in Visioning & Discovery). Everyone's plan looks different because everyone's current situation and vision for the future are different.

Plan Implementation

Once you agree that your financial plan is the right path forward, your planner will put it into action. This may involve opening new accounts, helping you move or consolidate accounts, making changes in investments, insurance, etc.

Regular Check-Ins

Especially in the beginning, your financial planner should be checking in with you 10, 30, 90 days into plan implementation to keep you updated on progress. Once your plan is in action, you should still be hearing from your advisors regularly on things that may affect your plan.

Annual Reviews

Your financial plan is a living, breathing document. As your life changes, so will your plan. Maybe there's a new grandbaby, and you'd like to get education planning going now. Maybe you've fallen in love with a small town in the Southwest, and you'd like to relocate there in the next few years. Annual Reviews are the perfect opportunity for you and your financial planner to talk about any life changes or new future wishes that need to be accounted for.

We've designed and tailored this process to work across life stages, adjusting for the continuum of client finances as they progress from early working years, through high-income-earning years, to pre-retirement years, into retirement, and then to legacy planning. Life is a continuum, and your financial planning process needs to adjust for changes in your life, goals, and circumstances.

The proven process can be applied across your life, as your needs, goals, and challenges will change during certain parts of your life. For instance, if you're early in your work career and just getting going on your financial journey, you'll need different financial planning tactics than you'll need when entering retirement. This is where our proven process comes into play.

Financial planning is a collaborative, iterative process. It helps you realize your life goals and ultimately your aspirations through a series of sequential actions and steps personalized to your unique circumstances and situation. By definition, a process must be repeatable and follow a series of steps in a pre-defined order.

Carson's proven process borrows from the collective best practices in the financial planning profession and builds upon them to fit different life stages while incorporating tax planning, current market trends, changes in public policy, behavioral finance, and technological improvements. When you look to build out the team that will help guide you on your path, they should be able to explain their processes, including the ways in which they will connect, anticipate, and collaborate with you and your family in the ever-changing landscape of life.

Finding the financial planner that works for you

A quality financial planning process starts with transparency. If you engage a financial advisor, you need to understand their education, experience, background, planning and investing philosophy, conflicts of interest, and compensation model. You should have clear guidance that your financial advisor is someone who puts your interests ahead of their own, which we call a *fiduciary* in our industry. It's a shame that people need to ask advisors this at all, but in our marketplace today, not all individuals who provide financial advice are required to be fiduciaries. That doesn't mean that all other financial professionals are bad, but it means you need to understand where they play a role.

If you hire an insurance professional, understand how they are compensated, the limitation of their duty to you, and that they're likely there to do one thing: provide you with an insurance product, not look at the entirety of your financial planning picture. Again, that's okay—provided they are transparent.

Most people can make their own educated decisions when given clear and transparent information. We need to treat people with dignity, not as if they're ill-informed and uneducated. Unfortunately, the financial services profession has diluted trust in many by hiding behind complex fee structures, long-winded industry jargon, and details hidden deep in compliance documents.

Behind any good financial planning professional there needs to be trust—not just that the person won't steal your money, but trust that they will do what's in your and your family's best interest, even when no one is around to check. Without trust and transparency, there can be no trusted advisor relationship.

You can't do it all alone

Now, if you're a do-it-yourselfer, you can also use a proven financial planning process to improve your life. But you should answer a few questions. Do you have the time, energy, knowledge, and desire to manage all of your financial affairs? What is the backup plan if you become incapacitated? Will you be able to stay up to date on all market, tax, legal, and other public policy changes that might impact your plan? Will you benefit from a third-party review?

Look, not everyone should delegate their financial planning decisions to a third party. Some people are willing to take this on themselves. However, for many, it's the right decision to delegate and hire a financial planning professional.

A financial planning professional can be like your coach. They can bring with them a process that's been demonstrated and proven over hundreds, thousands, maybe even millions of clients. For instance, growing up, could I have taught myself how to swim and tried to train for the Olympics by myself? Yes. But would I have had a better chance to make the Olympics and achieve my swimming goals by training with an Olympic head coach like Bob Bowman? Absolutely.

No matter whether you want to work with a financial planning professional or go it alone, this book lays out the financial planning and advice building blocks used to create the proven process financial plan. Remember, the financial planning process isn't that large electronic or printed-out document—that's the plan, the snapshot at that singular point in time. The financial planning process is ongoing and follows you through the different financial life stages. It keeps you on track to hit your financial goals—the goals that will help you achieve the financial freedom needed to reach your aspirations.

Process can be a powerful driver to help us reach financial freedom. Here are a couple of questions and takeaways that I have found useful as they relate to the importance of a good process:

Five key takeaways

1 Process can help us go from good to great.

2 Process does not guarantee success, but it provides a blueprint for us to follow.

3 A strong financial planning process must account for different needs and tactics across our different life stages.

4 Trust must be at the center of any good financial planning process or relationship.

5 Transparency is a key metric in both a trusted relationship and a successful process.

Five reflection questions

1 What is your current financial planning process?

2 What is one thing you would change about your current financial planning process?

3 What is a process you use in another area of your life that's been successful? Why do you think it has been successful?

4 How important are trust and transparency to your relationships with professionals like financial advisors?

5 Is it important to you how your financial advisor is compensated? Why?

Notes

6

How to Get More out of Your Financial Planning Process

Financial Freedom Framework

Your plan is going to change over time based on your age, life stage, or changing goals and aspirations. You shouldn't have the same plan in place at age 50 that you had at age 30.

B ENJAMIN FRANKLIN'S WORDS apply to many aspects of our lives, but perhaps they're no truer than when it comes to our personal financial decisions. If we make our financial decisions in the dark, without a clear plan, we're planning to fail. The financial planning process can help us create a plan, set goals, and achieve financial freedom, but only if we commit to it. This is challenging when we go it alone. Not only do we need to identify our aspirations, our goals, and the process, but we need to put that process into action.

As we saw in the last chapter, financial planning—like any other process—must be iterative and improve over time. We can't set a financial plan when we are 25 expecting that we'll put that same plan into action 40 years later when we retire.

My own financial plans have changed over the years. They haven't always been the same, and that's a good thing. Plans need to evolve and grow as you grow; they need to change as your desires, wishes, and life change. Life isn't predictable—that's one of the most beautiful and enjoyable things about it.

My financial planning when I was younger was really just to get by. I worked some construction. I was a lifeguard. I was a coach. I was doing all those things to survive. It wasn't about moving forward or looking five, ten, or 20 years down the line. As I started to develop after I got through college, I got the ability to go to graduate school, then to law school, then to business school. I have one master's degree in tax and another in financial planning. I've had a lot of school over the years, which helped me refine my own career trajectory. I started to realize that I could make a good living and think about other things down the line, but I also had some setbacks. While I loved law school—it was a fantastic experience—I ended up leaving it with almost $185,000 in student debt. That's something that could have completely derailed my life and given me financial challenges for the next 30 years. That's so much money. I remember looking at the amount I owed when I graduated law school and feeling so much dread. My stomach sank. My heart sank. I looked at that number and I'd never seen that much money in my entire life. I knew I had borrowed a lot, but seeing all of it at once was overwhelming.

I remember where I was when I wrote it down. I was   in my friend Mike Knickerbocker's basement. I was pulling together and writing down the totals from all the different lenders on a yellow pad. I looked at the number and thought, "How do you ever come out of that?" I was making around $60,000 a year at that time. I looked at the interest on the loans and I just didn't see a path out. I remember struggling with that for weeks.

I really wanted kids. I wanted a family. I wanted all of the American dream things—to own my own house, to have a dog. So I made a decision. I said that by the time I had kids, I'd have paid off this student loan debt. I made a very conscious decision to cut back tremendously on my spending. I had people who joked about my eating then—I would buy a whole ham and eat ham on white bread with mustard for an entire week. I decided that was the cheapest thing I could eat. I rented a room in my friend's house instead of having my own apartment. I sacrificed quality of life for a while and focused on paying down that debt. I even went and refinanced that debt with SoFi, because at the time they had the lowest interest rate. I didn't know much about them because they were fairly new in the market. Now they have national bank charters. The world has changed a lot for them too.

Amazingly, I focused on this for years. It wasn't an overnight experience, it was years in the making. Years later, in May of the year my daughter was born (in August), I was able to pay off those debts.

Law school and debt weren't the only things that changed my financial plan. I eventually met my wonderful wife Kathy when I was working in the Appellate Division, and she had a bit of debt at the time. But when I met Kathy, our goals shifted to things like, "How do we buy a house together?" and, "How do we save enough money to buy an engagement ring?" My planning started shifting to those shorter-term goals—I didn't have the longer-term picture in mind yet. I went from getting by day to day to setting a mid-term goal of paying off my student debt, to setting more short-term goals of saving enough money to do these things for somebody who I wanted to be with and cared about tremendously.

So I started setting up saving and investment strategies and explored how to accumulate enough money. How could I set aside enough each paycheck to be able to save for these goals? And again, I was able to check those goals off. Kathy and I ended up getting engaged, married, and paying for our own wedding. Then we were blessed enough to welcome our daughter into the world. The amazing thing about our daughter's arrival was that all of a sudden, we had a much longer-term view of the world. I started thinking that we needed to update our estate plan and our powers of attorney. We needed to start thinking about 529 college savings plans, about maximizing and enhancing our own retirement plans. It was time for us to explore how we were going to take care of our kids and ourselves, long term.

Those were pivotal moments in life that started to shift the focus and longevity of my plan. Things like 529s and retirement plans, which weren't important to me years before, became crucial. Fast forward to now: we have three kids and the planning around that—how to pay for diapers and daycare—has become part of this bigger plan.

I also realized that I was still being reactive instead of proactive. I hadn't really laid out my life aspirations, goals, and what I wanted to accomplish. It wasn't really until I established those things that I started to focus on how I wanted to be remembered and how I wanted my kids to look at me. What financial lessons did I want to instill in them? What did financial freedom actually mean to me? When I explored these things, I really started to get a true financial plan in place. Until then, I had pieces of planning, but I didn't have that comprehensive plan because I didn't have a guiding "North Star." I was engaging in tactics without long-term views of the impact. That's when things started to change for me—when I first felt that confidence in where I was going, and I knew the decisions I was making were the right ones.

As I got a plan in place, I started preempting some of the needs I knew I was going to have further down the line. I was able to save for a car instead of having to figure out how to pay for it when I needed it. This was uplifting and freeing to me. It started to open up possibilities in my mind for other things that I could accomplish—not just around finances, but around life in general. This helped me create a bigger purpose. Then I realized my goals didn't stop with me. They didn't stop with my wife. They didn't stop with my kids. I wanted to create generational wealth for my family so that my grandkids and their kids would also have the financial flexibility and stability to chase their dreams.

One of my financial goals is to have an impact on those who are less fortunate—who don't have food and water, who go to bed hungry or thirsty. That's the stuff that's started to keep me up at night, not how to get a $500 emergency bill paid. I've been fortunate enough to reach a place where I can open my mind up to the greater possibilities of impacting things out there in the world, especially for kids who had a similar struggle to me.

Controlling your sails

One of my closest friends and mentors, Erin Wood CFP®, always used a great analogy when teaching the power of financial planning. She would say that financial planning is like trying to sail in a windy bay. The dock in the bay represents our financial goals, and the wind represents all the things that can blow us off course. We can't control the direction the wind blows, but we can adjust our sails and plot a new course when things change. A good sailor and navigator can adjust to changing winds to get back home, while a novice might not be able to adjust, letting the wind blow the boat into the rocks of financial disaster.

To avoid hitting the rocks, we need to commit to a great process. But how? Behavioral research has masses of data on how to improve productivity, goal accomplishment, and process improvement. Goals are powerful tools. If you set goals, you're more likely to achieve them. And if you have a proven process to achieve these goals, that helps even more. But as Coach Bowman taught us, goals and process alone aren't enough. Many people set goals, lay out a process, but don't commit to taking action. Think of all the failed New Year's resolutions you've set with the best of intentions. A study out of Scranton University found that only 19% of people achieve their New Year's resolutions.[5] What often happens is people set goals with conviction but fail to execute.

To execute on your goals, you need to be productive. Researchers have learned two important lessons when examining productivity in small groups. First, if group members feel that they're indispensable to the group outcomes, they'll feel energized and work towards achieving a goal. For instance, if you were trying to push a rock up a hill and you realized that the group could only do it with your help, you'd feel motivated to help the group achieve this outcome. Additionally, research has found that if you believe that the group will recognize your contributions, you'll work toward achieving this goal, even though it might be more self-interested than altruistic.[6]

This is used in certain military training, in which a trainee who is first to quit an exercise receives social pressure from the group to keep pushing. This drives behavior on the other side, too. Your team will also see if you are the last to give up, and you'll be recognized with positive social rewards. As a result of both the negative pressure not to be the first to quit and the positive social rewards of pushing to the end, people are driven to work with extreme vigor towards the goal

So how do we act? As we just discussed, beliefs about the impact and outcomes of our actions can be motivators for performance. We want to know that our contributions are crucial to success and that they'll be recognized. We want positive reinforcement and recognition for our contributions. We also want to see that our contributions are indispensable to making an impact on our life. If we see all these things, we increase the likelihood that we'll act.

However, if you believe your situation is so dire you can't change it, you'll be less likely to act toward accomplishing your goal. In this case inaction will win out. We know from physics that things that aren't in motion don't start moving unless acted upon by an outside force. This is true for our financial situation, too. If we live in fear and don't believe that our actions and planning can change our financial future, we fail to act, instead relegating our lives to the status quo.

Research from the American Psychological Association shows that consistently monitoring progress towards goals increases your chance of success.[7] When you publicly share your goals and progress with third parties, the likelihood that you'll continue to make progress increases. The research also finds that the better you are at recording your progress toward a goal, the more likely you are to achieve it.

Now think about how we can put all of this in place through a financial planning process. The more you review, record, and discuss your goals, the more you'll increase the likelihood of success. And, to get adoption of your planning strategy and put your tactics into action, you need to see how your decisions and planning actions impact the outcomes. Lastly, you need to know there's a reward; you need to see the benefits of your work.

Our brains like to reward success and punish failure. Despite learning just as much from failures as successes, our brains try hard to deter us from repeating our failures over and over again. Research has shown that our brains are naturally wired to want us to chase tasks that give us rewards versus those that cause us pain.[8] This is also one good reason we can't get too focused on a single number, investment, or outcome as proof of success or failure in our financial planning process. Success is much more long term. If we view success or failure in terms of where our returns will be at the end of the year, we risk going down an ill-conceived financial path—because much of that is out of our control.

The facets of a financial plan

So often, when we talk about financial planning, people's minds go immediately to investment management. The truth is that investment management is one component of financial planning. A financial plan that's focused on getting you to your personal version of freedom has to encompass a whole lot more.

At Carson Group, we talk a lot about the Find Your Freedom™ Planning Promise. This is our way of showing clients that a financial plan is, first and foremost, about their unique vision of the future, and that the plan must take into account every area of their financial life.

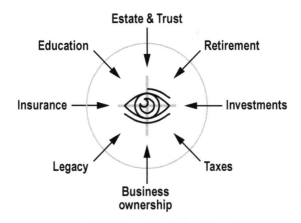

Deeper into the financial planning process

We all have needs. Our needs—whether they be food, clothing, happiness, connection, exercise, or love—motivate us to take action. This is the simple, yet complex theory behind Maslow's Hierarchy of Needs. The model—which you've likely seen before—depicts human needs across a spectrum of five categories. At the bottom are the physical needs—food, shelter, and clothing. Next is safety, both physical and in ways like job security. Next is a level of belonging and love, including needs for friendship, community, and connection. Next is esteem, where you find self-worth and become more introspective about your value. At the top is self-actualization.

You can't progress through these levels if you don't satisfy the levels below. The need to be safe and to have food is paramount to reaching a level of self-actualization. So as you progress toward that goal, you need to take care of your basics first.

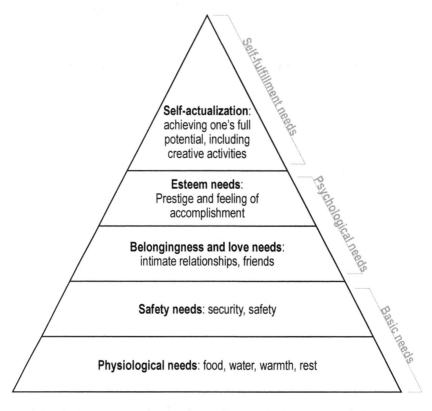

These same principles apply to financial planning and the process it takes to obtain financial freedom. You have to start off building up your base of core financial needs. This financial planning hierarchy also has five categories. And you can't reach the next without satisfying the ones below.

Simplify and organize

We call the first level "simplify and organize." You need to be able to meet basic expenditures like food, housing, health care, clothing, and transportation. Typically, this means some sort of budgeting, which isn't always an Excel spreadsheet tracking every dollar in and out, but rather a rough understanding of whether your income is meeting your expenses.

One way we can work on our basic needs is to balance and focus on expenses. This is true for most people from week to week, month to month, and year to year; we will have more control over our expenses in the short term than we will have over our income. However, long term, the real needle mover is to increase income. This means investing back into yourself.

Confidence and control

Ultimately the basic needs in your life are met by the interplay of expenses and income. As things start to get more complex, your planning needs and tactics will start to change. We call this level "confidence and control." Here you'll start looking at assets differently—not just as a way to meet current needs, but how those current needs impact your long-term journey to financial freedom. You can start working on increasing your savings and creating better savings habits; you can look at the types of investments you have and align them with your goals; you can start getting serious about retirement planning, reviewing insurance needs, and engaging in tax planning. These become complex cogs that form your financial picture. Not each piece is the same for everyone, and as you move through life your needs here will change.

Debt management might be crucial when you are just out of school with student debt and trying to get a mortgage, but less important to you once your mortgage is paid off and you are heading into retirement.

As you progress out of the basic need level of financial planning—where you have confidence, control, and you feel organized—you can shift your focus onto incorporating longer-term goals and needs (including wishes and wants) into your planning. This part of planning is no longer just focused on the day-to-day needs, but is driven by your aspirations. Here you can focus on things like funding your children's or loved one's college expenses. It can also involve getting more tactical with the type of health care you can afford by leveraging different insurance or savings vehicles, like a health savings account (HSA) or flex spending account (FSA) to help fund health care expenses. This next level on the hierarchy will likely include saving for retirement, getting the basics of an estate plan in place, and getting more strategic about charitable giving.

I would also contend this is where financial literacy and education become more important. There is a debate in the financial literacy and education world around when is the right time to educate. Obviously, there is no harm—there's actually a lot of potential good—in educating people at a young age. However, as humans, we start to learn more about things as they become more important to us. It's hard to get a 10-year-old to care about retirement planning education, but it's much easier to get someone who has $100,000 in a 401(k) to care about it.

Instead of doing things to get by, you have to understand the *why* and the *how* behind retirement planning. This can give you more meaning in what you're doing and help you better prioritize your goals and aspirations. Hopefully, you also have some financial flexibility to spend on things like vacations, entertainment, and the like. These are the wants and wishes in your life that bring you some degree of happiness and enjoyment.

Social belonging

At this point in your financial life, where you have more financial flexibility and are using that to enjoy yourself, you should have enough in place that you can shift your focus more on to the next level, which we call "social belonging."

Social belonging is about finding your place in the world and focusing your planning on the impact you want to have on those near and around you. You've saved, worked hard, created wealth and time for yourself, but you also have people who rely upon you and who you've created social connections with. Finding your tribe or community and identifying your role within it become crucial during this time. This could be your family, your church, or a group you do your hobbies with. This is a core stage of finding a sustained meaning in life while also finding time for fun and enjoyment. Part of this might be delegating tasks you once did, like mowing the lawn or managing your investments.

You've also likely accumulated assets and something of value that needs more serious estate planning, but estate planning is actually more about your family and loved ones than about the dollars and assets. Getting the right documents and processes in place protects both your wealth and the people you love.

You can now start to focus on the impact of your charitable giving. You could think about the legacy you might leave behind and how to maximize your gifts. Tax planning around assets and distributions becomes more important too.

Self-actualization

At this point the core of the planning is done and the last real phase is about "self-actualization." This is where you think about legacy and what you want to pass on. Additionally, it's a time for reflection and reviewing accomplishments. Did you reach your goals and aspirations? What are you proud of, what can you do differently?

The phase of self-actualization is what eventually leads us to financial freedom.

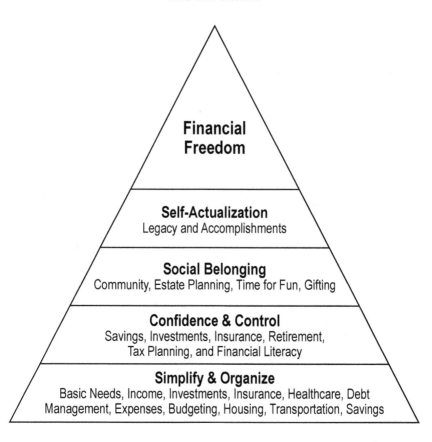

Financial freedom

As you can see from the graphic, the path to financial freedom starts with the basics. To achieve financial freedom, we must start by laying down a solid foundation in the "simplify and organize" stage upon which we can build. Investing in ourselves, education, and savings can get us on the right path, while debt and spending can get us off track. While we will dive into all these topics in more detail later on, here are a couple of questions and takeaways that I have found useful as they relate to the hierarchy of planning and goal setting.

Five key takeaways

1 Financial freedom starts by getting the basics of saving and spending right.

2 Simplify and organize your financial picture by taking care of your basic spending, budgeting, and income needs.

3 Gain confidence and control over your financial picture by creating a savings strategy, managing taxes, and coordinating both with your retirement planning.

4 Find social belonging by taking control of your finances.

5 Legacy and estate planning is often not about the dollars and cents, but about protecting and benefiting your loved ones.

Five reflection questions

1 Where in the planning hierarchy are you today? Simplify and organize, confidence and control, social belonging, self-actualization, or financial freedom?

2 What is your biggest concern about your financial situation today? Or in other words, what keeps you up at night?

3 What part of your financial plan or situation needs the most work?

4 On a scale of 1–10, how committed are you to improving your financial situation?

5 What is your favorite way to spend money? How can more financial freedom allow you to spend more time doing what you love?

Notes

7

The Continuum of Planning

66 If you do not know where you are going, every road will get you nowhere. 99

—Henry A. Kissinger

Financial Freedom Framework

Planning can be approached from an age-based perspective, but we can also think about it as a continuum that requires different planning for different phases of our life based on our trajectory, goals, and aspirations. Both are valuable for different people.

FINANCIAL PLANNING DEVELOPS as your needs change. It's a continuum because people's lives and needs are on a spectrum. Not every part of that spectrum needs financial planning. When you're younger and earlier in your career, your needs and desires are different than those of someone who is entering retirement. The financial planning advice, tactics, investments, and planning shift for you based on your needs. While not everyone goes through the same lifecycles and has the same needs, for many there are core elements that are consistent throughout life. Let's take a quick look at some core financial planning personas and the accompanying tactics that could be valuable across these life stages.

Unless you are born into wealth, are a child prodigy of some type, or inherit a fortune from your family or loved ones, most people start off their career relying on others for financial support. Even so, our lifetime earning potential is at its highest at this time. Our whole lives are ahead of us. We could start a company, find a cure for a disease, develop the next great advancement in technology, become a doctor, build houses, or add value to society in many other ways. Our ability to earn money throughout our lives is called our human capital. We'll discuss this in more detail later on in the book, as we ourselves— and our human capital—are one of our largest assets. As we move through life, we need to turn this potential to earn an income into actual money.

The entire secret of financial planning is this—make more than you spend. This generates savings. We invest some money we make now so that we can spend more in the future. This concept of saving today for the future is called consumption smoothing. We have a natural desire to consume now. For example, if you bring me food now, I want to eat it now. If you give me money now, I want to spend it on something I would enjoy today. We as humans have a natural bias and desire towards the now, not the later. This makes sense, because if I die tomorrow saving for a year from now will have been a waste. So, we tend to think that since *today* is the only certain thing, we may as well enjoy it. While there might sometimes be some truth to that, it operates against what we *know* is true in financial planning—that at some point in the future we might not be able to work for our money, so we need to save for when that happens.

As such, we want to save money when our human capital is highest so we can spend it in the future when our income is at its lowest. This can be illustrated in other ways too. Think about farmers—they don't just eat all the food they produce at once—they can it, freeze it, dry it, juice it, and preserve it, so it can last through the winter. This is about saving in times of plenty so we can consume in times of scarcity.

We'll look at this in two different ways: based on age and based on stage.

First, let's start with a look across ages, which is how most of us view our lives. It's important to realize that age is just a number and some people hit different life and financial milestones at different times. There should be no shame attached to the age at which you attain your goals. Some people run marathons in their 90s, some people never want to run a marathon. Some people want to buy a house and others prefer to rent. All of those are good.

Each decade of our lives is riddled with its own risks and problems, so it's important to know what to expect. Which decade can you afford to take more risk? Which decade should you really start to plan for retirement? Which decade should you focus on managing debt?

Your career and lifestyle look completely different when you're in your 20s versus when you're in your 60s—your financial focus and planning in each decade should look just as different. I've highlighted three or four financial tactics to focus on in each decade of your life, starting with your 20s.

Set yourself up for future financial success by living each decade to the fullest.

20s	30s	40s	50s	60s	70s
Self-Investment	Debt & Savings Management	Wealth Building	Retirement Planning	Income Transition	Making Money Last

Planning in your 20s

- **Invest in yourself**
  When you are just starting a career in your 20s, take time to invest in yourself. This might mean going back to school to earn a master's degree or professional certification. Take the time to grow your human capital, life experiences, and knowledge—it doesn't get easier to invest back into yourself later in life.
- **Build your positive financial behaviors**
  Start by saving. Put money into your employer's 401(k) or set up an IRA. Even if you can only put a few hundred dollars away, work on developing and automating your savings.

- **Take some risk**

  When you're young is the best time to take risk. It's true from both an investment standpoint and a life standpoint. When investing, look for equities and don't invest too conservatively—you have a long time horizon to let your money grow. Take risks in life, too. Look for startups and opportunities that will help you grow and flourish. I know many young people just want a sure thing in their first job, but a company that will grow and help *you* grow might be a better fit in the long run.

Rule of thumb for your 20s

During this decade, you should keep in mind that by age 30 you should have at least one to three times your starting salary stashed away for retirement. You should also aim to establish an emergency fund that contains three to six months of your living expenses in cash or an easily accessible investment with low risk.

Planning in your 30s

- **Debt management**

  It's vitally important to manage your debt obligations carefully in your 30s. If you have student, personal, or car loans, credit card debt, or a mortgage, you need to have a plan to pay them off—and which ones you'll tackle first. Some suggest that from a behavioral standpoint, you should tackle low-balance accounts first, but a financial planning approach suggests you tackle high-interest rate debt first. Either way, what really matters is that you don't overborrow.

- **Proper insurance coverage**

  One of the biggest risks for many people in their 30s is they're still acting as if they're invincible. This leads to many people being underinsured. Make sure you have the right health care coverage, car insurance, property and casualty insurance for your home, disability insurance, and life insurance. Especially as your wealth starts to grow—perhaps along with a family—your insurance and financial needs will continue to change.

- **Start building up retirement assets**
Hopefully your career is blossoming and you're able to set aside money. This means increasing how much you're saving for retirement. If you work with an employer that offers a 401(k), consider increasing your salary deferral. If you run your own company, look into setting up a SEP, 401(k), or SIMPLE IRA to help you set aside more money each year for the future.

Rule of thumb for your 30s

By your mid- to late 30s, it's ideal to be saving anywhere from 10–15% of your income each year for the future. The more the better. Remember that saving an additional 1% of income each year can lead to tens of thousands more in money saved for retirement. By the end of this decade, you should have at least three to six times your starting salary saved for retirement.

Planning in your 40s

- **Build your wealth**
In your 40s, you'll likely hit your peak earning years. Which means it's time to actually start building your wealth. Make sure your investments are properly aligned with your future goals and continue to be heavily invested in growth assets.
- **Cut back unnecessary expenses**
By your 40s, you've probably picked up some unnecessary spending habits or costs along the way. Now is a good time to review your overall budget, spending, and costs. Perhaps you have too many entertainment subscriptions, are paying too much for your phone bill, or your car doesn't fit your lifestyle. Any of these things could be changed to bring down your spending.
- **Take care of yourself**
The mid-life crisis can start to sneak up on people in their 40s. Many people feel burnt out or stressed with work and finances. It's important to take care of yourself. Set aside time for both your financial planning and wellness. Taking control of your finances can help you take care of yourself and reduce stress. Burning out

could negatively affect your health and finances and add additional layers of stress onto an already challenging situation.

Rule of thumb in your 40s

Your 40s are likely going to be your peak earning and working years. Focus on cutting back expenses, increasing your savings, investing heavily in long-term growth assets, and aiming to have between three and five times your annual income saved by your mid-40s. At the end of this decade, you should have six to ten times your starting salary saved for retirement.

Planning in your 50s

- **Retirement income planning**
  Retirement income planning should start in your 50s. This means sitting down and seeing how much you have saved, listing out your expenses and figuring out the income you can generate in retirement. Because if there's a shortfall projected, you still have time to restructure your plan. That could mean saving more or cutting expenses. It's also a good time to look at other retirement income sources, including a deferred income annuity, and review your investment allocation.
- **Long-term care planning**
  While long-term care planning isn't what everyone dreams about for their 50s, it's likely the best time to do it. With retirement starting to creep into your mind, one of the biggest risks you face in retirement should also be front and center: how to pay for long-term care. Long-term care insurance and funding strategies are best purchased and reviewed in your 50s. Once you get into your 60s, it can be harder to qualify for long-term care coverage. Take a look at it in your 50s and decide if it makes sense for you.
- **Family and next generation planning**
  In your 50s you might be getting pressure to care for both sides of your family—your parents, who are likely well into retirement now, and your children. Planning for how you'll help everyone in your family is crucial. Families need to discuss college planning

and funding as much as they need to discuss how they'll support and take care of aging parents. All of this planning needs to start with open and honest conversations at the family level.

Rule of thumb in your 50s

As you start to think about retiring and wonder if you have enough saved, a good rule of thumb is to have 25 times what you plan to spend each year in retirement. So, if you want to spend $100,000 a year from your savings in retirement, you should retire with $2.5 million. This amount doesn't include any income you might receive from Social Security or a pension, which could significantly lower the amount you need to save. By the end of this decade, you should at least have eight to 15 times your starting salary saved.

Planning in your 60s

- **Setting the retirement income plan in motion**
  You've spent your whole working career saving, investing, and paying off bills. Now it's time to turn your savings into retirement income. This decision requires a lot of planning because you need to make this money last for the rest of your life and no one knows how long that'll be. Working as long as you can and deferring Social Security are two ways to help ease longevity concerns. While many people call longevity a risk, it's a good thing. It makes other risks—like health care, long-term care, and inflation—more detrimental to the sustainability of your retirement income. Get a plan in place and know how you'll generate income, when you plan to retire, when to claim Social Security and when to put the plan in motion.
- **Re-evaluating work and meaning**
  Retirement isn't just a financial planning topic, it's a real and significant part of your life. Finances are just a means to an end— the end being your goals and what you want to accomplish in retirement. Make sure you take the time to envision what life will be like after you stop working. Look at what you want to do and consider phasing into retirement by working part-time. If you're

single, retirement could be more challenging for you since you leave behind the relationships you built at work. Staying engaged during retirement is important. It's crucial to have a plan on how you'll find meaning, happiness, and value in retirement.

- **Estate planning**

  While you should start your estate planning basics early in life, when you near retirement in your 60s, it's good to do a full overview of your estate planning. This can include reviewing your insurance to determine if it's still needed or if you need more. You also need to review your estate planning documents to make sure they're in order and that all your assets are properly titled. It's also important to do another beneficiary review, especially as assets start to get turned into retirement income. Remember that estate planning is not just about your money. It is about family, values, and leaving a clear path forward for your loved ones after you are gone. For instance, if you don't have a good estate plan in place, you can leave your loved ones in turmoil and chaos—fighting over what to do and even fighting over assets. In many cases with family fights over an estate, it isn't about money; but often fights break out over personal items, like mom's wedding band or a family painting. Make sure you list out your assets, with clear intentions as to which items go to which heirs. Clarity of your goals and communication can go a long way to protecting and caring for your family after you are gone.

- **Major life change planning**

  As you age, your life can change dramatically. This could be from divorce, the death of a loved one, the marriage of children, or the birth of grandchildren. All of these represent major life moments that require their own degree of planning. For most people, by the time they reach age 60 they will have experienced some major life moments that shifted their goals and plan substantially.

Rule of thumb in your 60s

As you head into retirement, try to understand the 4% safe withdrawal rate for retirement spending. The 4% safe withdrawal rate finding states that historically in the U.S., with a 50% bond investment and a 50% stock investment, you could afford to spend 4% of your investments per year and not run out of money for 30 years. This is a conservative approach, but it gives a good starting point for evaluating how much you can spend in retirement. Also, by age 67, you should have 10 to 25 times your starting salary saved—but note that this number depends on your spending goals and other income sources.

Planning in your 70s and beyond

- **Enjoying life**
  You've worked hard your whole life and should enjoy your retirement. Having a sound financial plan that shows what you can spend and how long your money will last can allow you to do just that. Many people worry about having enough money in retirement, so they hoard their money, refuse to spend it, and ultimately don't enjoy themselves. They're too fearful about the uncertainty of the future. But that doesn't have to be you. Having a plan in place can help you live the lifestyle that you want and enjoy your retirement.
- **Making money last a lifetime**
  A big part of planning for retirement while working is about saving, investing, and growing your wealth. Once you get into retirement, you need to monitor how your plan is doing and make any adjustments. Your situation, the markets, and your goals will change as your lifestyle and retirement change. As such, you can't stick with one plan from the first day of retirement to day 10,000 (or year 27 in retirement).

  Don't forget to plan and manage your required minimum distributions (RMDs) from IRAs and 401(k)s. Optimizing these assets can require new types of planning and tax strategies. As you start to spend down your money, keep track of the percentage of your assets you're spending. The 4% withdrawal rate that I wrote about before is a good way to help you monitor your plan over time. If your withdrawal rate from your assets starts nearing 8–10%, you might want to consider cutting back on expenses. On the flip side, if your spending drops below 3% of your overall assets, you could actually increase your spending.

- **Legacy and charitable planning**
  You should've started estate planning well before your 70s, but when you enter retirement, you'll have more time and energy to focus on leaving behind a legacy. Legacy planning isn't just about taxes and estate planning—it's more about meaning and impact. It can mean passing on security to family members, giving back time to your favorite charities, or funding worthwhile and meaningful initiatives you care deeply about. Giving back in retirement will keep you more engaged and reduce the likelihood that you'll become isolated and suffer from depression. Additionally, after you hit age 72 and need to take RMDs from an IRA, you have great charitable giving strategies, like qualified charitable distributions (QCDs) available. QCDs allow you to take a distribution in an IRA and send it directly to a charity to help offset your RMD requirements for the year and have it not treated as part of your taxable income.

Rule of thumb in your 70s and beyond

Now that you're in retirement, you need to track your spending and the longevity of your retirement portfolio. The biggest rule of thumb is realizing you might be underestimating your life expectancy. For instance, couples at age 65 have a greater than a 50% chance that one individual will live to 90, and an almost 25% chance one will live to 95. Plan to have many years ahead of you. Longevity isn't a risk—it's a gift for those who plan. Don't plan for the middle, plan for the end point.

By age 70, you should no longer be thinking about savings. Instead, it's time to think about income. If you want to make your money last, your withdrawal rate has to be reasonable—about 4–5% of your total wealth. If it gets up to 10% of your portfolio balance, you risk running out of money.

Different flavors for different stages

While age-based planning makes sense, it doesn't work for everyone. We should also think about life as a continuum that requires different planning for different phases of our life based on our trajectory, goals, and aspirations. An explorer will have far different financial needs than someone who sets out to have two children, a spouse, and live the suburban American dream lifestyle, or the couple that decides to build a housing empire.

As we detailed in the past chapter, the planning hierarchy allows people to focus on different topics and areas of planning as their situation matures. But let's look at this in another way: instead of focusing on the planning horizon, let's focus on where the person is in their life.

Foundational

For simplicity, your life can be divided into a number of planning stages. Early on in your planning, this is often the foundational stage, where you focus on the "simplify and organize" items of investing in yourself, generating income, budgeting, expenses, health care, housing, and debt management.

So early in life, we want to invest in ourselves so we can earn as much as possible and be able to work for as long as possible. This means training your mind and body to achieve this goal. Later in life, wealth without health is no life at all.

Once you get into your career, you really enter the first earning phase, or financial planning phase, of your life. I call this phase the "foundational" planning phase. In many ways you can do more harm than good in this phase. If you overburden yourself with debt, deplete your health, and get off track, it can be hard to recover.

Let's go back to the farming analogy. The farmer prepares the land, plans out the fields, and lays the seeds. But if they don't do any planning and don't realize they have bad soil that will dry out the seeds, then all the work the farmer wanted to do later won't matter because nothing will grow. They need to focus more on nurturing the soil so that they can grow what they want to grow, where they want to grow it, and in the way they want to grow it.

As I was writing this, my good friend Marques Ogden—who spent roughly six years playing in the NFL—messaged me. It's fitting that he messaged me as I was writing this section because his story is one of planting on bad soil.

Marques had the dream—he was drafted and paid well for playing professional football. But having no foundational knowledge of personal finance, he overspent, didn't save, didn't plan for the future. After his time in the NFL, he had to completely rebuild his career and financial footing. He asked me today where I was when he was in the NFL—and I told him I'm sorry, I wasn't in this line of work at that time. Even though we didn't know each other back then, I felt sincere in my response because I don't want there to be another Marques. I know there will be, but my goal in life is to give everyone planning foundations because everyone deserves a financially secure future.

Marques has built it back up, he reinvented himself—focusing on mindset and process. He rebuilt his business, got back on track, got great advice and support from loved ones, got his own mindset right, and now he is an amazing speaker, author, and coach. Marques gave me two quotes to include in this book– first he quoted Aristotle: "In times of extreme darkness, focus on the light." I love this, because no matter where you are in your financial journey there is light—you just have to find it if it feels dark. And secondly, he said, "You don't have to be the best to do your best." I don't think there is any better way to express foundational planning than that quote!

When you're in this foundational period, budgeting is important. Start to develop a healthy relationship with money by simply tracking your income and spending. Know what you make and bring in and where it goes. Managing debt in this foundational stage is crucial—you don't want to let the debt snowball and derail the rest of your life. Start by checking your credit score and educating yourself on the factors that go into it.

Another friend and financial services industry leader, Tyrone Ross, is well known for saying, "Educate before you allocate." In your foundational stage, take the time to learn—read books, study, and become somewhat knowledgeable on personal finance basics like definitions of stocks, bonds, crypto, and mutual funds. Another great friend and colleague, Erin Wood, also talks with me frequently about the importance of education in the planning process. We can only make decisions based on the information we have, so without transparency and education, we end up making incomplete decisions.

Next, you want to make sure you have a basic level of insurance in place. There isn't a need to do a deep dive into insurance planning just yet, so this will mostly be around having some mandatory insurance coverage like car, health, home, and disability insurance. This is all about protecting your future at this point. Many people have insurance for their phone, but not for themselves. You want to protect yourself and your ability to earn well into the future.

In order to grow your wealth and get on a path to financial freedom, you'll need to focus on three main things. First, manage debt and pay off any high-interest debt first—like credit card debt. If left unchecked, these items can snowball and put you behind for decades. Second, make sure your income is more than your expenses. You can't save and build towards financial stability if you are spending more than you earn. Third, you need to invest in yourself. This also includes things like health care and taking care of yourself. Not investing in yourself mentally, professionally, physically, and emotionally will come back to haunt you later in life.

While you are likely to be young during the foundational stage, that is not always the case. A major life event like a divorce, bankruptcy, or family death could cause someone to restart and focus back on their foundational planning elements. It is often a life event like buying a house, getting a new job, or having children that spurs on someone in this stage to seek out more financial guidance. Remember that the principles of the foundational stage remain throughout all of your life, but this is really the entry point into the financial planning process.

For instance, you can have someone in their 50s who is just getting started in their financial savings journey. You can also have someone in their 30s who built a great business and sold it to gain financial independence. While many people progress through these planning stages as they age, it is not a static path but a dynamic one as we live our lives.

Stability

The next stage in life is stability. In this stage you're established in your career and earning a good living. So, you've already made progress on income generation. There's some savings and accumulation of wealth going on. But growing wealth by gaining confidence and control over your financial future is paramount. Stability falls under the "confidence and control" planning step of the financial planning hierarchy detailed in the previous chapter. This step is about increasing savings, goals-based investing, insurance planning, retirement planning, and tax optimization.

At this point in life you likely have the foundational elements in place and you have a financial plan, but it's not fully complete. You could be in the early or middle stage of your career, but that's not always the case. Some people never get into—or make it out of—the stability stage, so there's a huge opportunity to address emerging needs, goals, risks, and concerns within the planning process. The concern here is that opportunities are being missed or wasted, and that a tuning up of the overall plan is in order. Risks and concerns about the future might be keeping you up at night. Worries about the market, retirement, health care, and savings might be weighing on your mind, even if you are doing many things right financially.

The most common example of someone in the stability stage is the couple in their late 30s or 40s with children. They're likely doing a lot of things right, but still need help. They're worried about family goals, personal goals, and retirement goals. So prioritizing goals becomes even more important. Most people can't save for or do everything.

You'll also want to increase your retirement savings. Contribute at least enough to get your employer 401(k) match. You also might be considering or setting up IRAs or SEP IRAs if you run your own business. You should do this while also continuing to manage debt. This might include exploring whether you should refinance anything.

This phase also includes many business owners who've built amazing businesses, but continue to reinvest back into their business instead of saving for their own future. This is often what helps make the business owner successful, but it can be a challenge to balance both the business and personal finances. Single professionals also fall into this category. At this point they need to start aligning values with their investment and financial picture.

Assets might not be substantial, but the ability to save and invest is. So the ability to get deeper into planning can add tremendous value to both your bottom line and mental well-being.

Strategic

After the fundamentals are taken care of and some stability is created, you're able to enter a new phase of strategic planning. Here you can get much broader and deeper with your planning. At this point you can start thinking about your community, education, gifting, and making time for the things you love. In essence, by creating a planning foundation you can focus on meaning and enjoyment in life.

To point out the differences between the foundational, stability, and strategic stages, let's think about building a house. In the foundational stage you get blueprints for the house, order the materials, set a budget, goal, timelines, and find the right builders to get the project done. Then you break ground and get started laying the foundation. Once you get into stability, you are putting up walls and a roof. You are making it a place that can provide stability. Then as you enter into the strategic phase, you can start thinking about flooring, paint, windows, kitchen appliances, and the things that will add to your enjoyment.

As people are entering the strategic phase of life, they're often saving for retirement, getting ready for retirement, or actually living in retirement. At this point, retirement income planning is more important, not just how much you have saved but how you'll spend it. This is where you can really focus on getting to financial freedom and aligning goals and timelines with aspirations.

During this stage you figure out where you are with your net worth and cash flow, and identify and address any holes you have. This is also the time to get strategic with your tax planning and other things, like what car to buy, which home to purchase, and whether you should have a health savings account.

You will want to beef up your insurance coverage. For example, when my wife and I purchased a home, we increased our life insurance coverage. We did it again after each of our children was born. Your coverage needs to change over time and you want to ensure you're not leaving your family without adequate resources should something happen to you. This also might mean doing a 1035 exchange of an existing policy to a new policy, in a tax-efficient manner. You might also consider setting up an irrevocable life insurance trust (ILIT) or transfering a life insurance policy, or funding up a permenant policy to create some diversification or spending flexibility in the future.

With retirement accounts, you might start to max out your accounts. This is really what strategic is all about, getting the most out of your opportunities. This means taking advantage of as many employer benefits as possible, tax optimizing year on year and looking into the future to reduce the lifetime amount of taxes you will have to pay. This also means building up your investments outside of just your retirement accounts.

It's now appropriate to hire a team of professionals so you can have a solid plan. This team should include an estate planning attorney to draft a will and basic documents, your financial advisor for financial planning, and maybe even a certified public accountant (CPA) to help with your taxes. But if you can't hire this dream team, you should at least grow your cash reserves to equal three months of your salary. Save approximately 10–15% of your income while focusing on tax diversification.

Strategic planning is much further along on the financial spectrum.

It means you have built the foundation, accumulated some wealth, and now can start being strategic about tactics, investments, tax planning, and the future. The focus becomes about maximizing retirement savings and switching from the accumulation period to the decumulation, or spending, period in retirement. As retirement is an entire shift in one's life, goal planning and aspirations likely need to be reviewed. Decisions about where to live, how to spend down retirement savings, and tax efficiency become paramount.

Another example of someone in the strategic planning phase is a person who came into wealth earlier in life. This could be a business owner, a successful professional, or someone who inherited money. This wealth could shift the person's life goals away from the daily grind of their current work toward a second, more passion-driven, career. It could also be a business owner who wants to shift their focus from running the firm to the next generation of leaders.

While it's not exactly the most comfortable topic, you start to focus on the challenges of aging in this stage—including thinking through what you might do in the event of your own incapacity. Will you need long-term care insurance to help pay for your care? Are you relying on family help? Also, what do you want your end-of-life care to look like? You'll want to dive into these topics with your family. This is where family meetings come into play. You can discuss these things with your family while also talking about your values, finances, and legacy, and if you own your own business, what planning for that looks like. Communication with family is key to leaving the legacy you want.

Strategic decisions around money, wealth, and passions need to be organized to get the most out of this stage.

Impact

Here, you can focus on an enjoyable life. Having foundational and strategic financial concepts covered, you can move to impact. The impact phase of life is very different. You now have time to reflect back on life. Stories become more important than numbers and data. How things make you feel and how they impact others become paramount to your decision making. At this point, you can reflect back on your path and your accomplishments, and start thinking about legacy. How do you want to leave the world? What do you want to leave for the world?

Impact can be an important part of everyone's life. It is not reserved for just the wealthy, rich, or retired. This is not always what people expect. A young person who built a business or inherited money can be in the impact stage. They could end up donating wealth or time back to charity, driving change and impact in their community. Giving back through charity, philanthropy, or social initiatives can be part of every life stage. I think this is important to instill in children at an early age. Every year before New Year we have our children pick a charity they want to support. This gets them into a mindset of giving back and caring about the impact that they can make in the world. It's amazing how these gifts stay with them all year. They tell their friends at school and our other family members—some of whom have even adopted the same tradition! Giving is contagious. When others witness giving, they want to give too.

This stage aligns with the self-actualization step in the hierarchy that focuses on values, reflection, and transition. Examples of people in the impact stage could be a successful business owner who wants to transition her business to her children, a retiree couple thinking about how to make a transformative gift to their local food bank, or even a young woman who inherits wealth from a grandmother and wants to take on a social issue in her community. All these people have an impact in mind. But they need to know their finances are in order and think about how their values and aspirations will be impacted by their financial decisions. This is both an introspective period in life and one to impact the rest of the world.

At this point, the dollars and numbers become a bit less important. You likely have achieved some level of financial security, and you could be retired or still working, but saving another dollar is no longer what keeps you up at night. Instead, you start thinking through legacy, impact, and philanthropic opportunities. Quality of life becomes paramount.

I mentioned my friend Tyrone Ross earlier. In addition to "Educate before you allocate," he's also known for saying, "Legacy is greater than resume." If your legacy includes charitable giving, the stability stage is

Sequence of Financial Decisions

Stage 1 - Foundational	Stage 2 - Stability	Stage - 3 Strategic	Stage 4 - Impact
Understand - Income, Cash Flow, Expenses, Debt	Understand - Net Worth, Cash Flow	Track Progress - Net Worth, Cash Management	Track Progress - Net Worth, Cash Management
Determine The Objective	Deductibles Covered - Vehicles, Home, Health	6 Month Cash Reserve + Upcoming Opportunities	Legacy Planning and Desires
Save $1,000	Obtain Needed Insurances - Disability, Life	Review Insurance Needs	Wealth Transfer Timing and Methods
Minimum Insurance - Health, Disability, Life	Employer Match + Free Money - 401(k), H.S.A.	Employer Match + Free Money - 401(k), H.S.A.	Alternative Investments
Employer Match + Free Money - 401(k), H.S.A.	Pay Off High-interest Debt	Pay Off High-interest Debt	Business Succession
Pay Off High-interest Debt	3 Month Cash Reserve + Near-term Expenses	25% Savings Goal - H.S.A., Roth, Employer Plan	Risk Management
Emergency Fund	Save 15% Gross Income - H.S.A., Roth, Employer Plan	Maximize Deduction Planning	Fiduciary Selection
Maximize Retirement Savings		Supplemental Tax-preferred Savings	Family Meetings

when you want to start mapping out your charitable giving and goals. The impact stage is where you start implementing that legacy.

The path to financial freedom

As we've shown here, there are many ways to describe the path to financial freedom. Some people find it easier to look at the planning process from "simplify and organize" to "confidence and control" to "social belonging and flexibility" to "self-actualization." For others, looking at planning across decades and ages can be beneficial to create a mental picture of what might happen at different times in life. For others, the ages and planning phases are less important than identifying what life stage you are in today. You could be in your 40s and in the impact stage if you started working young, were very successful, or found your financial balance early. All three of these categorizations can be used in conjunction to help guide you on your journey to financial freedom.

Planning will undoubtedly change for you over time. While any financial plan needs to take into account the certainty of today, it must also provide enough flexibility for the uncertainty of tomorrow. To wrap up this chapter, here are a few questions and takeaways that I have found useful as they relate to better understanding where you are in the planning spectrum:

Five key takeaways

1 Financial planning changes across one's life stages and ages.

2 Legacy often becomes more important than the dollars and cents of financial planning later in life.

3 An influx of wealth can quickly change the planning needs and complexity you are in.

4 Letting debt and spending get out of hand can keep you in the fundamental planning stage for decades.

5 The shift from accumulation to decumulation requires very strategic decisions for most retirees.

Five reflection questions

1 What phase of planning would most likely describe your current situation: foundational, stability, strategic, or impact?

2 What is the impact you would like to be remembered for or have?

3 Have you done a retirement income projection before and determined how much income you would need in retirement?

4 How many and who is part of your financial planning team today? What gaps might exist?

5 What is a life event you can see in the next five to ten years that would change your planning significantly?

Notes

8

Bucketing—A Commonsense Approach To Planning

<blockquote>
❝ Many drops make a bucket, many buckets make a pond, many ponds make a lake, and many lakes make an ocean. ❞

—*Percy Ross, business owner and philanthropist*
</blockquote>

Financial Freedom Framework

Bucketing is an approach to financial planning that helps us think about our wealth in "buckets" to visualize our retirement and give us a story for why we have each asset. We generally fund three buckets: one for today, one for tomorrow, and one for the future.

SMALL THINGS CAN become big things, which can move mountains. I love quotes, data, information—anything that shows how small actions can create powerful change. To some degree, this is also an instance of the butterfly effect—how a butterfly can flap its wings and create a storm elsewhere in the world. The whole idea of the butterfly effect is that a small, localized change in a complex system can have considerable effects elsewhere.

Small changes in how you approach financial planning can result in immense system-wide impacts elsewhere in your life. They can be the difference between a secure retirement, where you're not anxious about money, and a sleepless retirement, always wondering if you'll run out of money.

Small changes also need to occur over time to keep us on track. I often compare financial planning to trying to hit a moving target in the wind. The target is your goals and aspirations, or what you want to spend and accomplish with your finances. The target's moving because you don't know how long you will live, how long you will work, or when certain things will happen in life. For example, your retirement could last five years or 40. Some people never retire. Then there's *wind*, because things will change along the way. Your goals, timelines, laws, and public policy will change. We will also see changes and challenges we didn't predict, like those encountered in 2020 and 2021.

We can plan for uncertainty in the same way NASA sends astronauts to the moon: it takes a team, a plan, preparation, and adjustments—not to mention countless calculations. Like astronauts in space, we can't expect to reach our end target by going in a straight line. Instead, we need to have a plan to address the risks along the way and the ability to change course as our trajectory changes.

Now how do we do this in practice? While there are many different philosophies out there when it comes to investing and financial planning, I tend to gravitate to the bucketing approach.

Why bucketing?

Most of us have a jar of cash for something, whether it's for Friday night pizza or savings for an upcoming event. Keeping jars of cash for certain things exemplifies our natural tendency to put money into categories. A concept called *bucketing* takes advantage of that natural tendency.

Bucketing is an approach to financial planning that helps us think about our wealth in buckets to visualize our retirement and give us a story for why we have each asset. We generally think of three buckets: today, tomorrow, and the future. We can also further categorize these buckets as needs, wants and wishes, respectively.

That jar of cash for pizza is a form of mental accounting. Bucketing is just a higher-level mental accounting approach.

First coined in 1999 by Nobel Prize-winning economist Richard H. Thaler, mental accounting is how we organize and keep track of our financial activities. In mental accounting, we assign the money we have coming in and the money we have going out to different mental accounts.[1]

Money is fungible, and while we shouldn't care which dollar goes to what expense, we do. The way we categorize our money into these mental accounts could prevent us from moving money between them, even though they only exist in our minds. This could hinder our decision-making abilities and create inconsistent outcomes.

But bucketing can help curb those inconsistent outcomes. Bucketing has several benefits: it helps minimize the behavioral risk that we will sell out of the market when it dips; it's comforting because we don't have to worry about near-term volatility; it's easy to explain and implement; and it identifies why each investment is held, its timeframe and how and when it will be used.

Bucketing does three things differently than other types of planning. First, it sets out time horizons for your spending needs. Second, it aligns your investments with how you mentally account for money naturally. Third, it provides a systematic way to make adjustments to your plan over time.

Bucketing is what it sounds like. It separates out your goals and finances into buckets by time horizon. Under the strategy, your planning time horizon is defined by three or more distinct time periods (or "buckets"):

1. Today (perhaps one to three years),
2. Tomorrow (the next three to ten years depending on bucket one), and
3. Future (the remaining years and often at ten years or more).

Thinking about our wealth in buckets helps us to visualize and organize our finances. While the years above are helpful guides, the actual amount of money and years of income covered in your buckets will depend on your needs, goals, and financial situation. It also helps us align our investments to our goals, objectives, and aspirations. Here is a deeper dive into each of the buckets.

Deeper dive into bucket one: our needs today

Bucketing investments helps in a few ways. Our "now" bucket is for the short term—today or this year. When we look out at our spending, we're often looking at the near-term horizon of this year and next. We need to know that our needs are met and this bucket has the money we may need soon. We have to be able to pay our bills and get by. These expenses represent our needs—what we must have to live our life. If we don't meet our needs, we could get off track and not be as financially secure.

Even though this bucket is about needs, you can still spend money on discretionary items this year or next, but those discretionary items should be factored into spending from this bucket. These items could be cut or pushed off if you needed them to be, and if they can't be, they're likely needs. You can also have a need for next year that includes a vacation. Yes, it's technically a discretionary expense, but for next year it is a need to plan for and fund. There's a bit of an art to setting these categories, and they're not set in stone. That's part of the beauty of the bucketing approach—it's tailored to your needs, goals, and desires.

The bucket is designed to meet the expenses you know you'll need. If you're more likely to be alive for the next five years than you are to be alive in 40 years, you want to make sure you have funds for now, versus funds for 40 years from now. When you think about this time horizon, where do you want this income to come from? It likely should be an investment that's more secure and stable.

Bucket one is by design more conservative. It can house investments that align with your goals, needs, and short-term objectives, which will also change the makeup of the bucket over time. You likely rely mostly on your earned income and maybe a cash emergency fund when in the foundational phase of building wealth, versus someone who is in retirement—or in the impact phase—who might rely more on bonds, Social Security, pensions, and other income sources to meet their needs.

The now bucket is where you have safer, more secure assets with less volatility, which could include cash and certificates of deposit (CDs). The assets in this bucket are usually kept in a bank and there is little to no growth in them. As you are working, you can consider your income from your paycheck here. When you retire, you need to think about what income is replacing your paycheck. As such, buckets will modify based on people, goals, objectives, aspirations, and the planning phase they are in.

Let's do a quick exercise around bucket one.

Let's list out the item and dollar amounts you might project as your needed expenses for the next three years, which can include both planned and potential emergency expenses. Start with one year and then multiply it by three. Then consider how much of this you want to come from a secure and safe place.

Annual expenses you think of as needs

	Expense	Cost in $
1		
2		

3		
4		
5		
6		
7		
8		
9		
10		
Total costs		
Multiply by 3		

Annual safe income sources (income from work, annuities, pensions)

	Income	Value in $
1		
2		
3		
4		
5		
6		
7		
8		
9		
10		
Total income		
Multiply by 3		

Do you have a shortfall when you compare the two?

What major life event might change your income or expenses?

What type of emergency fund might you feel comfortable holding in cash to meet expenses if your income sources were to dry up?

Once you get a good grasp of bucket one, you can start to focus on the next buckets. But like we talked about before, it's about taking care of the foundation first. If you don't have a strong foundation, emergency fund, and safe income to meet expenses, you could find yourself in debt and without the ability to meet your near-term expenses and needs quickly.

The length of time represented by bucket one can vary because it depends on the person and their phase in life. A good rule of thumb is that this bucket can account for anywhere from one to five years. After five years, we're really heading into bucket two. But, for some retirees, this bucket gets larger than just the five-year range, and for some younger people, this second bucket is mostly filled by bond and fixed-income investments, with little else, and could be relatively small as their investment time horizon is long. A young investor might have a lot of money in bucket one, as they have cash set aside for emergencies and their monthly expenses, a little bit in bucket two, and most of their investments in bucket three. As such, the make up of your buckets varies over time. For a young investor, their paycheck meets their needs and they have longer-term investment objectives, so they are heavily weighted into bucket three. But, for someone in a mid- to late retirement stage, they might have more money in buckets one and two than in bucket three.

Deeper dive into bucket two:
our wants tomorrow

Bucket two takes a slightly different approach than bucket one. It's a little longer of a time horizon, so it allows us to take a bit more risk with our investment and income approach. These assets can be in the market, and can have some illiquidity. They are there to serve future wants and needs. However, if we have a want today, like purchasing a car, and we want to have the money to do that in five years, in five years that want will become a need. Then we'll have to put that car money from bucket two into bucket one. We have to understand that interplay when designing bucket two.

This also means there's no investment that always shows up in bucket two. The investments in these buckets are dependent on your individual situation. It's truly personalized planning. However, bucket two could include your mixed investments, fixed-indexed annuities, bonds, and CD ladders. The goal is to generate some income and return over the stated time horizon because we know these future wants won't be needs for another three to five years. We know our near-term and today expenses are covered. For some people, knowing that the next three to five years of needs are funded allows them to feel comfortable taking more risk in buckets two and three. For some people, this bucket could be for the first phase of retirement and is accessible when they need it. This bucket should be invested for conservative growth and help offset inflation.

For younger people, the "wants" bucket could be pretty close. It could be they want a nice car in a few years, but that want will become a need in two or so years. So should they save and invest toward that goal? How does that fit into their overall plan and impact their long-term goals and aspirations?

The most challenging part of bucket two is not designing it, but rather deciding how and when to refill bucket one. My approach is more like the NASA approach. Yes, you want guidelines, but you need to adjust over time. If your needs come faster than you expected, you might need to refill bucket one faster. If your needs get pushed out or your investments underperform expectations, can you push out wants further and stick to your needs? The plan is important, but so is the willingness to be flexible. For each person this comes down to their goals. Some are less willing to have flexibility, so this might limit the investment options in bucket two as volatility—even in three to five year ranges—cannot be as easily tolerated.

Deeper dive into bucket three: our wishes for the future

Bucket three is tied to our aspirations and long-term goals. Honestly, if you didn't do the work yet on your life's aspirations and what you want long-term, it's hard to develop a long-term investment and financial plan. This is why spending all that time defining values and aspirations is so important.

In bucket three we can start to dream. We can look at what we want our lives to be in the future, what we need to financially craft that vision, then start to align our value-driven investments and planning to the task.

Because bucket three is typically designed more for long-term wishes and goals, it's almost always more than five years away, typically more than ten years. This bucket is the one that's generally used for your last phase of retirement. This allows you to take more investment opportunities. This is where you can go heavily into long-term investment strategies—stocks, exchange-traded funds (ETFs), mutual funds, real estate funds, and other more illiquid investments. The safety here from an investment standpoint is that the U.S. stock market is more likely to provide a positive return to an investor in the long run than just over the next year. In essence, you have aligned the volatility and risk of the investment with the likelihood you'll need the expense (since it's more than ten years out) and the time horizon in which you will need it.

The other benefit of this approach is not having to worry about daily, monthly, or yearly volatility in the market now. If your long-term investments pull back next year, that's okay. You don't need to lose sleep about it because it's not the bucket you're using to meet your needs right now. This can help with what I like to call your return on sleep. Because you know you have a long investment time horizon, you can sleep better and not get as worried about the daily stock movements.

If you want bucket three to be more comprehensive, you can also look at other assets you own but might not be using any time soon. Your house, for example, could be a bucket three asset. It does help provide for a current need, but it also has equity that could be deployed at some point in the future. For many people, your home could be used for long-term care expenses, as a legacy asset, or even to supplement retirement income.

Another long-term asset could be business ownerships—your own business or businesses you've invested in. The liquidity of those businesses could be long-term investment assets in addition to the paycheck you bring home from them each year.

While most people think of this bucket as containing just the riskier or more volatile assets, it can also include those you want to hold for longer periods of time or those with less liquidity. For instance, a 30-year bond you plan to hold to maturity would fall into this category.

The length of time for this bucket will be dependent on your age, planning phase, and aspirations. The important thing about bucket three is to give these assets time to do what they are designed to do in your plan. This bucket is invested for long-term growth. As such, a 95-year-old might not have a lot left in bucket three besides legacy assets. That's beccause for some people, this is the bucket from which they'll leave their legacy money to heirs, spouses, charities, or institutions. But a 35-year-old might have a bucket three with a 60-year time horizon, filled with most of their investable assets.When you look at the bucket approach, it's important to understand why you own the investments you do. Certain assets are earmarked for certain time periods. The more secure assets are for more immediate needs and the more volatile assets for longer-term needs. In a lot of ways, the strategy plays on mental accounting concepts.

I often find the bucket approach to planning to be the most interesting approach because it helps define the "why?" of your plan. Bucketing strategies aren't plug-and-play, one-size-fits-all approaches. Many variations of the bucket strategy exist, but they generally follow a similar theme of time segmentation.

By segmenting your plan into distinct time horizons, you're also prioritizing the times you will need money. I like to describe the early retirement years or the prime activity years as the go-go years, the next timeframe as the slow-go years, and later in retirement as the no-go years. This tends to follow people's actual spending, travel and activity in retirement. While we are early in retirement, we might spend and travel more. As retirement moves on we might cut back a bit on travel and spending, until maybe we have a major health or long-term care event.

You also should prioritize spending a bit early in retirement as you have the highest chance of making it through your go-go years, and less of a chance of spending 25 to 30 years of retirement. As such, it's more important that you have funds available for the near term and more certain expenditures. Essentially, bucketing is a form of risk management.

The bucket approach provides a great way to tell the story of why you have the investments you have in your plan. However, it needs to be nimble over time to evolve and adjust to changes in laws, markets and goals. So, before you set out on a bucket approach, make sure you know how it will handle asset allocation and income generation over time.

It might all make sense to start, but will it last through the wind?

Five key takeaways

1 Small changes in your approach can have vast impacts on all areas of your life.

2 We don't know how long we'll live or work or when certain things will happen in our lives, so we have to plan for uncertainty.

3 The bucketing approach to financial planning allows us to visualize our retirement.

4 We have a natural tendency to put money into categories, and the bucketing approach takes advantage of that.

5 Buckets are categorized by time horizon (today, tomorrow, and the future) or by the time horizon of expenditures (needs, wants, and wishes).

Five reflection questions

1 What are some immediate things that you *need* to fund in the next few years?

2 What are some *wants* you'd like to fund in three to ten years?

3 What are some *wishes* you'd like to fund ten years or more out?

4 Have your goals, objectives, life aspirations, or planning phases changed recently?

5 What type of emergency fund might you feel comfortable holding in cash to meet expenses if your income sources were to dry up?

Notes

Part 2

Building on the Foundation

9

Be an Integral Part of Your Own Wealth Creation by Investing in Yourself

&&The most important investment you can make is in yourself. &&

—Warren Buffett

Financial Freedom Framework

Education has a strong connection to financial success, higher earnings, and the likelihood of being employed and avoiding unemployment. Investing in your education is an investment in your financially free future.

UNLESS YOU JUST plan to inherit money to live on forever, you need to be an integral part of your own wealth creation. That means all financial planning, wealth management, and paths to financial freedom start with you. The reality is that the single most valuable asset that most people have is themselves. As such, the key to building sustainable wealth over your life and achieving your financial goals is to invest in yourself.

So what does investing in yourself really mean? The answer is complex. Investing in yourself—not unlike financial investing—has two components. First, it has the growth component. This means you need to invest time, money, and energy in building up your human capital, or your ability to work and earn money. Second, just like with financial investing, you need to have an aspect of safety or preservation. This means making sure you protect your ability to earn over time. That could be through disability insurance, health insurance, or taking care of your mental health.

Let's start by looking at different ways you can invest in yourself to build and grow your personal wealth. Education has a striking correlation to higher income across the world. Worldwide, people have an average of just 7.8 years of schooling. Think about this in the context of research that shows that for each complete year of school attended, average income increases by 8.7%.[9] That's truly amazing!

There's some decline in return as schooling increases to, say, 18 years. However, even at 18 years of schooling, the average return is still at 6–7% per year. This shows that the demand for skills and higher education is still very high in the workforce over the long term.

Despite issues with the research—like it not accounting for many factors and data being hard to acquire—the connection is clear: getting more education helps increase wealth. Education appears to be even more important for women. World Bank data shows that, on average, women receive 1–2% higher return per year of additional schooling compared to men.[10] But education is a powerful wealth generator for everyone.

When you dive into the U.S. data specifically, you see similar trends. The U.S. Bureau of Labor Statistics shows two main connections between higher education and wealth. First, those with higher levels of education are more likely to be employed and avoid unemployment. Those with less than a high school diploma are almost four times as likely to be unemployed than those with a professional degree. Individuals with an associate's degree are almost twice as likely to be unemployed as someone with a professional degree. See a full breakdown in the following chart.

Earnings and unemployment rates by education attainment, 2021

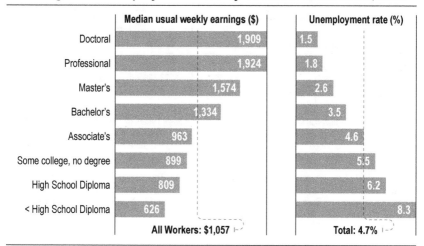

Note: Data are from persons age 25 and over. Earnings are for full-time wage and salary workers.
Source: U.S. Bureau of Labor Statistics, Current Population Survey

The chart also shows how much income rises with education. Those with a professional or doctoral degree earn more than three times as much per week as those without a high school diploma, and more than double what someone with an associate's degree earns.

Another way to understand how investing in yourself leads to wealth is to look at financial outcomes based on education. Research from the St. Louis Fed shows that those with an advanced degree earn a median income of $116,265, versus a median income of $76,293 for someone with a two- or four-year college degree.

Take that one step further and you see that their median wealth also changes substantially. For instance, those with a two- or four-year degree have a median wealth of $273,488, while those with an advanced degree have a median wealth of $689,100. The wealth-to-income ratio of a college-degree earner is about 3.45, but the wealth-to-income ratio of someone with an advanced degree is 5.58. Lastly, those who have advanced degrees are most likely to become millionaires, with 1 in 2.6 odds; whereas those with a college degree are about half, with 1 in 4.6, and those with a high school diploma at roughly 1 in 18.

Family Financial Outcomes Based on Education

Education*	Percentage of families	Median income (2013)	Median wealth (2013)	Wealth-to-income ratio**	Millionaires (family wealth)
No high school diploma	12%	$22,320	$37,766	1.43	1 in 110
High school diploma	50%	$41,190	$95,072	2.15	1 in 18
Two or four-year degree	25%	$76,293	$273,488	3.45	1 in 4.6
Advanced degree	13%	$116,265	$689,100	5.58	1 in 2.6

Note: Based on the education level of a family headed by someone 40 years of age or older. ** This ratio shows how much wealth each group has per dollar of income. For example, the ratio for families without a high school degree was 1.43, which means that, on average, for every $1 of income there was $1.43 of wealth. The ratio is a measure of how efficient people are at turning income into wealth.

Source: Boshara Ray; Emmons, William R. and Noeth, Bryan. "The Demographics of Wealth: How Age, Education and Race Separate Thrivers from Strugglers in Today's Economy. "Essay No. 2: Education and Wealth, Federal Reserve Bank of St. Louis, May 2015, pp. 4, 5, 9, and 13; https://www.stlouisfed.org/~/media/-Files/PDFs/HFS/essays-2-2015-Education-and-Wealth.pdf

These numbers show us that the more education you have, the more likely you are to remain employed, earn more income, and grow your wealth and savings.

Traditional education isn't the only way to invest in yourself. Trade associations and skilled labor education can also improve your financial situation. Designations and specific niche area training can be extremely valuable. For instance, in the financial planning world, those who have the Certified Financial Planner (CFP®), Chartered Life Underwriter (CLU®), or Chartered Financial Consultant (ChFC®) designations or similar have been shown to have increased earnings and success. So if your profession has designations and continuing education, you could increase your earnings.[11]

Education doesn't need to come from a traditional college system. You can learn by researching, reading, or taking free online classes. One area that I recommend you learn more about is finances and investing. If you're reading this book, you're off to a good start. Becoming more financially literate can also help to increase the possibility of having a successful financial future. Research published in the *Journal of Financial Planning* shows a strong connection between retirement income literacy and retirement satisfaction and preparedness.[12] The more knowledgeable someone becomes around finances, the more likely it is they feel prepared for retirement. Furthermore, research found that the more people engaged in planning, the more confident they felt about their own retirement.[13]

Investing in yourself outside of education

Investing in yourself is like investing anywhere else—at some point it could be a bad investment. You need not overdo education because you could risk taking out too much debt, falling behind and never catching up. Also, like with investing, you can diversify your investment in yourself. Let's look at a few other ways to invest back in yourself.

Invest in experiences

When we talk about financial freedom, we mean more than just money. Research from San Francisco State University found that people who spend money on experiences instead of material items are happier with their spending decisions.[14] This makes sense—when you spend money on travel and other experiences, you get to keep something for the rest of your life. It can help mold you and add to your perspective on the world. This added perspective can help you with your decision making and in some cases, even help you overcome biases or become a better worker.

I've always pushed the benefits of taking vacations, to take time away from work and focus on yourself. You need vacations to stay motivated and focused. Just like machines need time off to cool down and recharge, so do the human body, mind, and soul. Take time to recharge yourself by investing back into your future through experiences, travel, and vacations.

Hire a coach

Think about the best athletes of all time. Michael Jordan, Serena Williams, and Michael Phelps might come to mind. All three of these athletes achieved a high level of success in and outside of their sport. But they didn't do it alone. All three had coaches—really good coaches. In fact, all of them had multiple coaches over the years to help them focus and hold them accountable. Consider hiring a coach or finding a mentor to help keep you focused. I believe that mentors and coaches are very different and serve different roles. What they do at a fundamental level is hold you accountable, balance some of your emotional biases, and keep you focused.

Read

Time is the most valuable and scarce resource for most successful people. A Harvard study showing what it took to be a successful CEO tracked what CEOs did per week. They tended to delegate and work long hours, including at the weekend. But the one thing that most CEOs and other financially successful people found time to do was read. Tom Corley found, in his book *Change Your Habits, Change Your Life*, that 88% of financially successful people read at least 30 minutes per day.[15]

Bill Gates has said that the main way he learns new things is through reading. Warren Buffett says reading is how he gains knowledge. Elon Musk says reading is what taught him how to build rockets.

Why do so many successful people read? Knowledge, for one. Also, reading helps you solve problems you'll face in life. The reality is almost every personal and business issue that you will run into has been met by someone else, who then wrote a book about it. Reading teaches us how to succeed and overcome obstacles by learning from others.

Invest in yourself because you are key to your future financial wealth. Education, experiences, coaches, and reading can all help you build your income, diversify your skill set, and increase your knowledge, which will in turn give you a better chance to build your wealth and achieve financial freedom.

Checklist:

- How many books have you read in the past year?
- What books will you commit to reading this year?
- What are you doing to further your education?
- When was the last time you invested in an experience to build your career?
- When was the last time you went on a vacation to recharge?
- When is your next vacation and how will it add to your life experiences?

- Have you reinvested back into your professional skill set this past year?
- Are there professional education courses, continuing education, or seminars you could attend?
- What would be the best thing you could do to improve your professional marketability?
- Do you have a coach?
  If yes, what could you do better with your coach?
  If no, why don't you have a coach?
- Do you have a professional mentor?
- If you don't have a mentor, write down the names of three people in your life you'd like to have as a mentor.

Now reach out and get a mentor, take a new class, and invest back in yourself!

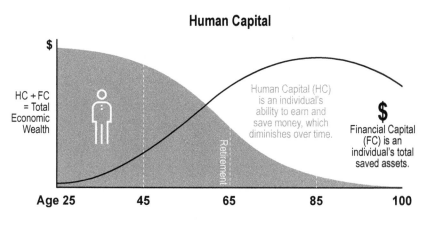

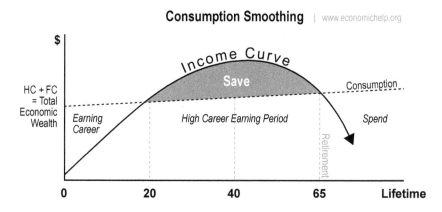

Five key takeaways

1 Education has a strong connection to financial success, higher earnings, and the likelihood of being employed and avoiding unemployment.

2 Investing in your education is an investment in your financially free future.

3 The demand for skills and higher education is still very high in the workforce.

4 The single most valuable asset that most people have is themselves.

5 Investing in yourself has two components—the growth component and the safety or preservation component.

Five reflection questions

1 What does investing in yourself mean to you?

2 How are you currently investing in yourself?

3 Have you pursued additional designations, certifications, and continuing education in your profession?

4 What are some experiences you've invested in that have developed you as a person? What are some experiences you want to invest in that you haven't yet?

5 How are you taking time to recharge?

Notes

10

Get SMART About Your Income

Financial Freedom Framework

There are many sources of income—our human capital or ability to work, our savings, our investments, and passive income. But there are five elements to getting SMART about your income: sustainability, maximizing, automation, reinvestment, and tax-efficiency.

LET'S TALK ABOUT your income. This is such an important conversation because it's usually the first number we're going to input in the financial model, whether it's a business plan, a personal financial plan, or a retirement plan.

Income isn't only the input in life, it's often the output—we get up, we go to work and the output we get back in return is our paycheck. We go to work for our income. But really smart, financially free people put their money to work for them and get their income from that.

There are many sources of income—our human capital or ability to work, our savings, our investments and dividends from them, and eventually our passive income if we can get to that point.

Here's an important reframing question: would you be happy if I could give you the highest income in the world? That's a nuanced question, because what if with that came the highest expenses in the world? It's possible your income and expenses cancel each other out and your life gets no better.

Now think of all the different options out there for generating income: market returns, dividends, income from rental properties, real estate investment trusts (REITS), lending, blogs, advertising, and side hustles. There are countless ways to get income, but it's not just how much you get paid, it's how you get that income. For example, if you think about equity versus your paycheck, they are very different things. Perhaps the dollar amount on the front end looks the same, but on the back end, the amount of disposable, usable, spendable income can vary tremendously because of taxes.

So, we often have to get SMART about our income. SMART income amounts to five things:

- Can we make our income **sustainable**? If you do something that generates a great deal of income today but it's not sustainable, it's not a great plan for income.
- Can we **maximize** our income?
- How do we **automate** the process over time so the income keeps coming?
- How do we **reinvest** the income that we get to generate more income?
- How can we be **tax-efficient**? You can have all the income in the world, but that doesn't matter if you pay 100% in taxes.

Let's dive deeper into each of these areas of SMART income.

Sustainable

If you look at the business world, you'll see companies with sustainable income often get higher valuations on the market. This means that people inherently look at sustainable income as a more valuable resource that makes for a more valuable business than volatile income. Sustainable income jobs are professions like teachers, as opposed to sales, for example. While volatile income can come with upside, we need to make sure that we have sustainable income throughout our lives because income ensures we'll be able to meet our spending needs.

We also have to look at where that sustainable income is coming from. Is that income coming from our work? Our investments? Our side hustles? In the last chapter, we talked about investing back into yourself so your human capital is as high as possible to generate a sustainable living from your work. But eventually we need to save money and put those savings to work for us, which can generate income later in life when we're unable to work, which for most people is in retirement.

One place we generate sustainable income is from buying into a business. Say, for example, we buy into a car wash, lawn mowing business, or distributor of wine and beer. Maybe we take a passive role in the company, or maybe we take a more active role as a manager, investor, and leader. All of this is geared toward generating some income or return so we can meet our spending needs and grow our wealth.

The downside of not having sustainable income is having to figure out how to meet our expenditures if our income disappears for a year. Asking ourselves whether we'll have a job next year is a basic question to explore, and if the answer is no, we'll have to figure out how to cover the costs we want to cover. We'll also have to figure out how to grow our wealth if we can't save because we don't have income coming in. This is the reason that we need to think about incorporating sustainable income—especially throughout the course of our working career.

We could also generate income from investable products. We put money into dividend-paying stocks and we expect the company to pay us back from their earnings for essentially putting our capital

Get SMART About Your Income

to work for them. They pay us back in dividends and over time this generates income. We could buy CDs and bonds, I bonds, and TIPS, some of which will adjust for inflation and mature at different rates or pay dividends along the way to generate income. Those are very secure types of income. Some of the challenges here include figuring out the rate of return relative to the opportunity cost of investing in the market, or identifying the opportunity or risk of inflation and whether it erodes the purchasing power of that income over time.

We can also look at insurance products. Life insurance and annuities can provide you with income and cash flow at different periods in time. While these aren't earned or taxable income, they're still income. Life insurance death benefits can be viewed as income for the surviving spouse when the insured passes away. We'll look at how to protect income over time later in the book.

We can also generate income from real estate, which has been a valuable source for many years. The reason being is its growth potential—the ability to use and maximize the land (build businesses, farm it, extract resources like minerals, trees, crops), and its income-generating potential—the ability to make money by renting it out.

Maximizing

Maximizing our income makes sense because we don't want to *reduce* our income, we want to maximize it. We don't think of maximizing income in just this year. When we're trying to increase our income, we're thinking about doing so over the course of our life over the long term, maybe even for future generations if we want to create income for our children or grandchildren.

It's important not to fall into the trap of going after the fast dollar. Instead we should think about whether to take half a dollar today, another half dollar next year, and another half dollar the year after that. Think of a forest from which you want to extract resources. This might mean cutting down trees, but you don't want to cut down all the trees because they won't grow back. Instead, we want to be strategic. We want to cut down what we need, but not so many that we destroy the ecosystem and it can't recover. The same thing is true for income. We can push and push and push—maybe you can work

129

24–7 for a year, two years, or three years—but you'll burn yourself out. You'll be unable to progress in your career. If you don't take care of yourself by taking time off, you might burn bridges, lose friendships, or leave your company, and your income will suffer.

Maximizing income isn't just about how much we get paid, it's also about when and how we get paid. There are entire books written that look at executive-based compensation and determine that many times, the best way to maximize our income is actually to push it off into the future. One way to maximize income is not to take all of our income today, but use tax-deferred strategies. This might be as simple as deferring some of next year's income into the future—which we often call non-qualified deferred compensation plans. This isn't available for everybody in every part of their career, but if it does become available, you should look into it. But you need to understand the tax ramifications and the risks, then compare those to the benefits of pushing income off into the future. Typically what you're gaining by pushing income off into the future is not having to pay taxes on all of it today. You essentially get an increase in that income because the company doesn't have to make the cash flow payment today.

One of the risks with this strategy is that these are unsecured amounts and if the company were to go out of business, you wouldn't have the income. That's a real possibility. There are some planning options you can do to mitigate that risk, but it still remains a risk.

Let's think about how we receive income and the form of compensation we're getting.

Are we asking for everything in cash or are we asking for executive benefits, company benefits, or increased services at work? Are we thinking about those perks—gym memberships, health care, day care, tuition reimbursement, increased 401(k) contributions, and HSAs? All of these are different ways to ask for more income and have more wealth being returned to us in a more efficient way.

Also think about equity. Beyonce famously sang, "Pay me in equity." Should you, too, ask for equity rather than ordinary income? Your equity-based compensation and long-term capital gains, if you are able to get them, are going to cost you less in taxes than ordinary working income. So in essence, you're maximizing your after-tax income. This becomes important in retirement, when you're identifying which accounts you need to pull income from and when you're considering what you should sell or keep; and whether you should invest in Roth accounts (for tax-free income in retirement) or traditional IRAs, and 401(k) accounts (for tax-deferred and taxable income in retirement).

Maximizing income across the board is about where it's coming from, in what form, when, and from which accounts and assets each year. Sometimes it's different in different years.

Automating

Put your income on autopilot so it increases every year. The first way you can do this is to ensure that you're negotiating the highest rates when you take a new job and that in your annual reviews you're bringing up your income and constantly renegotiating it to make sure you're not leaving money on the table. Build that into your processes and systems at work so it's not a one-off conversation. Ensure your income is adjusting for inflation and that you're being paid appropriately for your education and experience.

When it comes to retirement income, automate distributions from your retirement accounts, pensions, annuities, and life insurance policies to create that sustainable income throughout the course of your retirement. If you don't automate it, you might find yourself getting frustrated and spending mental energy and time on managing this income, and you're getting away from the benefit of income.

If that sustainable income you created includes assets like rental property, explore ways to automate the processes so you can scale and be more efficient with your income. If you spend all your time trying to deal with income and income-producing assets, you don't enjoy them. Many people get into the rental property world and try to manage the properties themselves and find it frustrating, time-consuming, and difficult. Often people leave the real estate world because they struggle with that. Or they learn that they need a good property manager, which essentially automates the process for generating their income.

So explore the pieces of your income, like rental property or distributions for your retirement accounts, that can be automated in a more efficient way to improve your overall sense of your income.

Reinvesting

One of my favorite lines that relates to reinvesting income is: "Put your money to work for you." You get income, save it, invest it, then generate income from dividends from stocks. But instead of taking those dividends and spending them, you reinvest them back into that company or another company, which allows you to reinvest them again and again.

You can do this across different income-producing assets. When you think about when your rental properties start generating income, you can then pay down some of your debt and reinvest back into the property to improve it. Maybe you can even put that income towards a new purchase. Often you can refinance those properties and continue to keep your costs down while generating more income. This strategy is used all across the real estate world to grow wealth and reinvest the income over time.

Successful business owners are excellent at reinvesting income. They generate income from their business and then reinvest it to grow that business, because if they don't, their business often won't succeed. It's very hard to stay in a state of equilibrium—you're either growing or you're shrinking. If you're not reinvesting back into the business, innovating, getting more efficient, building better products, and growing sales, eventually the business ends up in trouble. This is the same for individuals—if we're not growing our income, saving, and reinvesting, we will eventually face a similar issue because we'll have inflation, expenses, and other issues creeping in. If we haven't reinvested our income to grow it, we're not putting our money back to work for us.

Tax-efficiency

Not enough people ask their employers critical questions like:

- Do I have the ability to get equity here?
- Do I have the ability to shift some of my potential ordinary income to the 401(k)?
- Is there a way to buy life insurance or long-term care insurance tax-efficiently inside a C corporation?

- Are there additional benefits that I could get that would be just as efficient for the company but more tax efficient for me, like paying for parking, travel, or food? Can you pay for gym memberships?

These are all tax-efficient ways to save the company money and save you money while providing you more value than a higher cash base. Tax efficiencies aren't just about whether you should save in a Roth or traditional IRA, but having conversations about how you're going to be generating income and from what sources, and whether you can avoid taxation on some of those because they're non-taxable transactions.

So absolutely ask your current company about equity. And when you're creating side businesses and buying into other companies, think about whether you're getting equity, which can be treated favorably from a tax standpoint. When you're thinking about dividend-paying assets, should you put them in retirement accounts so they get tax-deferred growth, so that when you do reinvest those monies back into the companies that are paying dividends, they continue to grow undiminished by annual taxes?

Understanding tax-efficient distribution is incredibly important when we get to retirement because our income fluctuates each year. Some years, we need to push income to the next year. Other years, we need to accelerate income. Sometimes, to get better tax treatment, we need to give money to charities or bunch together contributions to 529 plans. We might need to increase business expenses in one year to reduce taxable income so that we can end up with more income over a longer time period. We have to engage in tax planning—which is one of the most important things when it comes to income planning. We have to look out over a five- to ten-year period to understand what expenses, what contributions, what money we should be leveraging to create the most tax-efficient flow of income possible.

Later in the book we'll explore how bunching charitable contributions together can actually save you money and increase your income by taking advantage of tax-efficient strategies, like QCDs. These are a tax-efficient way to give income from your IRA to charities, which can increase your total after-tax income in a given year.

SMART income in different phases

SMART income can apply to any part of our lives and across our foundational planning phase, stability phase, strategic phase, and impact phase.

Foundational

When we're in the foundational planning phase and we're starting to build our savings and our career, income creates the foundation of our financial picture. Income is what we're able to spend and reinvest. We're working to generate most of our income at this point while also figuring out where to put it. In this early-career stage, we want to put ourselves on a sustainable earning path so we can continue to increase our income over time. We try to create that sustainable income by building our career. We can then start building in the maximizing, automation, reinvesting and tax-efficiency in the other phases.

Stability

As we move into the stability phase, this is when we think about maximizing and automating. We explore the questions:

- How do I ask for better raises?
- How do I automate some of the income from my investments?

In this stage, you're able to nurture, develop, grow, and mold your income. In stability, you are established in your career, you know that you're good at what you do, you have some bargaining power, and you can see the longer-term view.

Strategic

The strategic phase is where we're reinvesting and renegotiating equity versus traditional compensation structures. We're buying into businesses and putting our money back into the equity markets. If we're getting dividends, we're buying more stocks and reinvesting. We're also paying attention to taxes because we know that retirement is coming up in the near future and we know that we might have high tax years. As such, we start engaging in strategic and proactive tax planning. In some tax years, we want to create lots of deductions, while in other years we might have lower taxes because we might not have as much income coming in. We are being more strategic about our taxes and our investments.

Impact

All of the SMART stages are in place in the impact phase. This is the phase where we're looking at how to make the income last the rest of our life. In this phase, we explore how to take all this income and use it to make an impact and leave a legacy for our children, community, and people we care about. Are we spending our income in a way that's creating enjoyment and financial freedom? Is the money moving us toward our goals and aspirations, or are we just generating income and buying meaningless things?

Where income goes is more important in the impact phase. This is when we start thinking about whether we should be transferring income to other people—our children, our grandchildren, and charities—while we're still alive. We are also considering whether to shift income-producing property to our heirs now.

In this phase, the other pieces still remain important. We still want to be tax-efficient and reinvest, but that might look different. We might now want to reinvest into our family, our community, and our church. And we want to automate as many of these processes as possible. We want to maximize our income and we want it to be sustainable for our retirement, and for our loved ones who come after us.

Income is almost always the first and last input of any financial planning equation. Income determines what we can spend and what we need to meet our goals and aspirations—to reach financial freedom.

Five key takeaways

1 There are five elements to getting SMART about your income: sustainability, maximizing, automation, reinvestment, and tax-efficiency.
2 Your income is usually the first number your financial advisor is going to input in the financial planning model.
3 But really smart, financially free people put their money to work for them and generate more income that way.
4 There are many sources of income—our human capital or ability to work, our savings, our investments and dividends from them, and eventually our passive income if we can get to that point.
5 Income isn't just about how much you get paid, it's also about how you get that income.

Five reflection questions

1 Where is your income coming from? Your work? Investments? Side hustles?
2 In what ways are you investing back into yourself to potentially generate additional income?

3 Do you have additional income sources that could sustain you if you lost your job today?

4 Are you asking your employer for more than just cash compensation? Are you asking for executive benefits, company benefits, or increased services at work?

5 What life phase are you in and how are you being SMART about your income?

Notes

11

The Power of Budgeting Across All Planning Stages

❝ Waiting for tomorrow's busy schedule to magically clear up so you can finally get around to creating a budget is probably not going to happen. ❞
—Ron Carson, CEO

Financial Freedom Framework

The point of budgeting is often to help us stay out of debt and make progress toward our financially free future. It helps us gain control of our spending and ensures we won't get off track. You can be as detailed as possible, or you can take a big-picture approach, but either way, you must make time to put together a budget.

THE WORD "BUDGE" makes me think of things that are stuck— they won't move. This makes me look at budgeting in two ways. The first way is negative—it feels like limitations, a negative version of control, and excessive attention to detail. But on the flip side, budgeting is the positive planning, tracking, observing, and prioritizing where your money is going. For some people, budgeting is agonizing because it comes from a place of limitations. For others, budgeting is freeing because it allows them to prioritize and understand where their money is coming from and where it's going. So we'll look at budgeting through both of those lenses.

The point of budgeting is often to help keep people out of debt and to help them make progress toward their financially free future by gaining control of their spending. The easiest way to describe a budget is as a spending plan for your money to ensure you won't get off track.

Budgeting starts by looking at your cash flow—what's coming in and going out. Then it makes assumptions about what you're going to spend in the future, putting some limitations in place to make sure that you don't overspend in one area and underspend in another. Budgeting will help you determine whether you have enough money to pay for bills, taxes, and insurance, and enough money to invest in your future by saving, buying stocks and bonds, and putting money away for retirement.

Budgeting looks different across the different life stages.

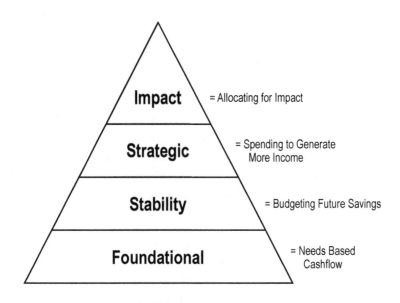

Foundational

Budgeting in the foundational stage can be very much about getting through the week, the month, and the year. Our budgeting timelines can be different based on the financial flexibility and freedom we have. If we live paycheck to paycheck, budgeting is likely playing an essential part of our life. We need to know the difference between $20 and $40 at a particular spend level. We need to understand what happens if we eat out too many times and spend too much money on entertainment. This could put other core aspects of our life, like our housing and our health care, at risk.

Stability

Budgeting in the stability phase becomes more about planning for the future, saving for retirement, and planning to pay for our kids' college education. In this stage, we can start doing things like shifting money from one expense to another and pre-paying high-interest debt. We can also consider refinancing and extending our mortgage to lower our debt payments and increase our cash flow for other needs.

Strategic

Budgeting in the strategic phase can include things like buying into other businesses, buying rental property, and increasing our travel expenditures to see countries and places we'd like to experience. It can also mean limiting our travel expenditures if we need to.

Impact

Budgeting in the impact stage is less about the daily, weekly, and monthly budgets and more about the allocation of wealth for impact. We consider how we're budgeting our resources and time toward things we want to do to leave a legacy. Time is among our most valuable resources, so in this stage, budgeting isn't just about dollars coming in and going out, we can also budget the time that we're going to spend.

I engage in a weekly exercise we at Carson Group call the "Six Most," where we write down the six most important things we want to accomplish that week. You can also do this daily and annually. In essence, it's a form of budgeting because I'm prioritizing my time and how I want to spend it. Just as we can prioritize our income through SMART income planning, we can prioritize our time.

I believe that as we move through our lives and move from the need to understand where our daily money is coming from—can we pay for gas or for dinner today?—to looking at monthly budgeting, annual budgeting, and lifetime budgeting, we're able to get more freedom and to start shifting our budgeting from dollars in and dollars out to budgeting for impact and time spent. Budgeting is not just about money, it is also about time and energy. My favorite thing about budgeting is not the actual budget, but the process it forces us to go through in order to prioritize our spending. By taking time to look at our cash inflows and outflows we can determine if we are spending money in a way that is really beneficial to our life goals.

In the impact phase, budgeting shifts to how we spend our time and the impact of our resources. It's not just focusing on whether we spent an extra dollar this week, but also on the impact we had with our giving. What was the impact we had by spending money on traveling and being with family? We can now exercise more control over our "time budget." Say we want to spend 30% of our week with family members, 20% of our week reading and writing, and 10% of our week giving back. We can now actually design our week the way we want to live it. That is time budgeting, and it's incredibly valuable as we move through life and time becomes an increasingly precious resource.

Budgeting starts with goals

I told you at the beginning of this section that I find budgeting to be distressing. I don't enjoy tracking every single dollar. But I know that's important for some people because that process gives them a feeling of control. Budgeting that way helps them understand what they need to do to operate and live their life within a framework of income coming in and going out.

This is why companies engage in budgeting. Budgeting is a crucial part of the corporate and business world. We have budgets in place to allow us to make decisions within a framework and to make sure that we're profitable in the endeavors that we embark on.

A good business doesn't just write down a budget and say, "Hey everybody, go make decisions inside of this budget. Here's a million dollars, spend it however you want, just give us a list of what you're going to spend it on." Instead, businesses say, "What do we want to accomplish this year? What are our goals and objectives?" Then they go back and ask whether they have the money to go down those paths.

Budgeting starts with having goals in place because if we don't set proper goals and know where we're going, budgeting is wasted time. Budgeting has to serve a purpose. Our goals help us understand why we're budgeting and create a framework to make better, and hopefully freeing, financial decisions over time. Budgeting also helps keep us in check so we don't fall off track and let debt spiral out of control, and ensures we continue to save. It can become a manager for our behavior.

In the end, budgeting provides us a systematic way of reviewing our income against our expenses to allow us to set realistic targets so we can make proper decisions about our spending behavior to keep us inside of that framework.

Budgeting can also free some people to spend more. I've spent time with people who weren't spending because they didn't look at their full financial plan or know what money they had, so they didn't know if or how to spend it. As they went through the process, they learned that they weren't spending on areas they truly cared about even though they had plenty of income and savings and they could increase spending to enjoy life more. That's the real power of budgeting—creating freedom for us. But if budgeting becomes constraining and restrictive, it can actually cause bad outcomes, like creating a negative relationship with money.

Big-picture budgeting might be easier for many people than putting together an Excel spreadsheet to track every single expense. We should know generally what we're spending in a month or a year and what monthly and annual income is coming in. And we should generally know how we're saving. Looking at the bigger picture can still create a framework for budgeting while taking us away from the tedious process of tracking every cent, where it's going, what account it's in, and how much we're spending in every place. In many situations, that type of budgeting is a misuse of time that doesn't add value to our future financial situation.

The method you choose comes down to your individual preference. If you get a benefit from structured budgeting where you track everything, do that. If you haven't yet gotten control of your finances and you've never done budgeting, that's actually a good place to start to regain control. But if you're somebody who thinks that way is too difficult, you can just look at the big picture, so you don't feel bad about spending an extra $200 on dinner or buying a nice car. Those things don't have to eat away at you. Spending should be enjoyable, not painful.

Some budgeting rules of thumb

50–30–20 budgeting model

Many people out there use the classic 50–30–20 budgeting model. It's a rule of thumb model that doesn't work for everybody, but it's a

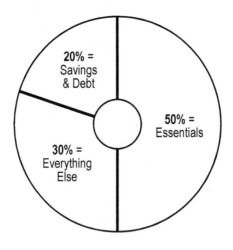

great place to start if you're in the foundational or stability phase. The rule states that you allocate 50% of your income to essential expenses, 20% to savings and debt repayment, and 30% to everything else. At a minimum, we need to be saving at least 10% (or more) of our income towards our retirement and future. We'd love that number to be as close to 20% as possible, but if you can't do that, start with 10% to help build that savings foundation.

70–80% replacement

As you reach the strategic and impact phases, budgeting might look different. In the strategic phase, you might be thinking about how to budget during retirement. You might start using the 70–80% of your income replacement method. Instead of worrying too much about what you're going to spend day in and day out in retirement, just think about what percentage of your income you need to replace. So if you're making $100,000 today, you're probably going to need 70% to 80% of that in retirement.

Why? Well, if we're saving 10–20% for retirement, that will stop when we get to retirement, so we can take that expenditure out of the budget. That gets us automatically to near $80,000 a year. Maybe we have some flexibility—we have a higher tax deduction for standardized filers, or certain income sources might not be taxed, like Roth IRA distributions—so we know that we can maintain the same quality of life we had pre-retirement with a rule like this.

Budgeting can be challenging. To make things easier, we've included many free resources in this book, like the simple one-page budgeting chart for you to track income, expenses, and a way to operate.

The power of budgeting

I had a friend who was living in New York City and was a really big fan of Starbucks food and coffee. Part of her daily routine was to go to Starbucks for breakfast and lunch. She didn't engage in budgeting or tracking her expenses, but at the end of the year, her credit card statement broke down her spending for her. Many of you reading this will have seen the chart that comes in your end-of-year credit card statement, showing your different categories of spending. My friend's credit card company essentially did the budgeting for her. When she saw the food and beverage category, she was shocked to find she'd spent almost $5,000 at Starbucks alone that year. She didn't think she spent that much money there, but when she thought about it, she was spending $15 a day for around 300 days. Until she saw it on the chart, she didn't realize it was impacting her finances as much as it was.

Thanks to her credit card company, my friend was able to visualize the total impact of her spending. It wasn't $5 here and there, it was the cumulative effect of spending $15 a day for almost a year. That allowed her to recognize that she was overspending and helped her identify where she could make small changes without diminishing the quality of her life. She actually went out and bought a coffee machine to put in her office. She thought she shouldn't, because it was expensive—a few hundred dollars—but when she compared it to the $5,000 that last year on coffee, she was actually saving. By being able to see the full picture and impact of the budget, she could make a positive change to her life.

We all probably have habits like my friend's, that add up over time. We all likely pay for too many subscriptions and don't pay attention to spending an extra dollar here or there, but sometimes when we can see that full picture, it allows us to take control of our finances, change our behaviors, and in some cases increase our quality of life. That can be the true power of budgeting.

Five key takeaways

1 The point of budgeting is often to help keep people out of debt and help them make progress toward their financially free future by gaining control of their spending.
2 Budgeting starts by looking at your cash flow—what's coming in and going out.
3 Budgeting looks different across the different life stages.

4 Just as we can prioritize our income through SMART income planning, we can prioritize and budget our time.

5 Budgeting starts with having goals in place because if we don't set proper goals and know where we're going, budgeting is wasted time.

Five reflection questions

1 Do you prefer a more detailed approach to budgeting, where you track every single expenditure, or more of a big-picture view?

2 Do you have a negative connotation of budgeting?

3 Have you ever looked at your end-of-year spending summary from your credit card? If so, which categories were your highest and where could you cut back?

4 Are you saving at least 10% of your income?

5 How are you budgeting your time among your work, family, and friends?

Notes

12

Caring for Our Greatest Asset—Our Health

66 Nutrition is king, fitness and exercise are queen, and when you combine them together, you have a kingdom. 99

—*Will Morales, personal trainer*

Financial Freedom Framework

Without our health, we can't do much. Planning to take care of ourselves by eating the right things, getting enough sleep, and working out are just as critical as going to the doctor and ensuring we have the right health insurance coverage.

H EALTH IS ONE of our most important assets. Our health allows us to chase our goals, dreams, and aspirations. Without health, we often end up with very little.

I've seen two people live their lives, saving for retirement. The first took good care of their health and didn't save very much. The second person saved and saved, invested for retirement, did all the financially correct things, but didn't take care of themselves. They didn't prioritize health. They drank too much, smoked too much, had multiple chronic illnesses. They had a stroke and ended up spending much of their retirement in assisted living and nursing facilities. The first person, who prioritized their health—worked out, managed their weight, exercised—was able to live a much more enjoyable retirement. They were able to live independently. They were healthy and happy and were able to spend time doing what they wanted to do.

Of course, not everything about our health is determined by our own choices—things happen. We could get in a car accident that's not our fault, we could contract a disease, or we could suffer from long-term effects of a global pandemic. Our health outcomes are a mixture of our decisions and biology. But that doesn't mean that we should leave our health to chance. Instead, we want to control and drive as much of our health as possible.

There's been consistent research showing a connection between happiness and health. Happy people tend to focus on living a healthy lifestyle—eating right, exercising, sleeping enough—and find personal meaning in life. Identifying our goals and purpose early in life can give us direction. There's research that confirms a connection between having a purpose and living a longer, healthier life. Our happiness, our health, and our longevity are all intertwined.

Maximizing our health care

Despite its importance, few people engage in planning for their health. They don't incorporate health goals into their financial plan, nor do they talk about them with their health care professionals. As such, we often don't optimize or maximize the value that we could get out of the healthcare system, because we're not being proactive enough.

Let's take a step back and think about how managing our health and creating a health care plan can benefit both our finances and quality of life. The basic foundation of this requires understanding what we're actually spending on health care. Go back a few years and review your health care costs. This could be painstaking because you have to look up how much you spent on doctors, hospital stays, prescription drugs, and other items you may not have tracked well, like over-the-counter medications.

I also argue that we should include things like gym memberships and healthy foods in our health care bucket. We often think of health care as only medical expenses, but we should think about it as caring for our overall health, which includes things like exercise, community, being happy, eating well, sleeping enough, and making sure that we get the medical advice and care that we need.

Identify the things that improve health

Start off by putting things in the budget that improve your health. This might be an area where you decide you should increase your spending. If health is a big priority in your life and you want to be alive and healthy in 20, 30, or 40 years, you need to invest in your health the way you'd invest in growing your financial wealth. If you want to lose weight, take care of your heart, and eat healthy, invest. Hiring a nutritionist to come in and craft your family's healthy eating habits might seem like an unnecessary expense, but if you're not going to make those changes without that help, that expense is actually an investment in your future and is worth every dollar.

Set health goals

Once we determine what we're spending and could be spending to improve our life, we can start planning. We start by setting health care goals. This could be goals like maintaining a healthy weight, ensuring you're going to your annual physical, getting your dental check-ups, exercising enough, and sleeping enough. We can also set goals for our future health—where we want to be in five, ten, or 15 years. We can't control every aspect of it, but we can set goals to work toward. That allows us to do better planning and execution along the way to make sure that we're making progress toward those goals. This type of goal-setting puts health front and center in our life, because oftentimes we neglect it, even though it might be the most important foundation to achieving our ultimate life goals.

Let me give you an example of this from my life. One year, like many people, I decided to make a New Year's resolution. My goal was to run at least one mile outside every day for a full year. I got this idea from a friend of mine who'd done it. I started in January, like anybody else starting their New Year's resolution. Guess what the weather outside is like in the beginning of January in Philadelphia? It's not that nice. It rains. It snows. And what happened to me? I got sick 26 days into the year and I couldn't continue because I didn't prioritize health. But I wasn't deterred. I restarted the next year, understanding that I needed to eat better, sleep better, wear the right clothes when I ran outside in January, be cognizant of the weather and how it would impact my body so that I could achieve my goals. When I started the next year, I focused on staying healthy throughout the time period. And guess what happened? Something amazing. I was able to run 3,004 consecutive days outside because I prioritized health as part of the goal.

If you don't prioritize your health, do you feel you'll be able to accomplish your long-term life aspirations? Will you be able to stay in the workforce for as long you want? Will you be able to work as hard and be as productive? Will you be able to spend the time with your family or travel as you want? If you don't prioritize health as part of your planning, you might not be able to accomplish anything because you won't be healthy enough to do it.

So after you set some goals—short-term or long-term goals—you need to write them down. Whether they be workout goals, eating goals, or funding goals, once you write them down, you can start to develop a plan to achieve them.

Making the plan with your team

The next step in designing our health care plan is to engage our team. Talk to our family about what we want, how we want them involved, the type of care we would want if something were to happen to us. We also need to talk to our providers—our dentist, our primary care physicians, our specialists—about getting a plan in place when it comes to proactive health care planning. Should we be doing different tests, engaging in certain types of preventative care, or doing other things to improve our overall health? Doctors actually have resources for this. They'll sit down and conduct consultations about your health and your plan, but oftentimes people just don't ask them. They prefer to engage in transactional approaches with their health care specialists. They go when something's wrong or they are due for their annual physical. Most people aren't getting the full list of the tests and procedures they need to be engaging in.

If that's too much work, you can hire people to help you navigate this. They can be that doctor on call who helps you set the plan for your health so you know the procedures, operations, and care that you're going to need across your life. But you also need to talk to your financial advisor and attorneys about your health care plan. You need to know if you have the right documents in place, the right health care agent, the right health care proxy, the right insurance, a personal directive, power of attorney, will, and funding to get you the type of care that you want.

This is where the rubber meets the road. You understand what you need from the medical side after talking to your doctors, you know what your goals are, you know what your budget is. Now you want to improve upon it and execute the legal and funding side with the proper planning tools to achieve your goals and live the healthy life that you want to live.

The planning tools for health care are much broader than you may have initially thought. When you first started reading this section, you may have thought we were just going to be talking about health insurance. Maybe you thought we were going to talk about health spending accounts (HSAs), Medicare in retirement, Medicaid throughout our lives and in retirement, maybe long-term care insurance. Absolutely, those are all great resources and tools, but we also have to think about the other things that we can be doing to improve our health.

Not enough people invest back into their health today. They talk about it, but people stop short of making investments to make a healthier lifestyle. While things like gym memberships, nutritionists, and chefs might cost thousands, when you think about what you spend in other areas of your life, how is this not one of the best investments you could make?

20s					70s
Health Insurance	Budgeting For Gym / Healthy Food	HSA Savings	Long-term Care Insurance	Medicare Choices	Medicaid

Health care decisions

You need to have proper health insurance when you're starting off in your career. This could mean short-term disability plus general health insurance plus dental insurance. Health insurance is important at any stage of life because we never want to be in a situation where we choose to neglect our health because of concerns about the cost. The trade-off between health and wealth shouldn't exist in the world today. Everyone should be entitled to quality, affordable health care that doesn't make them give up other things in life just to stay healthy. This is one of the most important things about picking the right type of insurance at any stage in life, especially when you're younger.

I've seen so many young people avoid going to the doctor, having surgeries, or getting care because they didn't have proper health coverage or savings to cover expenses above what insurance covered. In those moments they're trading off their health to avoid going into debt. It breaks my heart when I see some of those people struggling years later because they made that trade-off.

The right coverage

If you're lucky enough to work for an employer that provides insurance, remember to review the options. Sit down and analyze the differences between them during open enrollment. Are you considering a high-deductible health plan (HDHP)? What are the benefits and downsides of a HDHP? Ask your employer what the potential total out-of-pocket costs are. How much do you have to pay every time you go to the office? Understand what's in-network and what's out-of-network and compare all the available plans.

You have to remember that the lowest-cost premiums aren't always ideal. Oftentimes people shop based on cost, not on value provided. And if you pay a little bit more in premiums per week, per month, per year, and get more holistic health care coverage, but you don't have to worry about what you're paying when you go to the doctor, it allows you to remove that mental hurdle of considering the cost when you need to go in. That could be the right coverage for you. Premium cost does not equal the value of the insurance. Say it again with me: *premium cost does not equal the value of the insurance.* In general, higher premium costs likely mean that you are getting more coverage. For those of you who don't have a problem paying to go to the doctor and have additional savings, you should consider an HDHP.

I've been using HDHPs for years now because I love the value of being able to save in an HSA in addition to having my health insurance. In 2022, you can deduct roughly $7,200 that you put into a family-based HSA, and have it not included as your taxable income. Here's one of the great things about an HSA: you can invest inside of the HSA, grow it tax-deferred and pull out all of the money that was tax free going in to pay for qualified health care expenditures. If you do that for a decade, you can put $72,000 or more away into an HSA that is tax-deductible and can grow tax-free like a Roth IRA, and come out tax free to pay for qualified medical benefits. In essence, this is a triple tax play. It is one of the single best tax advantages found in the United States' tax system.

In order to be able to take advantage of the HDHP, you need to be able to cover the high deductible, fund the HSA, and still be willing to go to the doctor. It is not for everyone. If you're opposed to paying a high deductible every time you go into the doctor and you'd rather just know that those costs are covered heading into the year, that's a good reason not to pick an HDHP. If you don't have enough cash flow to fund the HSA or to cover the out-of-pocket costs with the high deductible, it may not be a good choice. This is because if you only go to the doctor a few times a year, it could be more expensive. Many people don't do this analysis. They don't review their insurance benefits at work and make an educated decision about them.

If you don't get health care at work, make sure you talk to somebody and understand what your options are on the public marketplace. What can you get under the Affordable Care Act? What can you get with private insurance providers? Also look at Medicaid or any other health care system you might be eligible for at that time. Without insurance, you'll still be able to get emergency room help if you desperately need it, but you might not be able to see other doctors. There are doctors who just won't take you unless you have insurance coverage. You're limiting your potential to get care and help if you opt out of having health insurance coverage. Many young people make this mistake by thinking, "I'm young, I'm healthy, I probably don't need insurance this year." But if you do need it, you're potentially trading off your health for the next 60 years of your life to save $1,000 today. Is that worth the risk?

Health care in retirement

As we get closer to retirement, we need to think about health care in a different way. We need to think about moving from the employer-based system to how we're going to cover health care costs in retirement. We need to analyze how our out-of-pocket costs will change. It's also important to understand how Medicare—Parts A, B, C and D—and Medigap policies work. Understand the out-of-pocket costs for those and that Medicare costs can vary based on income. So if you're going to have more income in retirement, you could see higher costs for Medicare. We want to have additional dollars saved to fund out-of-pocket costs in retirement. We might consider setting up an HSA to fund some of our Medicare premiums or out-of-pocket costs, or exploring other ways to fund health care costs in retirement. The present value a 65-year-old needs to fund health care costs heading into retirement is $250,000. For a couple, that could reach half a million dollars. For those in the upper 1–5% of costs, it can be significantly higher than that, as the costs of prescription drugs often go up.

In retirement, you might need other kinds of health care, like long-term care or assisted living, and those can make costs skyrocket. We'll talk about long-term care in Chapter 17, because while it's part of your health and end-of-life care, it's funded and managed separately from health care. Still, it's crucial to the success of your health in retirement.

Another aspect of health care in retirement is Medicaid. Medicaid can help cover many of your expenses and even long-term care costs, but you may need to spend down your assets before Medicaid will kick in.

As you think about where you want to live in retirement, you need to consider access to quality medical care. Look at the cost of doctors. Is there a network of professionals that you trust in your area? If you move to a new state, can you get the type of doctors and health care that you want in that new state? Or are you going to be traveling back and forth between where you lived before and where you live now for care? These decisions need to be considered before you relocate. But often, people don't set those long-term plans and goals, so they're often being reactive to health care, not proactive.

Another aspect of health care to understand is that for decades it has seen rates of inflation above the general annualized rate for inflation for other goods. So you might want to consider applying a higher-than-average inflation rate for health care cost projections. You're also going to have to make decisions about what type of Medicare, prescription drug coverage, and Medigap policies you're going to want to use. Hopefully you have trusted professionals around you who can help guide you though that decision-making process.

Lastly, it's critical to communicate your health care plan to others. Talk to your family members, but also your doctor, financial advisor, tax professional, and trust officer. Let them all know about your health care powers of attorney, health care proxies, or general powers of attorney. Let them know how your care will be funded by giving them your health care information. Make sure they know if you have a *do not resuscitate* or other health care directives in place. Communication to all these parties is important to make sure you get the outcomes you want.

Remember, health is wealth. If you don't invest in your health, you might not be able to achieve your goals and aspirations. So take advantage of the opportunity you have today to invest in your health for a true financially free and healthy future.

Five key takeaways

1 Health is one of our most important assets.

2 Our health outcomes are a mixture of our decisions and biology. But that doesn't mean that we should leave our health to chance.

3 There's been consistent research showing a connection between happiness and health.

4 There's research that confirms a connection between having a purpose and living a longer, healthier life.

5 If we don't prioritize health as part of our financial planning, we might not be able to accomplish anything because we won't be healthy enough to do it.

Five reflection questions

1 What are you doing to take care of your health currently?

2 Are you involving your health care professionals in your health goals and planning?

3 If you don't prioritize your health, do you feel you'll be able to accomplish your long-term life aspirations?

4 What are two to five health goals you'd like to plan for?

5 What challenges have you had in the past when it comes to taking care of your health?

Notes

13

The Changing Life Cycle of Housing

❝ Housing is absolutely essential to human flourishing. ❞

—Matthew Desmond, sociologist

> **Financial Freedom Framework**
>
> As we move through our lives, our housing needs and wants change. These desires are dynamic, not static. As such, our housing decisions will be complex and evolve over time.

H OUSING IS ONE of the basic, fundamental needs for all life. The habitats in which all creatures survive and live out their lives change over time. For example, certain types of fish might grow up in a stream, but then live out their lives in the ocean. Some bird species might start off in a nest, but leave and flock and fly across the country and nest elsewhere, then come back.

Humans also have a life cycle when it comes to housing. One interesting area of research looks at how income and family composition can be used to determine the style of house somebody is likely to have. The research finds that most people follow similar housing trajectories based on income, family composition, and career stage.[16] Housing prices, divorce, and wealth are also important determining factors. There are generally four choices for housing. One is charity, in which we rely on family, friends or actual charities to provide housing. Another is to be unhoused, which could occur due to finances, mental health, or other factors and is rarely somebody's desired choice. If you're reading this book looking for financial freedom, it's unlikely that either of those are among your housing options. Rather, you're probably deciding between renting or buying.

20s					**70s**
Renting	Buying	Upgrading	Mortgage Payoff	Downsizing	Assisted Living

We see very few young people—especially single heads of household (a single individual earning a living)—becoming homeowners. Most rent in the early stages of their life. Most pick a type of rental based on their consumption or need requirements. Single-household-income earners tend to rent apartments, which makes sense because they need less space at that point in their life. Their income is relatively low in the course of their life and their housing needs are more basic. Usually the decision will be based on location—whether it's located near work, friends, and things they enjoy doing.

However, as people get married, have children, or their income rises, the type of housing they need changes. Once you see these types of changes, people start to occupy single-family houses. Not everybody—some people can't afford it because of the significant upfront cost associated with home ownership—but as people's circumstances start to change, their decisions around homeownership change.

Research finds that renters in this middle life cycle tend to change from apartments to single-family homes, but almost all of them end up living in single-family homes if their income goes up, if they get married, and if they have children.[17] This is an incredibly interesting finding. What you also see is that housing decisions throughout the working years are mostly driven by household makeup (spouses, children), need for space, need to be close to their place of work, and affordability. They also depend on whether they can afford the down payment and the higher upside costs of paying to own a home.

Whether you're going to be a renter or a homeowner is distinguished less by housing preferences and more by access to resources needed to satisfy those preferences and changing dynamics. There are obviously renters who do have larger families that would prefer single-family homes to apartments, but can't afford them. There are those who are renting single-family homes who would prefer to own. But as we move through life, the homes we need and want change. Those desires are dynamic, so when we think about our housing decisions, we need to understand that they will change across our life cycle.

Diving deeper into housing decisions

One of the benefits of renting is that it's temporary. We could rent daily, weekly, monthly, annually, or sign multi-year leases. One risk that comes with this flexibility is that rental costs could change—sometimes significantly. In 2021 heading into 2022, there were certain cities where rental costs increased by 40% year over year. If you're living on a somewhat fixed income stream and your housing costs go up 40%, suddenly you're no longer able to afford it and have to relocate. So one risk with renting can be disruption to your life.

More prosperous individuals are more likely to pick home ownership. In addition, research has shown that across income levels, those who buy rather than rent accumulate more wealth over time. Part of the reason is because paying a mortgage becomes very much like a form of forced savings—your home will likely appreciate in value. That doesn't happen in every area and in every situation, but holistically across the country, home values tend to keep up with inflation and don't provide much more of a return after that, if you look at the Shiller Index. Forced savings or automated savings is a powerful wealth building tool. Dr Richard Thaler in his work around behavioral nudges found that these positive changes in our planning can have lasting long-term impacts. Remember, things in motion stay in motion. So if we can automate our savings, we keep saving. If we aren't saving, it is harder to get started and keep the momentum.

Your home will likely increase in value, and as you pay down the mortgage you're essentially freeing up home equity, creating value in the difference between the home price and the mortgage. So the home is growing in value and the mortgage is going down. To some degree, you can better control the certainty of your housing expenses by owning, because if you get a fixed-rate mortgage you know what your monthly mortgage payments will be for the next 30 years, whereas renting costs will likely go up each year. Due to inflation, home ownership actually becomes cheaper each year as a dollar in the future is worth less than today, but your fixed costs have been locked in with a mortgage.

As people move up in wealth, it becomes easier to accumulate a down payment and to stay in larger homes without feeling compelled to sell and "right size" to a smaller house after children leave. Increasing wealth gives people the flexibility to control their housing more than they could earlier on in life. People who don't get to that level of financial security and freedom, however, often right size or downsize to match costs with housing size and improve their finances.

Housing in retirement

Housing takes on a whole new picture in retirement. Housing in retirement is not only about the economic side and the need for housing, but the need has shifted from a growing family unit and a need for space to more of an economy of scale and what works for your lifestyle. Instead of being about location, location, location, in retirement the need for housing is more about cash flow, cash flow, cash flow. How is your house impacting your positive cash flow? Is it providing income to you in any way? Have you considered reverse mortgages? Have you considered Airbnb and rentals? Have you considered selling the house and downsizing to create additional equity for other uses? Or do you just want to live in your house and not worry about it as an income-producing asset?

You do have to consider how your housing needs might change over the course of your retirement. Will you need to move into assisted living? Will you need to downsize because your bedroom is on the third story of a three-story house with lots of stairs? Because when you're 82 years old, it might not be safe and you might not be healthy enough to climb those stairs every day. You might want to right size to a senior-friendly home that fits your housing needs—from both financial and functionality standpoints. We also see people who choose to relocate in retirement to be closer to family, closer to better health care, or in a more comfortable climate. These are important decisions that we need to make in retirement.

We need to think about the impact our housing situation and where we live has on our tax flow, and examine how high the taxes and health care costs are where we want to live in retirement. Is our general cost of living higher because we're living in an area where we're expected to be working—which is why we had the house in the first place? Do we need to better manage our cash flow by finding a cheaper place in an area with a lower cost of living?

Lastly, what's the role of our house later in life? Is it to fund all our housing needs in retirement? Is it something to be sold to help pay for long-term care? Or is it a vehicle to transfer wealth to our heirs? In that case, did you have those conversations with your children and do they actually want the house, or would they rather sell it while you're alive because they'd rather have the equity?

As we move through life, our housing decisions are crucial to the quality of life we'll have, to the fun and enjoyment we'll have, and to our family unit. Our housing decisions help us design our life. A large part of financial freedom is likely living independently in an area we enjoy. And while there are many factors that play into this decision— cash flow, location, family, access to health care—it's really based on economics and our life cycle. Ultimately, our finances and family will control most of the housing-related decisions—whether we rent or buy, and where we live. And again, those will change as we go through different stages in life.

If you decide to buy a house, this is a really important area to prioritize your spending and your goals. I know many people who've "overspent" on their house, but it was the right decision. When you think about how much time you're going to spend in your house and the quality of life that it'll bring to you, are you willing to overpay in that area and cut back on others? Or are you somebody who wants to minimize housing costs and spend more money elsewhere? There isn't a right or wrong answer to those questions, but there could be a right and wrong decision for you.

When you're making those decisions, consider whether you also want property and whether you want to leverage that property for businesses and development. Do you want to buy a fixer-upper? How much work do you want to put into your house? Do you want to be the one doing repairs or are you going to outsource those costs?

Eventually, you might get the opportunity to decide whether to get a second home or a vacation home. Then you have to decide on whether to rent it out, get a property manager, or manage it yourself.

Tax decisions come into play around all of those—renovations of your existing home, the growth of that home, when to sell it, how to sell it, and rental property that you might purchase—making it a very complex web of decisions.

Housing to me has always been about freedom. I've lived with other people, friends, family, in dorm rooms. I've rented the smallest, cheapest apartment possible—both during and after school—that had roaches that came out at night so I could be close to my work. And then I bought the worst house in the best neighborhood I possibly could, and spent three years renovating it while living there. And then I did that again. Both times I wanted to minimize my out-of-pocket costs to get into the neighborhood where I wanted to live. I prioritized giving up my own time and energy to build a house in which I wanted to live and raise my kids.

At one point in my life, I made the decision to keep costs as low as possible. I really didn't care about the quality of the house that I was in. Being single with limited income at that point, I was only concerned about having a roof over my head. I wanted to be close to work so I could easily be on time and work later. I wasn't concerned about having a yard, extra bedrooms, or a kitchen. I just needed a place to sleep so I could do a good job at work, which was the most important part of my life at that point, and grow my potential to earn more income.

When I got married, buying a house became more important. I needed space and a quality place to grow my family. As our family grew, we made the decision to move again because now there were five of us in a three-bedroom house. We decided we wanted more space. Even though we were pushing our financial capabilities, we made the decision to move into a larger house. And we never regretted that decision because it was about our family, not our finances. It wasn't about the house, it was about the children. If we could go back, we'd make the same decision to pick the larger house, even though it might not have been the best way to maximize finances.

But it's still important to understand how much house you can afford. Too many people don't think about repairs, property taxes, heating, cooling, and improving functionality and features of the house over time. We also need to have a plan to pay the mortgage in case somebody loses their job and we've always needed two incomes to pay the mortgage. This goes back to the importance of having an emergency fund, because one of the worst things that can happen is to fall behind on your mortgage and have debt compound. Our home is often called our castle. It's the place where we feel safe. If you end up defaulting on your mortgage and losing your home, it's almost like losing a battle. It's disruptive, it's painful, and it leaves lasting scars on a family. Protecting your family against that is crucial in any journey to financial freedom.

Housing—for all life forms—is so important that it is essential to protect it. But you also need to plan for it, understand how it changes across your life, and prioritize your decisions around it. Understand the financial impact of renting versus buying and how much home you can afford. Understand what income sources you have for housing. Understand whether you want to sustain your house in retirement and how that decision impacts your cash flow, quality of life, family, long-term care, and estate plan.

Five key takeaways

1 Our housing decisions are crucial to the quality of life we'll have in all stages of our life.

2 You can determine the style of house somebody is likely to have in the United States by looking at their income and family composition.

3 Our finances and family will control most of our housing-related decisions—whether we rent or buy, and where we live.

4 One of the benefits of renting is that it's temporary.

5 There's a financial impact of renting versus buying. If you have the means, oftentimes buying costs less in the long run than renting.

Five reflection questions

1 Are you in an earlier phase of your career and have more flexibility to rent?

2 Are you considering getting engaged, married, or starting a family?

3 Has your income gone up recently?

4 When you think about how much time you're going to spend in your house and the quality of life that it'll bring to you, are you willing to overpay in that area and cut back on others?

5 Will you want to sustain your house in retirement, sell it to fund long-term care, or leave it to your heirs?

Notes

14

Managing Debt as a Tool

66 The key is what the debt does for you—and it
should always be more than what you do for the
debt. 99

—Janet Alvarez, financial journalist

Financial Freedom Framework

Debt can be leveraged as a tool on your journey to financial
freedom. It's critical to note that debt itself isn't an issue, it's
letting that debt get out of control. Get control of your debt
and equip yourself with ways to use it as a tool.

D EPENDING ON THE household that you grew up in, the word
"debt" could be like any other four-letter word—bad, shunned,
looked down upon like it's a curse word invoking your parents' wrath
and scorn.

Almost everyone borrows at some point during their life in hopes
that borrowing will improve their situation. Like most strategies,
that's not inherently good or bad. Instead, debt is a tool that can be

used to help improve your life. But it can also be a tool that can be misused, with negative impacts.

The real issue with debt isn't the debt itself, but letting it get out of control. Debt typically isn't harmful in the beginning, but becomes harmful when it snowballs and compounding interest starts working against us, instead of working for us like it does when we're saving, investing, and reinvesting our returns. The exact opposite can happen when we're dealing with debt. Anybody who's looking for a financially free future needs to manage their debt. Out-of-control debt is one of those things that can take us off of our path.

Proceed with caution

Investing once doesn't guarantee future financial success, but borrowing too much once *can* very quickly ruin our financial future. Decisions around debt—because the pain, loss, and detrimental impact can be so immense—need to be approached with caution and a thoughtful and proactive plan.

You can argue that the worst type of debt is the kind we accrue in a reactionary way. If we understand the cost of the debt, how we're going to repay it, how much we're borrowing, and what the lost opportunity cost of that debt is, we can approach it in a positive way. However, if we make, or fail to make, decisions that inadvertently lead to debt, its accrual is reactionary. Oftentimes if we have to take out debt because we have no other choice, debt becomes harmful.

Good debt

So how can debt be good? Debt and borrowing to have the opportunity to grow something of value, or to acquire something of lasting value, can be beneficial. For example, if you borrow to go to graduate school to get a degree that pays you more, that makes you more highly sought after on the market, and that can keep you in the job force longer—that's good debt. You've used debt to invest in your future and your earning capabilities. If you borrow to buy a home—like many people with a mortgage do—so you can have a quality place to live that's growing in value while your debt is shrinking over time—that's good debt, creating equity. In this case, you're leveraging debt to create a house you want to live in, to improve your current lifestyle, and to accumulate wealth over time.

In other situations you might borrow from yourself, like from your 401(k), to be able to meet certain expenditures, instead of borrowing from somebody else. In the right situations, that can be good debt because even though you have to repay it, you repay yourself. Investment accounts can also be used as collateral for getting lower interest rates through custodial relations and banks. While there are some risks that come along with this, it can also provide huge benefits and value when done correctly. But before you borrow or put any property as collateral, including investable assets, make sure you understand the full costs, terms, and risks associated with the strategy.

Bad debt

Bad debt happens when we're borrowing to increase our spending over what we currently need.

Credit card debt can be used very beneficially as a way to pay for items throughout the month without having to carry around cash or a debit card. It can give us the flexibility of when to pay for those items. But if we carry that debt from month to month, it starts being more costly for us to buy something. And if it enables us to go buy things we might not need, like another TV to put in the basement that we never watch, coffees out when we could make them at home, clothing online when we have a full closet, more expensive jewelry that doesn't bring us any happiness—and we're unable to set a repayment plan—we could fall behind.

If our expenses, including our debt, start to outpace our income, this is where the snowball effect starts to occur. Then we can no longer keep up with the interest and principal payments of our debt. Then the principal and interest start to grow and all of a sudden, we're facing a mountain of debt with no strategy to pay it down.

Debt repayment strategies

It starts to feel like there's no way to escape that shadow and it starts consuming our life, our happiness, and our mind. We start dodging phone calls and collectors' bills show up in the mail. It completely reshapes our life because we didn't get control of it.

Once that happens to somebody, there are things you can do. You can start by getting a debt management plan in place and understanding how you are spending and prioritizing your debts.

The avalanche approach

There are two debt repayment strategies that can make sense here. The first is the avalanche approach, of which I'm a big fan. This approach is to attack high-interest-rate debt first, saving you money over time because it keeps the cost of your debt down. Prioritize paying debt with high interest rates first. So if you have one debt with 8% interest and another with 5%, pay down the 8% interest debt first. It might take longer before the different accounts you have open start to disappear, but this will be the most financially efficient way to approach it.

The snowball approach

The second approach, which some people like better from a behavioral standpoint, is called the snowball approach. This approach attacks the small balances first and then builds up to larger ones over time. This can help you get an immediate sense of progress and success, much like making your bed in the morning—it starts you off with a small win. Find the account with $300, $500, $800 balances before you go to the $10,000, $20,000, and $100,000 accounts.

Remember with either approach, you still have to make your minimum payments on all your accounts.

Once you prioritize your debts and your debt repayment, either starting with small accounts or highest-interest accounts, you can move on to the next stage, which is trying to stop or slow down the accumulation of more debt. You could do this by closing or freezing your credit card accounts.

Remember that closing out a credit card or loan could negatively impact your credit. Credit agencies look at the length of your longest outstanding debt in your credit history to determine your credit rating, so this is especially harmful to your credit if you close accounts that have been established for a long time.

Freezing your accounts is where you actually call your credit card company and the credit agencies and stop your ability to create new credit. You have to unfreeze your accounts any time you want to apply for new credit.

The importance of paying attention

Our credit helps determine whether we're eligible to borrow new money in case we need it and also determines the costs (interest rates) associated with borrowing new money over time.

Paying attention to your reports and credit score is an important element in managing debt. You can pull your credit reports from all the major bureaus—Experian, Equifax, and TransUnion—for free once a year. If you see your credit rate start declining and accounts you didn't know about on these reports, this could indicate fraud. These reports can also show you where you could consolidate debt if you have debt across too many different types of accounts. Consolidation and refinancing can be a valuable strategy to improve your credit.

Your credit cards also likely have a free FICO score check that you view at any time to monitor your score throughout the year.

A good rule of thumb when it comes to credit card debt is to keep your credit utilization under 30% of your credit card limits.

Getting to the root of the problem

Once you've determined you have debt, you have an approach to pay it down, and you've paused your debt, it's time to go back to what caused the problem to begin with: likely, your expenses are greater than your income.

So you have to go back to the budgeting conversation. If big-picture budgeting didn't work and small-picture budgeting didn't work, you have to implement a new strategy. Understand what you're spending on and why your expenses are more than your income. You probably have more capability to reduce expenses than to increase income right now. Over time, you can focus on increasing your income to surpass your expenses, but if you're already in debt, the answer is really going to be only in managing expenses. Do you have to relocate? Do you have to change your lifestyle? Do you have to cancel some of those ongoing expenses, like TV, streaming services, and food delivery subscriptions? Can you insource some of those costs to yourself, like making your meals, making your own entertainment, or going for a run outside instead of paying for an expensive gym membership that you only use once or twice a month?

Now, if you can't just get to the answer by managing expenses, you should go back to asking: how do you get new lines of income? How do you diversify income sources? Can you do a side hustle? Can you drive for money? Can you do pet sitting? Can you do freelance work? Can you start consulting or tutoring? Can you build something? Can you also have those conversations at work about raises, bonuses, and other ways to generate more money over time?

If none of these are working, you might get to the point where you're going to have to start working with outside sources of help. One of them is talking to your creditors themselves to see if there are different repayment options, different or lower interest rates, or even if you can negotiate down a lower amount you might owe in total. Remember, though, that forgiveness of legitimate debt can then constitute taxable income, so pay attention if debt is forgiven because you might owe taxes.

If your debt has been passed off to collection agencies, this could be scary, but you might have to make them an offer, negotiate with them to come up with a way to get the debt cleared, or work with a debt repayment program to figure out a way to repay. Go find somebody who does this for a living, and sometimes they will negotiate and make offers on your behalf.

Other times, you might be able to consolidate or refinance debt to get yourself back in a better situation. I told you earlier that when I graduated law school, I had almost $200,000 in student loans. I had some with incredibly high interest rates and others with lower interest rates. At that time there were companies coming on the market in the private sector that were allowing for student loan refinancing and I found one where I could cut my interest rate in half and make only one payment. This gave me the ability to repay my loan in five to ten years instead of 20 or 30 years. This motivated me to set a target to pay it off before my first child was born, and I got that done about three months before her birth. I got motivated by seeing that there was an actual path, because before I consolidated and refinanced that debt, I didn't see a way out.

Celebrate wins and envision a better future

It's important with any type of debt management strategy to celebrate your wins. If you pay off something, celebrate it. You put in work. You did something amazing. You got control of your debt.

Whenever we talk about debt, we talk about going back to figure out what the initial problem was. This also means envisioning a future in which we have our debt under control, we're managing debt, and we're committed to not ending up back at the starting line again with the same problems we had before. This can require us to outsource things. It can require us to hire a financial advisor or planner who can help us manage our inflow and outflow. Sometimes it's putting restrictions in place, getting rid of credit cards, freezing credit cards in a block of ice so we can only use them for emergencies, or changing what we buy out and what we build inside of our home. We could make our meals instead of eating out, we could ride share instead of driving every single place we go and paying for parking. This goes back to the fundamentals of budgeting. If we want to generate wealth, over time our inflows have to be larger than our outflows.

The positive side of debt

That was a lot on the negativity of debt, but let's take some time to discuss the positives. Debt can be referred to as leverage. It can allow us to spend money in other areas and increase our total wealth. This is why many people actually borrow to buy their house—they don't have the money to pay down the house. But every time that you continue to carry that loan, you're making a decision to borrow instead of paying it down. Generally speaking, I want to be able to invest throughout the course of my life, at the same time I'm borrowing. So I make that decision to invest in equities, to invest in the market, to invest in my 401(k), and not to pay down my mortgage. Every time I do that, I make a decision to borrow by not paying down my debt and continuing to borrow to invest. That's called leverage. Leverage is that ability to borrow at a lower rate than my long-term return will be to help me increase my total wealth.

Another strategy would be to take all of my money and pay down all of my debt before I start investing, but in most situations that will help me accumulate less money than balancing both.

Debt can help us buy a house, it can allow us to invest, it can allow us to get a car, it can allow us to go to school, it can allow businesses to expand. Debt is used all around the world to help grow economies and bring people financial stability. If we couldn't buy anything until we had the full amount of money, think about how hard it would be to be able to buy a home in this country, to be able to go to college with today's rates, or to grow a business.

Take a page from the smartest financial experts in the world—the best businesses leverage debt to grow. If you know that you can borrow at 3–4% and get a higher rate of return on that expenditure, you should continue to borrow to expand. This can be true in your personal life—you can borrow to grow the value of your wealth and the impact of your life.

With any financial planning topic, strategies with debt tie back to our long-term goals—what we want to achieve—and mixing that in with our risk tolerance, our risk capacity of where we are today and how we're going to get there. Debt can play a very important role in that journey.

Some people are more debt averse than others, and that always needs to be factored in. If you lose sleep over debt at night, consider paying it down. Come up with a plan to get rid of it. However, if you feel comfortable with debt, you know how you're going to repay it, you know what the risks are, you know what the costs are, and you know the opportunity cost of not having the debt, you can use that to advance your life and improve your financial picture.

Debt doesn't have to be a negative four-letter word, it can be a powerful planning tool to help us open up possibilities in life that wouldn't have existed without it.

Five key takeaways

1 It's important with any type of debt management strategy to celebrate your wins.

2 Like with any financial planning topic, debt management strategies tie back to our long-term goals.

3 Debt doesn't have to be a negative four-letter word, it can be a powerful planning tool.

4 Paying attention to your reports and credit score is an important element in managing debt.

5 The real issue with debt isn't the debt itself, but letting it get out of control.

Five reflection questions

1 How have you used credit and debt in a positive way?

2 Have you paid off a credit card or other account? How did that make you feel?

3 Has there been an instance where you've let debt get out of control? How did you get out of that situation?

4 Has there been a time where you were reactionary with debt because you had no other choice?

5 Envision a future where you have your debt under control and you're no longer accumulating debt. How does that feel?

Notes

15

The Art of Squirreling Away Money for the Future

❝ It is thrifty to prepare today for the wants of tomorrow. ❞

—Aesop

Financial Freedom Framework

We can learn a lot from squirrels, who actually have excellent savings habits. Squirrels have learned to become better savers by watching and learning from others. We can learn to save for the future from squirrels so our future selves will be taken care of.

YOU MIGHT BE a bit surprised to see saving so far into the book. Oftentimes people think that saving is one of the first things that we have to do before we can do anything else. But part of the issue with saving—the art of putting money aside for the future—is that it's more of a learned behavior than a natural behavior. In fact, most people tend to prioritize the now over the future. So if we're left to our own devices, we often just consume and consume and consume, and don't set things aside for the future. Most of our day is about current consumption—eating out and spending—and not stocking away for the future.

Hal Hershfield of UCLA conducted research that looked at brainwave activity in individuals when given prompts such as, "Think about yourself today," and, "Think about yourself in the future." They then instructed, "Think about somebody else today," and, "Think about somebody else in the future." The research found that the brain activity when you think about yourself today is amazingly different from the brain activity that takes place when you think about yourself in the future. When you think about yourself in the future, your brain reacts to that future self like it's a stranger you don't know.[18]

This is so interesting because you don't know your future self yet. You haven't connected with them—you might not even like them— so why would you put money aside for them? Just like you wouldn't put money aside for the retirement of a stranger on the street, you'll struggle to save for your future self's needs, wants, and wishes. The more time you can actually spend getting to know them, figuring out who they are, and designing their aspirations, the more likely you'll actually save for them and do the positive things to help create a good life for that person.

This is why saving has to be a learned behavior. We have to direct money away from our self today—which we know with certainty that we can enjoy now—and put it aside for somebody we haven't met yet. Then we have to trust that our life and planning will go in such a way that "future us" can use the money.

Now let's talk about another lesson here before we get into how to encourage and create positive saving habits. Besides connecting with future us so we want to save for them, we can also learn lessons from other creatures—like squirrels. Squirrels develop positive savings habits when it comes to storing their food for the winter. They become better savers by watching and learning from other squirrels. They even adapt the way they hide their food when somebody's watching versus when they don't think somebody is watching—they actually dig more fake holes when somebody's nearby then when there are just cameras on them. When somebody's nearby, they'll try to disguise where they're putting their savings so no one can take them.

Squirrels, on average, will save four times as much as they'll need throughout the winter. Part of this is they know some of it will get eaten by other creatures, some of it will get destroyed, and they won't remember how to get to some of it. And they also tend to save in different places all over the ground, in different trees, different holes, and safer, more difficult places to reach. They don't put all of their food in one place. In essence, they don't put all their eggs in one basket. Basically, squirrels have learned to diversify their savings across a multitude of different places to reduce the risk of loss over time. They've realized there's going to be some loss due to many factors (like rot or theft from other creatures), so they save more to make up for it. Our losses, however, are often things like inflation or market risk.

This is why savings are so important. They're the backbone to our financial future. If we can't get to the point where the money that we aren't spending is greater than the money we are spending, it's difficult to accomplish any of our other aspirations or goals. It's tough to become financially free if we don't create positive habits around money—including savings. Financial freedom only comes if we're able to develop the habits that lead us there.

Let's run through different ways to improve and develop positive savings habits.

Pay yourself first

This applies in every life phase. Pay yourself first because nobody else is going to do that for you. You have to fund retirement for yourself. When you get to retirement, you need to make sure that your withdrawals from savings are going to meet your needs first—not the needs of your kids, your grandkids, or your neighbors.

This is similar to when you're flying and the flight attendant says to put on your oxygen mask first in the event of an emergency. If you don't take care of yourself first and you can't breathe, you can't help anyone else. The same is true when it comes to savings and money—if you don't take care of your needs first, you're not going to be able to help others. It feels very selfish, but if we want to be financially free, we have to focus on funding our life first.

Come up with a plan for spare change

After you've started taking care of yourself—paying yourself first, saving and spending for yourself—then I want you to come up with a plan for the spare change.

When you go to the grocery store and you get a couple cents left over, when you end up with an extra dollar here and there, where are you putting that money? Is it getting lost? Is it just floating around the house? Are you putting it aside, towards something? Come up with a plan for that. Even if it feels like small amounts of money, it could be enough to put away an extra $100 this year and $100 next year. Then you can start investing that and letting compound interest work for you.

That little nest egg can become a much larger one. This is just about doing the small things right. It's about having a plan for the things that can slip through the cracks but that can really enhance your overall financial picture if you really focus on them.

You can also leverage technology. There are some great apps out there that offer insights into our behavior. Some also help us automate our savings to put aside and save spare change. Some apps and websites allow us to squirrel away that extra money and build positive savings habits. Technology can be a great benefit for us to help track our savings and turn this into additional wealth down the line.

Automate as much as possible

Automation is your friend when it comes to savings. The more you can automate your savings, the better off you'll be. Set up automatic deposits to your savings and retirement accounts when you get your paycheck. Get your tax refunds deposited directly into your savings account. When you put your savings on autopilot, you start to create this positive relationship with them, because it doesn't feel painful to put money away for your future self. It becomes natural and you get accustomed to it. It's out of sight and out of mind.

Dr Richard Thaler's work on automation has fundamentally changed the retirement savings landscape in this country and around the world. His research, which resulted in him being awarded a Nobel prize, showed the power of automation and what he called "nudges." This research showed that by automating savings we end up with more money over time than if we expect people to manage this entirely by themselves. As such, when we automate and build positive nudges into our planning we can supercharge our long-term outcomes.

Pay on time

This ties back to the budgeting discussion earlier in the book. Get accustomed to making payments when they're due and not after they're due. Automate those as much as possible too. Why do I bring this into savings? Because if you have a habit of being late or not following through with things that you have promised to do, like paying on time, this can leak back into your savings behavior and become very detrimental. If you start falling behind on payments, you might have to shift your savings over to meet your expenses instead of staying in front of your planning. It's not about budgeting here, it's about creating positive savings habits. Being late on your bills is creating a negative savings habit. That habit will leak back into the other areas of your life and can pull you away from creating positive savings habits.

Come up with a plan for unexpected money

Unexpected money comes from many places—inheritances, a sale of something random you found in your house (like a painting) that ends up being worth a couple thousand dollars, a larger tax refund, a stimulus check, or a bonus at work because it was a really good year. Whatever the case, now you have more money.

Many times, when people get unexpected money, they might buy something like a TV, or clothing, or go out to dinner to treat themselves a little bit. That's not necessarily a bad thing to do, but it's even better to have a plan for unexpected money. I'm not spend-shaming at all. If you want to use that money to treat yourself, and that increases your happiness in life, do it. But definitely understand the impact that spending will have on your overall plan, your long-term goals, and your aspirations. Ensure you spend that money in a way that will give you the most enjoyment, and not in a way that you'll be upset about in three weeks. Research by Nobel Prize winner Dr Daniel Kahneman showed that once you get to a certain base level of income, the new dollars you earn above that do not increase happiness as much.[19] Furthermore, if you focus on how you spend money, on time saving activities, on others, and on experiences, you can be happier. In essence, research has shown that buying time and spending on others are what can promote happiness.[20]

Clear delineation of needs, wants, and wishes

Have clear breakdowns between your needs, wants, and wishes and how they relate to your long-term goals. This could also help create positive savings habits—especially if you realize that you have future needs and wants that will be greater than your needs and wants today. Maybe you see that you're going to have kids going to college, kids getting married, a desire to purchase a vacation home, or a desire to relocate to a house with a pool. Then you know that your future spending is going to be higher so you need to save more today.

The better you can create a picture of your future self, set clear goals and aspirations, and understand your needs, wants, and wishes, the better you can design your savings, bucket your savings and investing together, and tie them all together in one cohesive plan. This will help you align your goals with your needs, wants, and wishes.

Automate reinvesting

Another important saving habit you can create is to automate your reinvesting, or as I call it, "resavings." People usually think about this as reinvesting, but resaving is really what we're doing. If you get dividends paid out of a fund or stock, you're saving it via reinvesting. If you can create an automated investment approach that's on a glide path where you know that the allocations are correct, you have a process to review them over time, and you reallocate when appropriate, you can keep those funds invested, reinvest the growth, and continue to automate and build positive savings over time.

Make saving a family affair

Saving isn't something to do in a silo. Creating positive savings habits matters for you and for your family. Create a family atmosphere where savings can be discussed and encouraged, where you can build these positive relationships across multiple generations. Make it a family project. Many people, especially as they move into the strategic or impact phases, might become somebody else's bank. Your family might rely on you for money—either for borrowing or for spending. If you don't help create positive savings in the next generation, and if you become their bank, you'll be stretched too thin and might not be able to meet your own spending goals. You'll get away from paying yourself first and will be paying others first. Create an atmosphere where you can talk about savings in your household without shame.

You can do this by tying it to annual events. Think about end-of-year planning or tax season, birthdays, or other holidays. Maybe even create a savings atmosphere around a holiday that doesn't have anything to do with savings, like Halloween. For Halloween, you fill up a bag with all of this candy and consume way too much. You could talk about the benefits of spreading out our consumption. On Halloween, or the day before or after, you can put some money into a bank or savings account or in the stock market. Spread it out over multiple investments to diversify. Then in a year, check your balances again. Then again the next year. Over time, the next generation will learn the power of positive savings tied to a holiday designed for overconsumption. Halloween can be a blast and be fun, and you can turn that into a foundation for positive savings.

Don't be afraid of change over time

I always tell people, only stay on the course if you're on the right course. But how do you know that? Challenge what you believe to be true and if you can't defend it, change your course.

I see so many people still with bank accounts paying almost nothing when there are other accounts just as secure paying a higher rate for their money. They're leaving money on the table because they aren't willing to take the time to shop around and make a change.

Shopping around is always important. You need multiple different views and pricing so you don't get caught off guard and take the first option—price, advisor, or offer—out there. If you've been doing this for decades, challenge yourself to find something better and if you can't, then great—you made the right decision. But often we fall into the ease of doing what we've always done. That doesn't mean that it's harmful, but there could be something better out there. Change can be your friend and your enemy. But if you're proactive about change, you can find ways to improve your total financial situation and help you down the path of financial freedom.

Avoid lifestyle creep

Everyone's heard of trying to keep up with the Joneses. With lifestyle creep, our income goes up—we get a raise, a cost of living adjustment at work, then we go spend that money. We buy a bigger house, a nicer car, nicer clothes, and go out to eat more often. We keep making more money, but we don't seem to be getting any more freedom in our life because we're spending at a rate equal to our increasing income.

There's been lots of research showing that people in the highest-wealth countries are the happiest. But there's not a lot of research showing that people are much happier after they meet their basic expenses. A new dollar of income doesn't equate to the same increase in the level of happiness. We actually get decreasing happiness with every dollar we earn over our basic expenditures.[21] One study showed that above $200,000 of income, almost all happiness gains from earning more money start to disappear and people start becoming less happy with each dollar earned as compared to the previous dollar.[22] So we focus too much on generating more wealth to spend when we should focus on things that can actually increase our happiness.

We also have to figure out how to get new increases in wealth into savings before we spend it. Save the bonus. Save when you get a 4% cost of living increase. Figure out what that money is and have that automatically go into a savings or investment account. Move the money before lifestyle creep starts to happen.

Reframing the entire savings picture

We often think about savings as fixed dollar amounts—save an extra $10 or $100. I've talked about it throughout this entire chapter. But we should also think about savings as a rate—just like how we think of a rate of return. We want a good rate of return from our investments and should want a good savings rate. We should be able to pinpoint what our savings rate for each year is. We should know whether last year we saved 3% or 12% of our income. Then we should challenge ourselves to move up from 3% to 5%, then to 7%, then to 20%. So eventually we could be like the squirrel and save enough for our future selves to enjoy the quality of life and financially free future that we want.

Reframing the conversation to focus on a savings rate can help you gauge what you're going to need in the future for your needs, wants, and wishes back to an actual number you can aim for, versus just saying you'll do better or save an extra few dollars. Saying you'll do better isn't specific or actionable enough. You need an actual action item. When you identify that target savings rate, you can review it every year while moving through your career. This can be incredibly effective.

Hopefully this chapter has given you some ways to improve your savings habits, to pass positive savings habits on to the next generation, and to create an atmosphere where savings is encouraged. And I hope you learn from the squirrels and diversify your savings to mitigate risk, and that you save more than you might need for your future self, so they can live a financially free future.

Five key takeaways

1 Financial freedom only comes if we're able to develop the habits that lead us there.

2 Pay yourself first because nobody else is going to do that for you.

3 Negative habits, like not paying bills on time, have implications on our savings.

4 Savings is a learned behavior.

5 We have to connect with our future self in order to better save for them.

Five reflection questions

1 What are some positive savings habits you've developed?

2 In what ways did your family impact your savings habits (or lack thereof)?

3 Have you leveraged technology to help with your savings plan? What apps have you used? Which ones did you like and which ones didn't you like?

4 Have you ever come into unexpected money? How did you spend or save it? Do you wish you had done something different with that money?

5 Have you gauged what percentage of your income you're actually saving? Is there a target percentage you're aiming for?

Notes

16

Have Your Cake and Eat It Too—Through Investing

GG Investing isn't a game to be won. At the end of
the day, it's a way to achieve your big goals. *DD*
—*Sallie Krawcheck, co-founder and CEO, Ellevest*

Financial Freedom Framework

Investing is really about your values and where you want to go in
life. It's a critical element on your path to financial freedom, and
you have to be disciplined and stay on your course so you're not
overreacting to short-term market trends, volatility, and fears.

M ANY PEOPLE MISUNDERSTAND investing. They think it's
just putting money aside, but it actually runs much deeper
than that. It goes all the way back to our values, who we are, and the
impact that we want to have on the world. The idea is to identify your
core principles, have a sense of what your goals are, know your risk
tolerance, and have those all align with each other.

In essence, when we're investing, we're giving our money away to somebody else to shepherd, to have an impact on the world, and ultimately to bring us back some of the monetary value that was created by that impact. Somebody once told me that a lot of investing is like planting trees that you might never get to sit under. I loved that. It's about putting value back into the world. And when we lend our money to other people through investing, we're telling them that we want a positive return on our money—that there's a cost to use this money. The riskier your business or value proposition is, the more return you want back. This is the fundamental negotiation that is inherent and ongoing in all investing. Often, this is where people fall short—they don't think about the impact their investments are having.

Think about if somebody walked up to you and said, "Hey, I really want you to invest money with me," and you said, "Great! What are you going to do?" And they respond with, "I'm going to go out and burn down all of the forests in the world and destroy all the trees." And you say, "Why are you going to do that?" An investment in this company might generate a positive return for its investors—because maybe they found minerals and precious metals after tearing down all the trees. But you might pause and say, "You know what? I might not want to invest in this endeavor. I don't know that I care what the return is from a capital standpoint because what does that matter if we destroy all the trees in the world?" Before you invest, evaluate and consider the following: what words would you choose to describe the company? Are these words represented by themes in its social posts? The company should be trying to position itself against competitors. Is it doing a good job of differentiating itself? Does its value proposition align with your values?

With investing, you do care about the impact, but not everybody cares about the impact in the same way. So many people don't align their values and their long-term goals with their investing behavior. The reality is we don't have to have one or the other—we can actually have both. One of my *least* favorite sayings out there is, "You can't have your cake and eat it too." My response to that is that's the only purpose of having cake—to eat it! Of course we want to have our cake and be able to eat it. And that's the purpose of aligning our goals, our values, and our aspirations to our investing over the course of our lives.

Behavioral biases to overcome

It's important to note that when it comes to investing, there are many biases and behavioral triggers that could set us off course. We'll identify these and some of the ways to mitigate or remove them from our investing strategy.

The bandwagon or herd mentality bias

This is where we see everyone running toward the cliff, so we run toward it too, or where we see everybody looking up so we also look up. It's natural human behavior to react as others around us react. If everyone around us starts moving one way, we all move that way. In investing, if we see everybody else investing in a certain way, we want to hop on the bandwagon. Another issue that ties closely to this is FOMO—fear of missing out. We hear about a new investment or something happening out there in the market and we want to be part of it—we don't want to get left behind.

Misunderstanding diversification

Owning several stocks that are very similar or highly correlated is not diversification. For example, if you own stocks that all have to do with internet gaming—the chip manufacturers, the gaming companies, the console distributor—you may think you are diversified but you just own one value chain. Neither is picking several target-date funds inside your retirement plan. Ensuring you understand diversification and working with an advisor to ensure you're properly diversified is the easiest way to mitigate the impact of this.

Stay rich mentality

People who are wealthier get in a "stay rich mentality" where they want to maintain their wealth relative to people around them. So when there is any downturn, they feel threatened and try to protect that wealth but end up paying a high cost. They might start to chase investment trends or fads, and end up with a bifurcated portfolio that is half super risky investments that often don't work out. They spend a lot of money to protect their portfolio when they would have been better off just being true to their plan.

Buyer's remorse

This happens when people have investments and they don't know why they have them. Perhaps they picked something because it was returns-based, but don't have a rationale as to why they picked it or where it fits into their overall plan. Then when that investment goes down 10–20% they might start to feel buyer's remorse and make bad decisions that could lead to them pulling money out of the market. Working with your advisor to ensure you're in investments that align with your goals and that you know the role they play in your overall portfolio and plan is a way to mitigate this.

Investing across the stages

Let's look across our planning stages and figure out how investing should play a role in each.

Foundational

As the name of this stage indicates, you want to think of it as building a foundation where you're getting the hang of the fundamentals. At this stage, you're early in your career and you're just starting to invest, so your time horizon is long. As such, you should be fairly aggressive in your portfolio, depending on your risk tolerance. At this point, many of us should be 100% into equities and building our emergency fund, which should be about three to six months in cash for expenses in case something comes up where we need the cash to survive and it's not locked up in an investment we don't have access to. At this stage, volatility might actually be your friend because in downturns you can buy more shares. You don't want to be checking your account when there's volatility and going to cash because you're going to miss the rebound. You also want to take advantage of your 401(k) match with your employer because that's essentially free money. If you are in a position to exceed your 401(k) contributions, you might want to consider putting that excess contribution into Roth accounts.

In the foundational stage, you might say you're not very well-diversified. You have two potential assets—cash and equities—and you're taking a lot of risk in the market. But the risk and the diversification here still matter.

Remember, you can diversify across asset classes—so bonds, real estate, insurance, and equities, cryptoassets, wine, and art. But you can also diversify within an asset class. If you're in the market, there's still value in diversifying your investments across different types of companies: dividend-paying stocks versus growth stocks, technology sectors versus oil sectors versus health care sectors. This adds a layer of risk reduction. Some diversification can actually help you reduce volatility and increase your total return assumptions. The reason is that when you're early on in your career—and in your saving and investing—you can take a lot of equity risk, which does expose you to volatility in the market. Your stocks can go up and down any given day, but you have time on your side. The longer that you stay invested in the market, the more likely it becomes that your wealth will grow. The longer you are invested in the market, the narrower the range of potential returns on your assets—meaning if you're in the market one year, you could see a 40% drop or a 40% increase. When you look at 20–30 years in the market, you won't see your overall returns dropping 40% or going up 30%. That range of options on your average return will narrow over time and in essence become less risky the longer you stay in the market.

This is the stage where robo-advisors and a set-it-and-forget it approach could be appropriate. Today robo-advisors are technology-driven investment accounts you can set up to put a percentage of your assets into different investments. But as your needs start to get more complex—you start to need estate planning, insurance, college funding solutions, trusts, or tax planning—a robo-advisor is no longer appropriate. The ideal situation is that this type of technology supplements the human aspect of planning, rather than replacing it altogether.

Stability

By the stability phase, the good behavior that you started to develop in the foundational stage should kick in. This is where you develop a plan and you've already started saving for it. You should continue to have a set-it-and-forget-it approach and not look at your investments because the less you check on your investments, the better off your investment behavior will be. The more you try to trade, the worse you're going to be. You have to pick a good strategy, feel comfortable with it and stick to that strategy, because so long as you stay the course, you're going to give yourself a greater chance of achieving your financial goals and legacy.

This is the stage where the bucketing strategy we talked about in Chapter 8 comes into play. You'll work with your advisor to ensure your bucketing plan matches your risk tolerance and that all your buckets are set up and funded correctly in times of growth so that you're bringing in investments from buckets two and three and refilling those buckets to make sure you stay in the stable zone. You want to ensure you're altering your buckets and investments to match any family or financial changes. In this stage, you'll also want to talk to your advisor about rebalancing your qualified accounts at least annually and, depending on the types of portfolio, maybe even

Find Your Freedom

quarterly. Rebalancing annually can help you determine whether you're going to harvest your tax losses or gains and how that ties into other financial planning techniques, like your charitable giving.

In this stage, we also want to automate as much as we possibly can. The problem with forgetting to automate months, even up to a year at a time, of putting money into our investments is we miss out on a really good year of returns by sitting on the sidelines.

The other side of this is we want to keep buying. There's volatility and potential reductions with the dollar-cost averaging strategy—that ability to continue to buy over time, versus trying to hold and save up a big sum of money and then dump it all into the market at one time. We get timing risk with that.

We're also waiting to invest in many of those situations because we're holding on to money instead of investing, which could actually bring down our total return over time. As we get money, we typically want to put it into the market, which is why automatically depositing money into our 401(k) and other investments becomes important. We're trying to build stability and wealth.

In this phase, we're probably looking at fairly simple asset allocation mixes between bonds, stocks, and our emergency fund. Maybe in our 401(k), we're looking at ETFs and mutual funds and building our diversity across our equity portfolio. Maybe we're looking at some international funds to mix in because we want some of that long-term growth potential.

But, just like in the foundational stage, we're still in an accumulation mindset. Our contributions at this point are important. Taking risk in the market is important because time and compounding growth are still on our side. We haven't discussed the power of compounding growth yet and it goes back to the time element. Let's just say we have $100,000 and we invest for 30 years and get an average of 7% return, but we stopped saving and we just see where that $100,000 goes. We get tremendous value. Compounding investment growth is one of our best friends, and it's why we want to take risk early on. By risk, I mean we want to go into the markets and be where the higher returns over a long period of time will be.

At this stage, it's a good idea to start working with an advisor as your situation is likely more complex. In this stage, you might switch

196

jobs and need to do IRA rollovers. Keep maximizing your 401(k) matches at work, keep contributing to a Roth account, and continue to be invested in a majority of equities.

Strategic

As we move to the next phase of our life, we start to shift from accumulation to being strategic about turning that accumulation into income and the tools we use to do that. We start to get more strategic with both asset allocation and asset location. Asset allocation is the mix between stocks and bonds, real estate, and other asset classes we want to consider investing in, and then the way in which we diversify within those asset classes. Asset location is where we hold these assets. Is it in our Roth account? Is it in a taxable account, like a traditional IRA or 401(k)? Is it inside of a trust or some other type of investment or insurance vehicle? Exploring the tools that can provide income is important in the strategic phase, as is understanding the interplay of these, how they impact our long-term wealth, the asset protection from a liability standpoint, and the taxes that come into play.

Change is inevitable in this stage, and we'll likely have the first conversation with our advisor about how we want to live out the rest of our life. Volatility now becomes more important because our retirement is closer to us. Time is still a huge benefit to us because we might be 55 years old and have another 40 or 50 years of investing ahead of us. So we don't want to leave the markets entirely, but we do have to understand the issues with sequence of returns risk—meaning that having to pull money out of our investment portfolio to meet our spending needs could reduce the ongoing ability of our portfolio to continue to meet these withdrawals. If we get bad returns when we have to pull our money out, it can deplete the portfolio faster than if we get bad returns at the end of our retirement. Average returns no longer matter as much, but the sequencing of returns becomes more important.

Those five years right before and right after retirement are often the years we need to be the most conservative with our investments, understanding that we can actually increase back into equities over time. We can have what we would call a rising equity glide path—the total percentage of assets we have in the equity market could increase and we can take on more risk as we move through retirement. The amount of time that we need to have these assets is shortening. We've gotten through those first couple years in which a really down market cycle could deplete a long-term retirement portfolio. This goes against the status quo of subtracting your age from 100 to determine your asset allocation between stocks and bonds. So if you're 70 years old, according to that old adage, you should have 30% in the market and 70% in bonds. But this declining equity-to-bond asset allocation has been shown to be less sustainable than an increasing equity allocation over time.

This also runs counter to our behavior because we think we should get more and more conservative as we age. Now, if you're 75 and upset about the equity market and constantly worrying about it, then yes, you should change your allocation back to your values. And if your value is, "I don't want to be upset every time we invest in the equity market and it's volatile and I'm in my 70s," then you need to plan around having enough money and the right allocation for your risk tolerance.

Impact

This is where you start to plant trees that you'll never sit under. You start to look at the impact your investing is going to have. Is it aligned with your values? Are you trying to pass on a portion of your wealth to your kids at a certain dollar amount? Are you trying to pass on a portion of your wealth to the community to have a certain impact? How are your investments going to both reshape the world you live in and continue to make an impact on the world you leave behind?

The focus becomes less about the total returns year in and year out, but the impact that those are having on your family, your legacy, and the world. You also have to think about how these assets are being presented and cared for. There might be a time where you're no longer the one who owns this asset—it's going to pass to somebody else. Does that person understand the purpose of the investment? Will the person who will eventually own that investment understand what you were doing with those professionals and the impact you wanted to have on the world?

If you don't communicate your wishes to other people, you won't have the impact you were trying to have. Maybe you really cared about your investment portfolio, how you crafted it, and the impact it was having and it goes into a trust. Then the trust officer wasn't given clear direction on the investment strategy and they act as a prudent trust officer would and pick a new allocation that's better suited for the slightly different stated goals in the trust. If you didn't correctly identify and define your goals for the trust officer, now some of your impact is lost.

At this point in life, you're so far away from just being concerned about the return and the risk. It's all about the impact. It's all about what this allows you to do. Can you live a successful retirement and a financially free life? Can you have the ability to give back to charity and transform your community? That's what investing becomes about.

This is also the stage where if you've spent your career building a business, you'll want to consider those business assets and how those will pass down.

The last word on investing

Now there are some other pieces of investing that we should think about. First, investing is personal. It's about each individual. But we can do it at scale and we can automate it. Every investment portfolio doesn't have to be new. We can work with the investment strategies that are out there in the world and gear those to our specific needs. So we can think about things like our values and write those down, then build a portfolio that aligns with them. We can understand what our goals are to reach certain milestones in our life and create an investment portfolio that's aimed at hitting those goals. But always remember, past performance does not guarantee future performance. So even though something might have worked in the past doesn't mean that it will work again.

Getting comfortable with risk at an early age

We also need to understand how much risk we are willing to take on. We might start out as very conservative young investors, but should get comfortable with taking risk and understand that our time horizon is in our favor. As we age, our risk tolerance will probably have a bigger and bigger impact on our allocation. But it shouldn't be the only determining factor.

The ability to meet our goals isn't in cash

We also have to understand our needs, our goals, our wishes, our wants, and that we likely won't achieve those if we're all in cash. Are we going to be able to meet our goals and aspirations if we're 70% in bonds? The answer is often no, if you're 30 years old. We've got to take risk. We've got to educate ourselves and understand the role of investing in our goals.

The difference between risk tolerance and risk capacity

There's also a fundamental difference between risk tolerance, or how upset we get about loss when the market pulls down 10%, and risk capacity, or what risk we can actually take on. I might be very risk averse, but I might have millions of dollars and I don't need the returns from the market. The latter is risk capacity—what I can actually handle if the market went down by half. Risk capacity can help us decide how we want to invest. If you're somewhat conservative and you realize you have the risk capacity to take on higher-risk assets, you might be willing to do it because you know that you're going to be okay. And the better you understand the interplay of your tolerance and capacity, the better you can marry them together with your goals and aspirations. Then the stronger and more confident your planning will be and the more likely you'll be on the path to financial freedom.

Investing is a journey in itself

Many people might be looking at this chapter saying, "Well, I really thought Jamie was going to give me that stock pick and hot investing tip." But that's not what investing is about when we're looking at financial freedom and wealth building. We've got to think of the accumulation part of it, that we can get returns over time by taking on risk and being in the market. We want to automate it as much as possible and pay attention to our risk tolerance. We want to know where these investments are having an impact on the world and the location of our investments from a tax-planning perspective.

As our accumulation phase starts to grow and we start to near retirement, we need to understand the impact that the decumulation time period will have on our investment philosophy. We might have to de-risk a bit to not run into sequence of returns risk and run out of money from having down market years.

Volatility is inevitable, but don't miss the rebound out of fear

We also have to understand the impact of volatility and diversification on our portfolio and that sometimes volatility can be a good thing from a long-term investment standpoint. Sometimes diversification can actually help us improve our returns and lower volatility. Even if we're doing a good job investing and being diversified, we have to remember that volatility will happen and we have some ability to ride it out. We don't want to just go all cash as soon as there's a bad market year and miss part of the recovery.

Investing, again, is about your values, where you want to go in life, your path to financial freedom, and being disciplined on that path. Don't overreact to short-term market trends, volatility, and fears so much that it puts you on another path where you'll never meet your aspirations or get to financial freedom.

Five key takeaways

1 Investing goes back to our values, who we are, and the impact that we want to have on the world.
2 Many people don't align their values and their long-term goals to their investing behavior.

3 When it comes to investing, there are many biases and behavioral triggers that could set us off course, including the herd mentality bias, not understanding diversification, the stay rich mentality, and buyer's remorse.

4 The longer that we stay invested in the market, the more likely it becomes that our wealth will grow.

5 We have to pick a good investment strategy, feel comfortable with it and stick to that strategy, because so long as we stay the course, we're going to give ourselves a greater chance of achieving our financial goals and legacy.

Five reflection questions

1 How are you aligning your values and long-term goals with your investments?

2 Do you have an investment strategy? How would you define it?

3 Do you tend to look at your investment account balances frequently? Why?

4 Have you automated your investments?

5 When you come into extra money, what do you tend to do with that? Do you spend it or invest it?

Notes

17

Using Insurance as an Economic Tool to Mitigate Risk

𝕮𝕮 Ultimately, life insurance is for somebody your clients love and care about. It's the ultimate gift that your clients can give. 𝕯𝕯
—*Matt Lewis, vice president, insurance, Carson Group** *

Financial Freedom Framework

If you have a financial plan without insurance, you don't have a financial plan at all—you have pieces of a plan. Having the proper insurance coverage is a key element of financial freedom.

L ET'S GO BACK to one of the first stories I shared in this book. The perfect example of people who needed life insurance and didn't have it. As I put this down on paper, my eyes tear up thinking about my family. My dad, who fell off a ladder while working on gutters and

---

* Matt Lewis is a non-producing registered representative of Cetera Advisor Networks.

roofing, was our sole and primary breadwinner. And my mom, who was running the company with him, didn't have the skillset to hang gutters. If you can't hang gutters, you can't earn money running a gutter company. My mom was left with two children and without the ability to meet all of our financial needs at that time. We didn't have life insurance in place. We didn't have a financial plan or an estate plan in place to help us move forward.

My mom had to pick up the pieces and will herself forward. She is very resilient. But think about the impact that having the proper life insurance to take care of us would have had on our young family. It would have made my mom's life easier, happier, and more secure. It's exactly what my dad would have wanted had he had the opportunity to sit down and have this conversation with somebody and understand how life insurance could fit into the picture.

If you have a financial plan without insurance, or if you have a financial plan with only insurance, you don't have a financial plan at all—you have pieces of a plan. That's like having only a steering wheel and no car.

Often you hear horror stories of the insurance world and its sales-driven nature, but insurance isn't a good or bad thing. It's an economic tool intended to help mitigate the risk of certain events and the personal and economic damage that they can cause.

Think about ten people who all think that in a year from today, they will have a $100 expense. However, only one of those ten is actually going to have that expense. They could do a couple different things:

- First, they could take the risk of not saving enough and not having the money set aside for the expense. But let's say that expense was really important—it could cost them their home or their life. So they have to fund it. The level of the risk and expense in the future matters.
- Second, all ten could come together and say, "Only one of us is going to need this $100 in the future. Let's put in $10 apiece to cover that expense for whoever needs it." That is risk pooling— when we pool the risk together and fund it as a group because we know the outcome will occur, but we don't know when or for whom.

Compare these two options to everybody each saving $100. In essence, $900 of that would be going to waste, as the group of ten would put $1,000 aside and only one of them would need $100. This is the basic aspect of insurance—it doesn't get rid of risk or reduce the likelihood that it will occur, but it helps mitigate the economic impact of certain risks.

One of the best examples of how this works is life insurance. On a basic level, we're replacing the income of the deceased breadwinner if they were to die before the end of their income-earning. One of my friends always said, "If you had a machine that would make $1 million over the rest of your life, would you get insurance on it?" Most people would say, "Of course I would get insurance on it!" Well that machine is you. Insuring yourself is one of the most important things you can do when we're talking about getting down the road to financial freedom.

If we don't protect ourselves and our income, we can't save or build on the foundations of our planning to grow our wealth and utilize it to make a meaningful impact and leave the legacy we want.

There are different types of life insurance to consider. Looking at them all can feel overwhelming. And when you dive into each subcategory, it can get even more complex. These can include:

- Life insurance.
- Health insurance.
- Property and casualty insurance.
- Errors and omissions (E&O) insurance.
- Short- and long-term disability insurance.
- Long-term care insurance or annuities.

Life insurance

Options to consider include term, level-increasing premiums, level-decreasing premiums, permanent policies, whole life, universal life, variable life, and variable universal life policies.

Our insurance needs will change over the course of our lives. We typically need more life insurance early on in the foundational stage when our human capital and earning potential are at their highest. In most situations, we're buying life insurance on the life of the primary earner to cover their lost earnings if they were to die at an early age. In essence, we're trying to preserve the economic security of the family and loved ones through life insurance.

Health insurance

Health insurance helps us keep ourselves on track—from both a financial and life goal perspective. We know that people with health insurance are more likely to get preventative care and end up living longer, happier, and healthier lives. We also know that people who end up in bankruptcy often have big medical bills—for surgeries and other medical procedures. The more that we can cover those unexpected costs when they occur through health insurance, the better we can keep ourselves on a financially stable pathway. If we don't put protections in place, that bad storm, bad injury, or bad illness that takes us out of the workforce could set us behind and drain our emergency fund, cause us to spend down our reserves, or tap into our retirement plan. Then 15 years after saving and doing everything right, we're back to square one.

There are other risk-mitigation tactics in other areas, but not when it comes to health risks. We can't transfer health risks to somebody else, but we can transfer health care expenditure risk to somebody else by buying the correct type and amount of health insurance.

The role of longevity risk

Longevity, or the ability to outlive your money, is often called a risk. But it's not a risk, it's a risk exacerbator. Longevity is a great thing— we get to live a long time, which is one of the goals of life. We want to survive. The human body, mind, and soul are conditioned to live and find ways to survive and overcome obstacles. We're incredibly resilient beings—we sometimes literally will our cells to continue to go on. We overcome disease and injury to survive because we have a driving desire to do so.

But if we live a long time, inflation, spending, health care, long-term care, and market risk become bigger issues because longevity exacerbates those. Inflation is a compounding risk—it's not a huge risk year to year, but over a 30-year period it's a powerful factor that can reduce our quality of life as it reduces the value of $1 over time and our spending power declines.

We can buy long-term care insurance or annuities to transfer some of the "risk" of living a long time onto somebody else, very similar to the story of the ten people who pulled together the $100. You can do the same thing with longevity risk through long-term care insurance and annuity products in order to minimize some of the risk of outliving your money. This is exactly how Social Security and pensions were designed, with people looking at life expectancy, market risk, inflation, actuaries, and understanding how long particular groups of people might live and designing products to help transfer that risk and pull that risk together over masses of people.

While there might be some negative connotations attached to insurance, it can be incredibly powerful and helpful.

We've laid the foundation for why insurance is important and how it fits in. But there's not one particular insurance product that everybody needs. As we talked about, life insurance protects a life. While it can be used for different things—like investments, college planning, and estate planning—at its fundamental level, it's about the underlying life that it's insuring.

Tying insurance to goals

Before you go out and buy insurance, you need to start with all those things we talked about before—your goals, dreams, and ultimate aspirations. If you don't know those things, you don't know if you need a particular product or not.

To figure out whether you need life insurance, you can start with a basic question: is there somebody who will suffer financially if you are no longer around? A family member? Your business? A charity?

Your alma mater? If the answer to that is no, I'd argue you don't necessarily need life insurance. Now there are tax benefits and ways life insurance can be used to effectively transfer wealth, but not at its foundational level.

We can think about life insurance as providing income to the surviving spouse and children. We can think about it replacing income. We also want to think about life insurance for the spouse who is not the primary earner because their income also needs to be replaced. A big mistake often made in life insurance is thinking it should only be for the primary earning spouse.

Today, often both spouses are working outside the home, but if you have a spouse that's working inside the home, you can ask the same question: if that person passed away, would somebody suffer financially? The answer is going to be yes, because they do so many things for the household.

You can also use life insurance as I did with my very first policy. I bought a home and I wanted that life insurance policy to cover the mortgage if I were to pass away before my wife, so she wouldn't have to worry about it. We definitely pushed the limits of what we could afford with our first house because we loved the area, we wanted to have kids in that house and wanted to build it to be our home. Since we went down that road, I wanted to make sure my wife could sleep well at night, knowing that we had this insurance coverage so she wouldn't have to worry about paying the mortgage by herself if I were to pass away.

Often in businesses, life insurance is a valuable asset and strategy to help protect the business in case one of the owners, key employees, or stakeholders passes away. This strategy ensures the business can hire their replacement, pay out ownership interests, and pay off creditors if need be.

Lastly, life insurance can be incredibly valuable when we think about charity and giving. It's a great way to fund a legacy that's tax free to our heirs, a charity, or our school. And it can be a lot more in some situations than if we tried to make cash gifts, because the value of the life insurance policy builds up over time.

Life insurance helps create peace of mind for loved ones and the insured. It helps protect the heirs from having to lose both someone they love and their financial security. And it doesn't always have to be permanent life insurance, we can have temporary-term insurance because some people don't need a lot of life insurance once they retire. Their assets have already been accumulated and now they're in the decumulation phase. If they don't have an insurance policy, their legacy will be made with the assets they've accumulated.

It's important to understand that the benefits of life insurance and the need for life insurance can change over time. If you're looking at life insurance in particular, explore whether you need term insurance, temporary insurance, permanent insurance, and the purpose of this policy. Make sure you're not just being sold a product that's positioned as a be all and end all for all things. Life insurance can be good, but there's a cost. Everything costs something. What's your trade-off? Maybe that you lose flexibility or the policy can be expensive. Maybe there are inflexible premiums. Maybe there's limited growth in the underlying policy or cash value over time, if you have a permanent policy. Maybe the insured isn't healthy, or they're older and it costs too much to buy the level of protection that they need. Maybe it's unclear why you're buying a certain policy versus another.

There can be conflicts involved in insurance, so it's always important to ask your insurance agent or advisor about that. Understand how they're compensated. Many people in the insurance world get paid a commission, which isn't a bad thing, but you have to understand that there can be a conflict relating to the sale of a product if it's not being done inside of a holistic plan. Ensure your needs, wants, and wishes are being identified and that you're not over-skewing towards insurance because it's the way that the person you're working with is compensated.

But then the question always comes up: "How much life insurance do I need?" While we're focusing on life insurance now, all types of insurance can go through this process. Evaluate what risk you're trying to offset and how much of it you want to offset. You don't always have to offset the full range of the economic impact through insurance. You can self-insure parts of things, like deciding to fund half of your legacy for your surviving spouse through life insurance, but not all of it because you're also going to leave them a home and retirement assets.

You can decide to only fund half of your long-term expenditures through long-term care insurance or a hybrid life insurance policy and self-fund the other half through Social Security, distributions from retirement accounts, or state funding through Medicaid.

It's usually good to look at a way to determine the amount of life insurance you might need. Some good rules of thumb are five to ten times your income, especially when you're younger, and a present value analysis. You can also do a financial needs analysis and a capital needs analysis.

A present value analysis looks at the present value of all your future income and the economic impact that would have on your surviving spouse or beneficiary. This might be challenging, as maybe your income increases over time. A financial needs analysis looks at what your survivors or beneficiaries would need in order to get by if you were gone. A capital needs analysis will determine what your company or partners would need in the event that you die, and also buy out provisions, if you're looking at life insurance for your business situation.

There are many riders and features that can be added to life insurance and we're not going to go through all of them now, but it's important to ask about them. Ask about the riders you can get to protect against inflation or to create lifetime income. If you're looking at a permanent policy, ask what type of market and savings opportunities you have inside of the policy and what risks are associated with it.

Insurance and estate planning

It's important to think about how insurance fits into your overall estate plan. Insurance can help provide liquidity for your estate. It can help with trust planning. You can take a life insurance policy and put it in an ILIT so it's not part of the taxable estate from a federal estate tax standpoint. The death benefit can then be excluded from the estate when set up that way. You're able to transfer wealth out of your estate through an ILIT so it's not subject to federal estate taxes and the death benefit isn't subject to ordinary income taxes for heirs.

Life insurance can also pay for funeral expenses, estate charges, the executor, and the court and probate fees if you have any. It can help fund a legacy goal or leave money to a charity. Life insurance has tremendous value when it comes to estate planning.

Life insurance and your business

If you're a business owner, the most important aspect of life insurance comes by way of funding buy-sell agreements with partners. This can be the best, most tax-efficient way to fund buy-sell agreements to help with business continuity planning. This can also be done between key employees and owners, where everybody ends up purchasing a policy to insure against the death of another key stakeholder of the business. This is a cross-purchase buy-sell agreement, where each one of the members is purchasing a policy on somebody else's life. Let's say each of four partners purchases a policy on another partner's life. The formula for this is $(N - 1) \times N$. So if we have four, we get $(4 - 1) \times 4 = 12$. These four partners would need 12 life insurance policies to fully fund their cross-purchase buy-sell agreement. Then when one person dies, each of the other owners has enough money to buy out and liquidate the deceased partner's interests.

You can also make an entity buy-sell agreement, where the entity purchases all the life insurance that will pay out to keep the business running and provide liquidity to the deceased owner's or key stakeholder's family to buy out their ownership in the company. This way is more efficient because if you have four partners, you'd only need four policies that the entity purchases, instead of 12 that the partners purchase.

The total amount of insurance is essentially the same between the two, but who owns the policies, pays the premiums, and gets paid upon the death of a business partner or owner is different.

Annuities and longevity planning

We dove into life insurance pretty deep, but it's important to talk about the role of annuities in longevity planning. I briefly mentioned how annuities can provide lifetime income across numerous individuals that allows us to pool risk and provide less money into a pool than if we all had to fund the "risk" of living to 95 or 100.

Risk pooling and mortality credits are an efficient way to deal with longevity risk. There are many different annuities on the market, but one I like in particular is the qualified longevity annuity contract (QLAC), which can only be purchased inside of an IRA. It's very restricted due to government regulations and rules, so you don't have to worry about as many odd riders and costs attached to it. It's straightforward compared to other types of annuities.

You can purchase a QLAC inside of an IRA and have it start at age 85 and pay out for the remainder of your life. You can exclude it from the value of your IRA prior to reaching age 85 so it's not subject to required minimum distributions. This can be an effective way to deal with the possibility of running out of money.

QLACs aren't the only type of annuity. There are also deferred income annuities, single premium immediate annuities, and variable annuity policies. They can all play a different function inside of your financial plan. But like with anything else we've talked about in the book, the type of annuity you choose starts with why you're buying it. You need to ask yourself: "Can I afford it? What are the risks? What are the benefits? Who else benefits? How is the person selling me the annuity compensated? How does it fit into my overall plan?"

Also, be sure not to get overly invested in any one strategy or product. Understand there could be penalties for pulling money out early. Your principal and capital could be locked up inside the annuity, but there are also benefits to having lifetime income for your retirement income planning.

I often say annuities are oversold and underutilized. They have incredible insurance benefits to retirees, but they're over-positioned as a solution to everything. So you have to make sure that you understand the benefits before you buy one. If you have a negative perception of annuities and you're reading this right now, challenge yourself to look up research by Dr Moshe Milevsky, Dr Wade Pfau, Christine Benz of Morningstar, Dr David Blanchett, and Dr Michael Finke. Many people have negative perceptions of products because they've heard bad stories, but that doesn't always mean the products are bad—often they were just used poorly.

Even if you look them up and decide you still feel uncomfortable, that's okay. You're allowed to have feelings about products and strategies and build your plan with or without them. That's the great thing about personalizing a financial plan.

There are annuity suitability rules that you can look at to understand the basics you need to start with. But you have to go further than annuity suitability rules before you buy one. You have to engage in a fiduciary planning engagement that ties all this back to your needs, wants, and wishes, and determine how this product fits into your comprehensive plan. As with other insurance products, there's no single, magic bullet solution. Products play a role, but they're not a plan. When you use products correctly as part of your financial plan, they can help you get to where you want to be.

Reviewing your insurance investments

Be sure to test your plan by regularly reviewing your insurance. Make sure you have the right type and amount of insurance. If you need, you can sometimes exchange insurance policies through something called a 1035 exchange to get more coverage or better policies.

Review whether you've incorporated your insurance—your car insurance, house insurance, E&O, or umbrella policy—into your financial plan or whether they're one-off decisions that you made outside of your financial advisor.

I'll argue that the best insurance policies are wasted money—and I'm trying to be dramatic when I say that. The best insurance policies are when we pay for something we don't end up needing. I want to pay for life insurance that I never end up needing. I want to pay for long-term care insurance that I never end up needing. I want to pay for disability insurance that I never end up needing. I want to do all of that because I want to protect my family. I shouldn't look at insurance as a cost, I should look at it as an investment to protect me and my family on my way to financial freedom.

Five key takeaways

1 If you have a financial plan without insurance, you don't have a financial plan at all—you have pieces of a plan.

2 Insurance is an economic tool intended to help mitigate the risk of certain events and the personal and economic damage that they can cause.

3 Insuring yourself is one of the most important things you can do when we're talking about getting down a road to financial freedom.

4 Our insurance needs will change over the course of our lives.

5 People with health insurance are more likely to get preventative care and end up living longer, happier, and healthier lives.

Five reflection questions

1 If I were to die, are there people who would suffer financially? My family? My church?

2 Do I have a negative connotation about insurance? Where do I think that came from?

3 Do I own a business that would be financially impacted after my death?

4 Are there other goals I could utilize with insurance products, like funding college education?

5 Do I know how the person selling me an insurance product is compensated?

Notes

18

A Framework for Making Informed Decisions About Retirement Planning

66 More money is lost through poor planning than anything else. 99
— Erin Wood, senior vice president, financial planning and advanced solutions, Carson Group

Financial Freedom Framework

There are three critical pieces you need for successful retirement planning: your own definition of retirement, a plan to save for retirement, and a plan to spend your wealth down. All of those, however, will be based on your individual goals and aspirations.

WHAT DOES RETIREMENT mean to you? From an accounting standpoint, the definition of retirement is when an asset no longer has a useful life. But most people think about retirement as the period of time in life when we spend time doing the things that we want to do and we can leave work behind. Maybe we continue to work. Maybe we travel and spend time with family. Maybe we volunteer. Whatever it is, retirement is the time in people's lives where they get to make an impact. Retirement almost takes an opposite approach to its definition.

Retirement is different for different people. If you're looking at this chapter wondering how I'm going to cover retirement for all the different people out there, you can stop wondering. I'm not going to do that. Retirement is a broad and deep topic. There are numerous books out there that go into retirement planning.

Instead, we're going to approach this conversation by setting up a framework for making informed and educated decisions around retirement planning. To do that, we're going to look at retirement through three different lenses: defining retirement for you, saving for retirement, and how to spend that wealth down. These are the three fundamental pieces we need to understand to create a framework for creating a retirement plan.

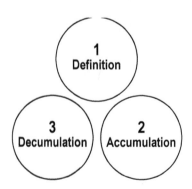

First, we need to define retirement for you. We can't plan for your retirement if we don't know how you define it. We have to dive into the details and understand what retirement planning is to you in order to create a plan that can help you reach your goal and aspirations.

Second, we'll go into saving for retirement (the accumulation phase). This is where we're strategic about putting money aside in our 401(k)s, IRAs, and investments; saving, and managing our expenses so we can grow our retirement nest egg in order to meet the meaning of retirement that we defined. If we don't define retirement and have a sense of where we want to go, there's no magic number for retirement. You can't just save a million dollars and think you're good to go. Depending on your goals, you might need to save much less or more than that. That's why it's important to have a North Star, determined by your goals, so you can save to move towards it.

Lastly, after we've saved and accumulated wealth, we need to know how to spend that wealth. This is the retirement income distribution (decumulation) phase of retirement. We get to retirement and we know what we need, want, and wish to spend on. Now we have to figure out how to efficiently take that money out of our retirement and investment accounts to ensure it lasts our lifetime and we can do the things we want to do in retirement.

Defining retirement

I opened this chapter asking you how you define retirement. Many people view retirement as a time where they don't work anymore, whether they leave voluntarily, are pushed out, or are physically unable to do their work. At that point, they must rely on their savings, on family, on the government, and on their employer-provided benefits to get by.

For others, retirement is when they free their mind from the shackles of having to go to work every day. Retirement can be a mindset as much as it's a time you no longer work.

Retirement continues to evolve. Retirees' lives are continuously changing. They're not consistent from the first day to the 35th year of retirement—it's a continuum. Retirement can be what you want it to be if you take the time to envision and define it. Then you can develop a framework for success and financial freedom and start saving and planning for that.

There is perhaps no better way to truly demonstrate financial freedom than by saying, "I work because I want to. I love it and I don't even need the money any more." This sounds like somebody who is completely free. These people are free from having to work to meet their fundamental planning needs—like their house, health care, taxes, and savings. Once you start to get to this level of freedom, you can picture a retirement that's not just goals-based, but aspiration-based. Being financially free means that if your aspiration was to be a great explorer, then you can travel, go on cruises, hike, and camp. You can bring your family, friends, and others along with you. The only way you're able to do that is if you first envision and define it, so you can plan for it and have the financial freedom to achieve it.

One way many people start to envision and define retirement is to think about their friends and family members who have retired. This is a normal way to process any envisioning or planning exercise—start with the things that you have some experience with. For most people, retirement is just a single period in their life. You're not going to go through it multiple times.

While it's normal to look at those around you to envision what retirement might be like, it's important to recognize that retirement for you is going to be vastly different than it was for your grand-parents and parents. That's good, because it means you can design the retirement you want based on your desires, goals, wishes, wants, and needs. Retirement should be developed for each individual who's worked so hard to create a financially free future. It should be designed to allow them to spend time doing the things that make them happy.

Retirement researchers often argue with me about the most efficient retirement savings and distribution strategies. They often explain in detail with long Excel spreadsheets the best way to design retirement from a financial standpoint. But the reality is the financial aspect is only a small piece of the puzzle when it comes to a happy retirement. You can create a different plan that makes you happier, but is less financially efficient. You can spend more money on certain things or put less money into your safety bucket but still meet all your expenditures in retirement. If you do this and it allows you to live a happier, more secure, more stress-free life, then you've done the right thing.

That's the power of bucketing—it allows you to envision where your money is and how it aligns with your spending needs in retirement. It's the power to look at your needs, wants and wishes. It's the power to look at investments over a time period and to be comfortable with your plan, rather than stressing over whether it's the most efficient solution out there. There could always be a more efficient plan to save a few dollars and get higher returns over a longer period of time, but if that means taking on additional time, risk and complexity, and in some cases less freedom to do things, you might be happier without it.

A successful retirement is being mentally free to do the things that you want, to achieve the financial freedom to spend time how you want instead of spending it working to get by.

To envision your personalized retirement, start by writing down what you want to be your top three retirement priorities. Is this being healthy and spending time with family? Or not running out of money? These are big-picture things, not things like wanting a house with three bedrooms instead of two. These big-picture things are things that if you don't achieve you couldn't have a happy retirement. Would you still be happy if you weren't healthy? If you ran out of money? If you didn't get to see your family?

Now under each of those three priorities, write down three things you can do to help increase the odds that each will happen. For example:

- If your priority is to be healthy in retirement, what are three things you can do to achieve this?
- If a priority is not to run out of money in retirement, what are three things you can do to achieve this?
- If a priority is seeing more of your family in retirement, what are three things you can do to work toward that?

After completing this exercise, you'll have a list of nine things you can do to work toward your top three priorities to make retirement successful for you. This is a shortlist action plan that we made without talking about money. Instead, we talked about big-picture priorities to help us define retirement, and what we need to work on to have a successful retirement.

Another way to envision retirement is to ask your kids, your spouse, your friends, what they think a successful retirement might look like for you. Ask your spouse, "If you could create a retirement for me, what would it look like?" The people around you sometimes know you better than you know yourself. Their answers might give you insights that you might not get on your own.

If I were to do this, somebody might say, "Jamie, you know that one of your favorite things is getting to spend time on the water fishing, but you didn't mention anything about that. If you never went fishing again in retirement, would you be happy?" The answer is no. So right there was a good insight to add into my plan. Now I know that I need to factor in a fishing budget and that I should live close enough to the water to drive there. Or better yet, maybe I want to live on a lake stocked with fish. Either way, I can start envisioning the more granular details of what retirement looks like for me based on input from the people closest to me.

If you are in a long-term relationship, make sure your partner does both of those exercises. Retirement isn't the same for everybody. I've talked to couples where one spouse has a clear picture of retirement and the other has a completely different picture. They have different visions of how they'll spend their money and what they'll do, but that doesn't mean those versions of retirement can't coexist in reality. It just means we need to know what success looks like for each partner so we can better build a plan that focuses on achieving their goals and aspirations. We don't want to focus so much on building the ideal retirement for the partner who is the financial decision maker and breadwinner that the other one ends up unhappy, which has been a problem in the financial planning arena for a long time. Planning for the family unit is crucial for success.

Envisioning and planning for the future shouldn't feel like a chore. If it does, we probably still have some foundational planning issues. It's hard to get to retirement planning if you haven't taken care of the foundations. If we're waking up worried about how to pay bills, we can't get to really good retirement envisioning because our focus is on today. But we have to get that baseline planning done today so we can start to focus on our future selves.

Different ways to save for retirement

After we define retirement for ourselves, we can set up a framework for saving to get there. We discussed saving in Chapter 15, and everything said there remains true, but here we'll set up that framework for different ways to save specifically for retirement.

We often talk about the three-legged retirement savings stool—the government leg, the employer leg, and the personal leg. It's actually more dynamic today. It's more like a chair with four—sometimes five—legs because we also include home equity and other income, like that from a side gig, into our retirement picture.

Let's work through these different ways to save for retirement.

Personal savings

We could put this money in many different places—brokerage accounts, taxable accounts, the stock market, private investments, into CDs and bonds, cryptocurrency, or our house. This is our money to decide how to invest, save, and spend.

Ultimately your retirement savings should follow some of the tenets of good long-term saving and investing.

Diversification

We need to ensure we follow principles of diversification when investing and saving for retirement. This doesn't mean that we need to diversify among all different asset classes (like wine, real estate, and cryptocurrency), but that we focus on asset location across accounts from a tax perspective. While our investment philosophy can be driven by our risk tolerance, the growth levels we want, where the market is, and the long-term returns we want, our saving philosophy should be driven by how to have after-tax money. Meaning that we've already paid taxes on the money and we get to invest it after-tax in our brokerage or taxable account. We often get long-term capital gains on our equity investments in those accounts, and we're getting preferential tax treatment on long-term capital gains on our after-tax investments in a non-qualified retirement plan.

Tax-deferred investment growth

We want to think about how to get tax-deferred investment growth while at the same time generating a tax benefit today. This is where 401(k)s, IRAs, 403(b)s, HSAs, and pension plans all come in. They allow us to save for the future, invest for retirement, grow, and protect our wealth. These accounts have tremendous tax benefits because the government decided in the 1970s that it was important to encourage retirement savings by giving tax benefits and creditor protections inside qualified plans covered by the Employee Retirement Income Security Act of 1974. This was so that people would feel confident enough to save for the future.

Tax-free investment accounts.

We want to look into tax-free investment accounts, like a Roth, where we can put money in after taxes so our investments grow tax free. There could also be certain types of life insurance policies where we can put in after-tax money for death benefits for our surviving spouse, estate, a trust, or heirs to get income free of federal and state taxes. We can also look at strategies with our HSA, which are actually tax deductible and can be invested to grow tax-deferred. The growth and principal can come out income tax free when used for certain medical expenditures in retirement, like Medicare premiums, surgeries, and prescription drugs.

Taking advantage of compounding growth

We want to plan so that compounding growth becomes our best friend in saving for retirement. For example, if somebody starts saving $1,000 a month for ten years with a 7% growth rate and then stops saving after ten years, the money continues to grow. That person actually ends up saving $12,000 a year for ten years, and ends up with $173,084 at the end of the ten-year period. If this money then sits for another 30 years with no more savings, they will end up with roughly $1,404,835 at the end of that 30-year period. This is the power of compounding growth. The earlier you start, the more money you'll accumulate by the time you reach retirement. Also in this scenario, if you're getting that 7% growth 20 years in, the growth on those assets will end up being more than the amount you put into them.

Let's look at this one other way. The person who starts saving $1,000 a month from age 25 to 35 can stop saving from 35 to 65 and they'll end up having *more money* than somebody who starts saving at age 35 for 30 years. The person who saves $1,000 a year for 30 years ends up with $1,219,971. They also saved $360,000 compared to the person who saved $120,000 but started earlier. What this means for planning is that when we save a few thousand dollars earlier in our career, we need to ensure we leave it invested for retirement. If we don't, it's called leakage. This happens when people take the money out of their retirement account when changing jobs and spend it instead of rolling it over into their new employer plan or IRA. They lose out on potentially hundreds of thousands of dollars for retirement.

Time in the markets

Investing in the markets becomes less risky over time in the sense that the range of return outcomes tends to narrow as the time horizon lengthens. Raw S&P 500 data shows if you were investing for one-year rolling periods, you could see swings in U.S. stocks up 61% or down 43% and an average rate of return, median, in that period of 14.1%. But start moving your time horizon and see what happens:

- With three-year rolling returns, you could see a high of 33%, a low of –16%, and a median of 12.3%.
- With five-year rolling returns, you could see a high of 29.6%, a low of –6.6%, and a median of 12.8%.
- With ten-year rolling returns, you could see a high of 19.5%, a low of –3%, and a median of 12.2%.
- With 15-year rolling returns, you could see a high of 19.7%, a low of 3.8%, and a median of 10.9%.
- With 20-year rolling returns, you could see a high of 18.3%, a low of 4.8%, and a median of 11.4%.

With **three-year** rolling returns, you could see	▲ high of 33%	With **ten-year** rolling returns, you could see	▲ high of 19.5%
	median of 12.3%		median of 12.2%
	▼ low of −16%		▼ low of −3%

With **five-year** rolling returns, you could see	▲ high of 29.6%	With **15-year** rolling returns, you could see	▲ high of 19.7%
	median of 12.8%		median of 10.9%
	▼ low of −6.6%		▼ low of −3.8%

With **20-year** rolling returns, you could see	▲ high of 18.3%
	median of 11.4%
	▼ low of −4.8%

So you start to see that your average rolling-period return didn't change much—it hovered in the 11–13% per year range, on average.

But you went from facing the possibility of a loss of over 40% in a single year—looking at a one-year investment time horizon—to a worst-case scenario (based on U.S. history) of 4.8% average return if you stayed in the market for 20 years. This becomes more of a story of volatility than it does of chasing returns.

This confirms time is on your side when it comes to investing for retirement. We know it's best to start earlier, leave that money alone, put more away, and take more risk in the market early in your investing career, because you know that you can ride out a lot of that volatility by the time you get to retirement.

Employer-based savings

The employer's role in retirement planning has shifted over the past 50 years—back then the employer took a much more central role in retirement planning and savings. Today that burden has shifted more on to the individual. Employers now offer savings plans with automatic enrollment and matching, but most of the onus falls onto us to put enough money aside, to pick our investments inside of the accounts, and to make sure we're saving and investing enough.

Your employer might offer a 401(k), 403(b), or a pension plan, and the most important thing is to maximize the benefits that you're getting from these year to year and over the course of your career. This means having those conversations with your employer, your HR department, and your financial advisor. Understand what the plan is offering and what you're getting as a retirement savings benefit. Often 401(k)s and 403(b)s have matching contributions—so if you put money into the plan, your employer will match what you put in. If you get a 6% match up to the first $100,000 of your compensation, you put in $6,000 and your employer puts in $6,000—that's $12,000 a year going into your 401(k). If you can do that through your working years, you'll end up a millionaire by the time you retire.

Companies offer other benefits to help you save for retirement, like health care coverage. Like we talked about in Chapter 12, if your employer offers you HDHPs, take a look at HSAs. Explore whether you should be putting money aside to cover health care expenditures in retirement while getting a tax deduction today.

Some companies offer things like health care for retired employees. Other companies offer pension plans where they fund the retirement account for you and you get to distribute it once you retire.

Some companies will even offer long-term care funding options such as long-term care insurance policies. Other ways to leverage employer-savings options is to ask for deferred compensation, through which you delay receiving some of your income until retirement. Often you can get tax benefits by doing this.

When you're the employer

When your employer offers good benefits, you need to take on the burden of ensuring you're maximizing them. But if you're a small business owner, the conversation changes. In this scenario, you're likely both the owner and the employee. Are you saving for your own future and giving your employees the opportunity to save?

In some cases, setting up retirement plans to help people save for the future can create tax benefits for your business. It will also help you be more competitive in the marketplace, as everybody's looking for total compensation—not just salary. How employers help them save for the future is part of that.

If you haven't looked at small business planning options, start with that. Ask an advisor to walk through the options for plans—whether it's a SEP IRA, SIMPLE IRA, or 401(k)—and how to maximize them to get the most out of them for both you and your employees. Also ask the advisor about creditor protection and managing costs appropriately.

Social Security

Social Security in general is funded by our Federal Insurance Contributions Act (FICA) and Self-Employed Contributions Act (SECA) taxes. These are the equivalent of 12.4%, so 6.2% from the employer, 6.2% from the employee, and if you're self-employed, you pay the whole 12.4% up to the taxable wage base each year. This is an annually indexed number, so it changes from year to year.

We fund Social Security by working and paying into the system. Our benefits are then calculated based on how much money we earned and contributed to Social Security over our working years. Social Security represents the largest source of retirement income today. For roughly 62% of retirees, Social Security is their single largest source of income. Social Security represents more than 90% of income for almost one-third of retirees. As a total income source for retirement it represents more than one-third of all retirement income. And today over 94% of the workforce pays into Social Security.

Social Security is the largest government program from a financial and tax standpoint. I'm a strong proponent and defender of the Social Security system. I've often argued that Social Security is one of the most efficient financial instruments ever built. It operates with a tremendously low overhead, as evidenced by the Social Security Trustee Report every year. But it does have funding issues today.

We need to understand those funding issues and make smart decisions around claiming Social Security. The system does need the government to fix its funding issues. At the end of the day, Social Security is a math problem—money coming in and money going out—but the true challenge of fixing it is a human problem. Not a human problem in the sense of the politics that keep good solutions from being implemented, but one that forces people to make impossible choices when benefits that one-third of retirees rely on as their only source of income are cut—choices like whether to pay for rent, food, heat, or health care. We remove the safety net that millions of

Americans have paid into, included as part of their retirement savings plan, and expect to be there.

To me, Social Security is an incredibly important part of the retirement planning stool and we need to make smart decisions around funding it, claiming it, and integrating it into our overall financial plan.

Anything short of fixing Social Security in the long run would be so detrimental to current and future retirees in this country because people aren't saving enough in their personal savings or their employer plans to offset the loss of Social Security. If you're reading this, Social Security might be an important part of your retirement picture and I'd be remiss if I didn't mention that it's facing a funding shortfall by 2034, when benefits could be reduced. It would also be remiss of me not to explain that Social Security is arguably the single most important retirement savings and income vehicle that we have in the United States today.

I often talk about Social Security as the automatic savings bucket because it's where we're putting away up to 12.4% of our income (up to the taxable wage base) each year throughout our working years. It's a huge part of our annual spending when you think about it that way.

For a lot of people, Social Security is the first tax they see taken from their paycheck. When you see those FICA taxes come out of your first paycheck, you're probably thinking, "Why am I paying FICA?" But then you realize you're actually putting that aside for retirees today and yourself in the future.

Retirement income planning

Social Security is a great segue for us to talk about retirement income planning. I've said this before, but I liken this to trying to hit a moving target in the wind. The target, again, is your goals and aspirations in retirement that we defined at the beginning of this section. And you're trying to hit those through various tactics—you're trying to take withdrawals from your 401(k), from Social Security, your IRA, your HSA.

But that target is going to move because we don't know how long we're going to live. Longevity remains a risk for retirement income planning because we don't know whether retirement will be five, ten, 30, or 45 years, and we don't know if we have the money to make it through a 45-year retirement.

The things that could push us off course—the wind—are things like public policy changes (tax law change, policy relating to Social Security and Medicare), market fluctuations, and funding status of retirement accounts. We need to be flexible enough to change with these things.

Retirement income planning is about taking all our financial goals for retirement, our income needs and expenses, and putting that together in one financial picture with the risks that will come along. Those risks are longevity, inflation, health care, long-term care, sequence of withdrawal risk, public policy risk, currency risk, and behavioral biases. Then we tie that all together by distributing the money to both meet goals and address risks. That becomes our secure retirement income plan.

When we're working, it's all about saving, not spending (or SNS). We're taught our whole life to save instead of spend. But when we get to retirement, we're talking about spending, not saving. So we have to flip our mental switch. Now we have to think about generating income from Social Security, our employer plan, and our personal savings in a way that meets our needs, wants, and wishes for an unknown time period, through volatility and risks. It's incredibly challenging. So challenging that many people lose sleep over it. They stress about running out of money, about health care, about what inflation will do to their retirement. A really good retirement strategy helps remove some of that concern.

We talked about the bucket approach earlier, but I'm going to go through two other approaches to generating retirement income.

Safety first (flooring)

The safety first, or flooring, approach to retirement, is in many ways a two-bucket approach. It says you want to meet all your basic expenditures, so you go out and find investments and other financial vehicles, like annuities and Social Security, to meet all of your planned expenses. Then anything you have left over after that, you're okay investing because that's discretionary spending.

Basically, this strategy looks at things in two buckets: required spending and discretionary spending. I put all my safe assets—annuities, pensions, Social Security, CDs, and bonds—against those essential spending items. Then my investment portfolio can be used to meet my discretionary spending items throughout my retirement. Often what people do in the essential bucket is create lifetime income sources so we can't outlive those.

Systematic withdrawal approach

This approach has you pull out a percentage of your total portfolio over time to meet your spending goals. The most well-known version of a systematic withdrawal approach is the 4% withdrawal. This approach, based on 1994 research by Bill Bengen, states that if you had a 50% U.S. large cap stock and 50% U.S. government bond portfolio, you could withdraw 4% of that each year (adjusted for inflation) and not run out of money over a 30-year retirement in the U.S.[23] This has often been dubbed the "safe withdrawal rate" because it was historically safe to pull 4% out of that portfolio without running out of money. Now 4% isn't a magic number that applies to every portfolio in every country, rather it applies specifically to that 50/50 U.S. stock/bond portfolio. It was also based on historical data, and one thing to remember is that past performance doesn't guarantee future performance. Still, the 4% finding is useful to help us gauge what a sustainable distribution percentage might be over a 30-year retirement.

This is a good approach for many people, but others think it is more analytical than real life and doesn't tie into their goals. That's why we have the bucketing approach.

Bucketing

We've covered this in Chapter 8, but for a quick recap, bucketing is a time-based and time-segmented approach that tries to align needs, wants, and wishes over a period of time. It then essentially assigns assets to those time periods based on risk.

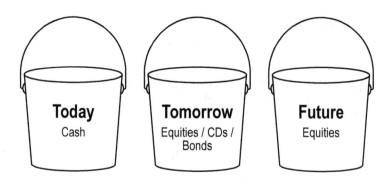

Our safest assets go in bucket one, so we know that for the first three to five years we're taking care of our basic expenditures. Then in bucket two we have a more balanced portfolio with a mix of equities, CDs, and bonds. We can start taking a little more risk in bucket two because we know we won't need this money for a few years. Remember that time is our friend when it comes to investing, and the likelihood of the worst-case scenario happening is reduced the longer we stay invested.

We won't need the assets in bucket three until more than ten years down the road into retirement. These assets might be riskier from a volatility standpoint because they're equities in the market. But equities actually become less risky over time because that range of potential outcomes lessens ten, 15, or 20 years down the line. This allows us to tie our goals back to our investment philosophy.

Retirement planning wrap-up

We have to start retirement planning by defining what retirement means to us. We've got to get disciplined and focused on saving in multiple ways for retirement while getting tax benefits today and leaving that money alone to stay invested for the future.

Then when we get to retirement, we have to decide on the right philosophy for us to distribute our money through a retirement income planning strategy—safety first (flooring), systematic withdrawal, or bucketing. We have to explore which one really helps us get to our desired outcomes, as all of them have some value to different people.

I believe the bucketing approach can be leveraged across the other two strategies. Some people want the safety of knowing they built a large floor of income. Some people prefer the analytical approach of looking at total returns and ways to distribute systematically.

Ultimately, retirement planning is entirely personal. There are thousands of different strategies and tactics to enhance the retirement plan, but they're far too concerned with the details if you haven't defined what it means to you to be financially free and you haven't taken care of the basics today. When you do both of those, you can enhance your retirement picture, save for the future, and have that happy, healthy, and sustainable retirement that many people are trying to achieve.

Five key takeaways

1 There are three critical pieces you need for successful retirement planning: your own definition of retirement, a plan to save for retirement, and a plan to spend your wealth down.

2 Most people think about retirement as the period of time in our life when we spend time doing the things that we want to do and we can leave work behind.

3 If we don't define retirement and have a sense of where we want to go, there's no magic number for retirement.

4 Retirees' lives are continuously changing. Retirement is different on the first day than in the 35th year.

5 You can design the retirement you want based on your desires, goals, wishes, wants, and needs.

Five reflection questions

1 What does retirement mean to you?

2 What would you do if you didn't have to work anymore?

3 Thinking about your family members and friends who have reached retirement, what did their retirements look like? How do you anticipate your retirement will look different?

4 What will be your top priorities in retirement? Not running out of money? Being healthy? Spending time with family?

5 What would your kids, spouse, and friends say if you asked what they think your successful retirement might look like?

Notes

19

Getting Surgical with
Tax Planning

—Benjamin Franklin

Financial Freedom Framework

There's a distinction between tax preparation, which looks backward, and tax planning, which takes a more proactive approach. But in tax planning, it's critical to look back at what you've done in the past so you can identify gaps and engage in better tax planning.

D EATH AND TAXES, as the famous saying goes, are the two things in life we can expect no matter what happens.

However, while we die only once, we experience taxes each and every year—sales taxes, income taxes, estate taxes, or excise taxes—no matter how we live our lives. As such, we need to be much more surgical about taxes than almost any other area of planning.

Taxes are interesting because they come in two different formats: our tax filing, when we're being retroactive and looking back; and tax planning, which is more proactive and forward-looking.

Tax filing and preparation are important. That's why there's a whole industry of certified public accountants and tax planning professionals to help us file and prepare our taxes each year. And it's no surprise that people seek out help when it comes to taxes, because the tax code is so complex. The intersection of the law, the tax system, and our personal situations can get very complex. We often need help navigating the complex system that is the United States tax code.

Tax planning is a more proactive approach to taxes. This isn't about filling out paperwork and reporting back what already happened, it's about looking into the future in relation to the other planning we've done.

Interestingly enough, the tax picture often gets more complex, deeper, and more interesting to somebody with a keen eye to pay attention to the tax system. For instance, early in our careers, when we're not earning much money, we're often not paying much in taxes. There's also little we can do to manage our taxes up or down at that point—we don't own a lot of property investments, we don't have savings in different types of taxable accounts. In essence, we go to work, we earn income, and we pay state and federal income taxes on it.

As we move up in our careers and life stages, our financial pictures get more complex and so does our need to engage more in tax planning. In the stability and strategic phases, we want to start to plan out our tax savings, from both retirement savings and investment standpoints, and how to minimize taxes in retirement.

As we get toward the end of our lives, we want to plan to make an impact on the world in a tax-efficient way. This determines how we'll use charitable giving, how we'll design our estate and how we want our assets to pass on to our heirs. These decisions will start being directed more by playing within the tax system, trying to minimize taxes so we can maximize our spending, our wealth, our retirement, our legacy, and our impact.

Your taxes and financial planning

I always tell people, if you're working with a financial advisor or you have a financial plan that isn't trying to get you to pay the least amount of taxes that you're legally obligated to pay, you don't have a good advisor and you don't have a good financial plan. Taxes can be such a big part of our planning. They can be a huge cost each year— if we ignore them, or only engage in tax prep work, we could be losing thousands of dollars a year. That could be the difference between a financially secure retirement and a retirement filled with sleepless nights not knowing if we can make ends meet with what we have. That distinction can come down to being smart with taxes.

We all have to think about some of the big tax planning situations that can happen in our lives. Remember taxes are unique to you, like your fingerprints. As such, the tax strategies and tactics that you're going to use to enhance your situation will depend on your income levels, where you live, the type of work you do, the types of expenses you have, and the type of family setup that you have. They will also depend on whether you're in school, if you have medical expenses, and how old you are. All these factors come into play in your tax planning.

There are thousands of tax planning strategies out there—just listing them could fill up a dozen books—but your strategy goes back to your journey to financial freedom and your planning process. There are some elements I recommend to focus on: know where to get started, get some help, keep good documents, and then make a plan to improve your taxes. We'll look at each of these points, including six different ways that will help you achieve the last one.

Getting started

Part of the tax-planning process is knowing where to get started. One good way to do this is reviewing what happened already. This helps to create consistency in our process. We should look at last year's returns so we can understand where we're coming from and our situation. From there we can start to improve upon our situation. We can start to understand if we missed certain deductions, whether we had expenses we didn't deduct, if we're taking too much money in income, if we're gifting the wrong way, and whether we're managing our RMDs in the most efficient manner possible. Once we start seeing those holes in our tax plan, we can start making longer-term enhancements just by reviewing where we've been.

In looking back, we might see that we're creeping over into a higher income range most years; pushing up our ordinary income taxes on that marginal amount of money can mean we lose some deductions, because our income is so high. We can identify whether we're better off deferring some income into the future, and maybe that means higher retirement contributions, more gifting to charity, or being more aggressive on certain business deductions. But we can't do that type of planning unless we've created a baseline.

Working with professionals

Once we've looked at last year's return and identified areas to improve, we need to find a way to make those improvements. Here's where we should work with an advisor or an accountant, because it's too complex for us to know all the things that we don't know. The IRS is constantly changing rules and the government is constantly changing tax laws. We've had four major tax bills in the last four years as of this writing—the Tax Cuts and Jobs Act, the CARES Act, the SECURE Act, and the American Rescue Plan Act—that have consistently shifted the rules and therefore the planning we need to engage in.

Document, document, document

We need to ensure that we're doing a good job gathering and tracking all of our tax forms and all our business and personal expenses. One major way we're derailed from a good planning process is by not keeping good documentation. We need to document, document, document.

Making a plan to improve (and six different ways to do that)

Once we've looked back, found the right help, and documented our expenses and processes, we can start planning for how we're going to improve our taxes in the future.

Let's look at six ways you can improve your tax situation moving forward. Keep in mind that two things key to our overall financial planning—diversification across both taxable and non-taxable accounts and saving money in retirement accounts—are key to tax planning over time.

1. Deferring income into the future

We want to take income from high tax years when we're working, and spread that out to low tax years when we're not working, like in retirement. Some companies offer non-qualified deferred compensation plans in which you can defer compensation that you earn next year into the future, with a trigger event (like retirement, leaving the company, becoming disabled, reaching a certain age, or death) required before you have access to those funds. This can allow you to not take that income as taxable income next year and only take it as taxable income when you receive it, maybe 30 years into the future.

This can help you reduce your short-term taxable income, grow your wealth by deferring it over time, and then pull that deferred income into taxable income in the future when you have lower taxes.

With any income deferral strategies, you need to balance cash flow and tax rates today, while also paying attention to what your future tax rates might be. Your future tax rates could potentially be higher, which could potentially offset the benefit of this approach. Even so, this is a valuable strategy for minimizing taxes.

2. Accelerating income

In low-tax years, you might consider accelerating income. A low tax year can occur after we've switched jobs and didn't work for a few months, we lost a job, or we were in sales and didn't have the best year. If these things happen, we might consider ways to accelerate income to this year. We might not be able to do that by working more hours at our main job, but we could go get a second job to bring in more income this year because we still have ranges within their tax brackets.

There are other ways to accelerate income into this year. One way would be to sell a business, which could be both a good business decision and a good tax decision. When we sell businesses, we have the conversation about whether to defer income to the future, spread out the sale through installments over many years to limit the tax impact on the sale, or accelerate income into this year because we have other high income years coming in the future.

Other ways to accelerate income are to sell real estate, sell investments, do Roth conversions from our traditional IRA or 401(k) accounts. When we do a Roth conversion we're taking tax-deferred money in a 401(k) and converting it to money that will be tax free sometime in the future. We can pick a time, like today when taxes are lower, to do this. If the tax laws change, our income is down, or we have lots of deductions, doing a conversion in a low tax year—as opposed to pulling money out in a high tax year in the future when we're in a higher bracket—can be a valuable tax planning strategy.

3. Required minimum distributions

RMDs interplay with tax planning. Once you reach age 72, you have to take RMDs from your IRAs, 401(k)s, and your qualified retirement accounts (except for Roth IRAs). The amount you have to take is based on your age and IRS Factor Table each year. You take the previous year's account balance and divide it by that Factor Table number to determine your required minimum withdrawal amount.

RMDs are so tied to taxes because those withdrawals are taxable income. In essence, RMDs are forced taxable events for retirees because the government wants its tax revenue. It's given you the benefit of deferring all this income into the future, but now you're over retirement age and you need to start spending this money—or at least start paying taxes on it.

People don't like taxes. They like forced taxes on money they thought was for their future even less. Now, we have taxes coming out of our retirement accounts, we have higher taxable income because of our forced withdrawals, we've lost our control and flexibility if we didn't do prior planning (like Roth conversions to minimize the amount of money we had in RMD-subject accounts like traditional IRAs and 401(k)s). As our RMDs are getting higher and higher as we move through retirement, this starts to impact other tax areas, like the taxation of Social Security and higher Medicare premiums. The Medicare IRMAA surcharge, while not a tax, feels like a tax. The intersection between RMDs and other taxes is so strong that if we fail to do this planning, we could be costing ourselves tens of thousands of dollars in additional taxes.

4. Tax-loss harvesting

Tax-loss harvesting is the ability to offset capital gains with losses each and every year. People who engage in tax-loss harvesting usually take December to look at their investments and see what went up and what went down, and aim to offset any losses with their gains.

When tax-loss harvesting, keep in mind the 30-day wash-sale rule, which states that, after selling an investment at a loss, you can't buy substantially identical securities within 30 days. This rule effectively prevents you from "locking in" a loss to offset any gains and immediately buying back the same asset.

You start realizing that this shouldn't just be done in December, because stocks and investment assets don't just move up and down in December. You should be engaging in tax-loss harvesting throughout the course of the year. Some of the best times to capitalize on these gains and losses might be in the middle of summer or spring.

One of the issues that many people have with doing tax-loss harvesting planning is understanding when and why to do it.

5. Bunching

Bunching is a strategy where you pull a bunch of expenses or contributions into one year to increase the likelihood that you'll be able to deduct them. For instance, if you spread out charitable contributions over ten years and you're a standard filer, you'll likely get no tax benefits from your charitable giving. However, you could pull all ten of those years together and instead of giving $1,000 a year over ten years, you give $10,000 in one year. You increase the chance of going above the standard deduction amount and being able to itemize, gaining a tax benefit.

Bunching can also be done with business expenses, medical

expenses, and 529 contributions to create a larger state income tax or federal deduction in a given year.

Bunching is the opposite of deferring or accelerating income, in that it's about spreading out (deferring or accelerating) or bunching together expenses. Both are good to talk about when it comes to tax planning. There are certain expenses that have a cap on how much can be deducted per year, so we'll want to defer those into the next couple of years so we don't have an expense we can't deduct just because it happened this year. If we wait one more year, we'll be able to deduct it. This creates a powerful planning opportunity.

6. Multi-generational impact of our taxes

We need to think about how our taxes affect our heirs and whether we're leaving money on the table because we failed to plan.

For example, let's imagine you're a 65-year-old with lots of income-producing rental property. You're at your highest earning years and likely going to stay in the highest tax bracket for years to come. But you have five different kids and all five of them are much lower-income earners.

A good way to manage taxes would be to gift some of those income-producing properties to the children so that the income would move to them and be taxed at lower rates today. This requires many things to fall into place—that you want to gift the property away, that you're not currently subject to the gift and estate tax, and that you're willing to give up ownership of the property. But if all those things fall into place, the impact and legacy you'll have on your family can be maximized by transferring income-producing property to the next generation earlier than you'd planned.

We can also explore the opposite situation. Say now that you are a 75-year-old with a large $1 million IRA. But all the income and savings that you have come from that IRA. You've got a kid—a doctor who earns enough to put them in the highest tax bracket—who's going to be the beneficiary of your IRA. Leaving that IRA to your wealthy child is going to subject it to the highest possible income taxes. If you're in this situation, you need to think about how to convert it to a non-taxable asset—a Roth or life insurance—for that heir. Life insurance can be a tax-free death benefit to heirs and, if you use the right policies, you can pull from them in retirement, income tax free. Many people don't think about using life insurance from a tax diversification standpoint, rather they just think of the traditional use to protect their income while they're working.

So tax planning can also encompass the next generation—including planning for estate and gift taxes, looking at trusts, looking at how our estate itself will be taxed, and exploring tax-efficient ways to leave wealth to heirs.

Tax planning becomes more and more important as we age, as our assets grow, as we start looking at retirement, required minimum distributions, Roth conversions, and leaving wealth to our heirs.

While death and taxes are both certain, death is something that's guaranteed only once. But taxes? Taxes are guaranteed every year. So proper tax planning is vital.

Five key takeaways

1 Taxes come in two different forms: our tax filing, when we're being retroactive and looking back; and tax planning, which is more proactive and forward-looking.

2 We often need help navigating the complex system that is the United States tax code.

3 As we move up in our careers and life stages, our financial pictures get more complex and so does our need to engage more in tax planning.

4 We can make an impact on the world in a tax-efficient way.

5 If we're working with a financial advisor or have a financial plan that isn't aimed at getting us to pay the least amount of taxes that we're legally obligated to pay, we don't have a good advisor and we don't have a good financial plan.

Five reflection questions

1   Have you reviewed your last tax return yet? Does anything that might improve your situation stand out?

2   What is your system for tracking all your business and personal expenses?

3   Do you keep up to speed with tax law changes?

4   When was the last time you engaged in tax-loss harvesting?

5   Are there ways you and your family can shift income-producing property to be beneficial from a tax perspective?

Notes

20

The Power of Community

❝ Alone, we can do so little; together, we can do so much. ❞

—Helen Keller

> **Financial Freedom Framework**
>
> Communities can play a vital role in your growth as a human being. But they can also hinder that growth. Surround yourself with the right people and teams to achieve your life goals and financial aspirations.

As Dr Martin Luther King Jr. once said, "We are caught in an inescapable network of mutuality, tied in a single garment of destiny. Whatever affects one directly, affects all indirectly."

You might be a little bit surprised to see a chapter on community in a book talking about financial planning and financial freedom, but the reality is that human beings strive for community. We need it to be healthy, happy, and, eventually, financially free.

Community might not be exactly what you think it is. If you break down the word "community," you get "common unity." Community is typically a group of individuals connected to each other by one or more common attributes.

As our lives change and we move through different phases—when we're younger, working, and retired—our communities might change because those common core elements might also change throughout our lives. Some of us hold to demographic, social, economic, religious, or value-based communities that might not change as much over time. For instance, some people stay in their church their entire life. Your family is a form of community that might evolve and change, but remains the same unit for most of your life.

But think about other types of communities that change more frequently. For example, your work community is probably constantly evolving as people come in and out of the workforce. When you think about online communities on Facebook, Twitter, and LinkedIn, they're constantly evolving and changing, in terms of both the medium and the type of information that's relayed.

You might think about your neighborhood and where you live. Neighborhoods change—people move in and they move out—and the community develops and modifies based on the commonalities of the group that lives there at each time.

We're probably involved in many more communities than we might think.

There are broad communities and more narrow communities. There are communities that we actively choose to be part of, and others that I call "accidental communities," which are communities we didn't seek out but that we find ourselves in.

Some communities we feel incredibly passionate about, and others might make us feel lonely, isolated, or unsafe. Communities are almost always described with the connotation that they're safe, warm, welcoming places where we're surrounded by others who lift us up and carry us forward. But the reality is that while communities can be positive and uplifting, they can also be dangerous and stunt our growth. They can create bad and harmful habits in us. They can actually bring down both our physical and mental health.

The reason we're discussing community is we want to make sure that we're not falling into accidental communities that are harmful to our well-being and our journey to financial freedom and mental and physical wellness. Instead, we want to focus on the communities that are positive and raise us up and allow us to be better, to achieve our goals, to see the possibility of things that we didn't believe were possible.

Let's try an exercise right now. Write down five to ten communities you're a part of. You might initially think you're not part of five communities, but I can tell you that almost everybody alive is part of at least five different communities—your family, friends, religion, nationality, work, former work, maybe a sport. Then the next step is to write down a 1—10 rating for each community, with 1 representing a community you actively chose to be part of, and 10 a community you did not choose. For example, you'd rate your family a 10 because you didn't decide to be part of that community, you were born into it, whereas your friends would be a 1.

This is an interesting exercise to challenge our mind, to see that we pick certain communities while others occur more naturally. I also want you to take some time and reflect on something you get out of each of these communities. Do you feel welcome? Do you feel loved? Are you part of an art community where you learn and are inspired to create and build? This helps us narrow in on the function that each community plays in our life.

After you see what's positive about your involvement in each community, I want you to go further and identify one thing that you'd improve about each community experience for yourself. Is there one that you feel forced into? One you don't feel welcome in or a part of? Is there one that encourages negative behaviors, like a group of friends that spend too much money, drink too much, and stay out too late? Do you have a group of friends that are negative and pull you down and criticize things? Are you part of a local community that doesn't live a healthy and fulfilling lifestyle?

We need to challenge the ways that we think about community. Going one step further, it's also a really big myth and misconception that communities should immediately feel like home. Some of the best communities should not feel like a reversion to the past, like you've walked into your house and everybody knows you. There's research from psychologists that gravitating toward communities that feel like home can stunt our growth because we're looking backwards, not forwards.

Find communities that challenge you to grow

We should be looking for communities that not only make us feel that we're safe, but that challenge us to grow as individuals. One of the best things about a community is that others in the community can show us how to do things that we never would have been able to do without them. When you see someone succeed inside of a community, it builds that belief that you can succeed too. Think about that in life: a time when somebody did something that you didn't think you could do, but then you saw them do it and you said, "Wow, if she can do it, then I can do it, too." It gives you that belief in yourself because you can benchmark off of others in your community. Since you have a common unity, if they accomplish something, you know you can too.

We have to find communities that uplift us, not just hold us to where we were before. If we're trying to go on a journey to become more financially independent—we want to save and invest—we need to find communities that will help us do that.

What are our aspirations? And are we around those that have similar thoughts, ideas, and aspirations? On the investing side, there have been communities like the Bogleheads, who follow the works of John Bogle, Vanguard, and low-cost investing. They come together in an online community and discuss investing. There are investing chapters that meet all across the country to discuss do-it-yourself investing and recent trends in the market.

Colleges get investment clubs together in which people talk about finances. Financial planning chapters exist all over the country where people come together to discuss proper and healthy financial planning and coaching.

Think about how important your finances are to your life—are you surrounding yourself with a community that encourages and promotes positive financial behavior? If you don't have that type of community, do you want it? People don't always want a community around particular aspects of their life. For instance, when I was big into running, I didn't run with other people. I viewed running as "me time." It was time for me to reflect. It was time for me to exercise. It was time for me to be alone and away from the rest of the world. I needed that personal time.

However, as I mentioned before, communities change, we change, our needs and wants change. I ran the Boston Marathon during the year of the bombing. The bombing was a tremendous tragedy, but it brought together both the city of Boston and many of the runners who had shared that experience. After going through such a tragic and terrifying time, I felt much closer to the running community. I felt that I was a part of it. I felt like I had experienced something that gave me a shared unity with them. After that, running wasn't just about me going out to exercise and meditate anymore, I found a home. While I wasn't seeking that, I found an accidental community from the shared experience, not because of my own decision. But then I embraced that and now I love the running community. I love talking to people about running, their training, what races they're going to do, how they got into running, and why they love it.

Community can be built in your work environment too. Recently I was talking to a financial advisor, who works with us here at Carson Group, who said, "This is the first time I've ever felt like this in my life; this is just so special and so amazing." I asked them what was special and amazing. They said, "I don't feel alone anymore."

This was because they were now around other advisors who had this common goal and unity in putting clients' interests first during financial planning, coming together to make an impact on the world.

While creating that feeling for everybody was not the primary goal at Carson—that was more about simply doing the right thing—we started to create a community of people who wanted to be there because others were raising the bar and doing better and better. It was very inspiring to hear we're having that impact on a person.

Community across different stages

While this chapter is a little bit shorter than other chapters, the aim is to help you understand that as you begin your foundational planning—and as you move through life—you should think about how communities around you can help raise you up and create positive financial behaviors.

As you start to accumulate wealth and become a little bit more stable, you're surrounding yourself with individuals who are also growing and learning about finances, spending, and saving for college.

When you start moving into the strategic phase, are you sitting down and talking to people who have experienced retirement and have been strategic about investing and taxes?

As your wealth grows even more, are you immersing yourself in the charities and communities that you want to impact? We often hear stories about people saying, "I want to make an impact, I want to give back, I want to help raise up a community in my estate." But those people never actually spend any time in that community. They don't go down and meet the people and engage with them and talk to them. If you want to have an impact in a community, spend time in that community first.

Your financial advisory team is a community. Are you surrounding yourself with the team—the planner, the tax CPA, attorney, investment specialist, insurance specialist—that's creating positive financial behaviors and a safe place for you to grow on your journey to financial freedom? This is a purposeful community that you get to develop.

But a lot of people fall into accidental communities with their team—they pick up an advisor here, an investment there, or they develop this habit from family and friends. They don't take control of that aspect of their community.

It's important to know the difference between the communities that you create and the ones you don't, and to design the communities you want to help you become a better, healthier, and more stable person.

One parting challenge

The last thing I want to challenge you to do is examine what role you play in your community. I never used to think about communities like this until I had to start leading teams, leading organizations that are overseeing nonprofits, leading communities of advisors, and leading a family.

I realized that I play different roles in different types of communities. My role as a father and brother within my family community is different than that of a boss, and it's different than my role as an educator teaching thousands of financial advisors about retirement income planning, and it's different than leading a nonprofit board. I have to use different skill sets and function differently across these different communities. Not every community needs me to be a driver. Sometimes they just need me to listen, create, and manage.

Think about your role in the community and the role of your communities. If they're not uplifting you, make a change. Remove yourself and find the right communities to get you on your path to financial freedom.

Five key takeaways

1 Community is typically a group of individuals connected to each other by one or more common attributes.

2 Communities can play a vital role in your growth as a human being. But they can also hinder that growth.

3 As our life changes and we move through different phases, our communities might change.

4 We're probably involved in many more communities than we might think.

5 We want to make sure that we're not falling into accidental communities that are harmful to our well-being and our journey to financial freedom.

Five reflection questions

1 What communities are you part of?

2 Of those communities, which ones bring you the most joy?

3 Of those communities, which ones push you outside of your comfort zone and help you be better?

4 What community makes you feel unwelcome and unsafe?

5 In which community do you feel most welcome and why?

Notes

21

Making an Impact Through Efficient Charitable Giving

GG Those who are the happiest are those who do the
most for others. *DD*

—*Booker T. Washington*

Financial Freedom Framework

Charitable giving can be energizing and meaningful. You
can give back to causes you're passionate about and make an
impact. But oftentimes people give in inefficient ways. You can
give in a way that is just as impactful but that saves you money
in the long run.

A T THE BEGINNING of the book, I talked about how I don't
like giving and receiving gifts. It brings back bad memories and
it has always felt uncomfortable. But when you shift the conversation just ever so slightly to giving to charity, my mindset shifts
completely.

I love the impact of gifting to charities, to your church, to your school, to local food banks, or to those in need. It energizes me and is often one of the most meaningful things I do with my money.

Like many people, as my wealth has grown over time, I've felt more freedom and opportunity to give to charity. Initially I began giving because I was asked. My school would email, and I would send them money. I'd pass somebody on the street in need and they'd ask for money and maybe I'd consider it and give some. I'd go to church and put money in the basket.

I started to realize that I was only giving to those who had access to me and were asking. It was all reactive giving. I hadn't done the exercise or set the framework of what giving means to me and how to incorporate it into my financial plan.

I had to take a meaningful step backwards, and I had to ask myself, why do I want to give to others? What is the purpose of my giving? The only reason I asked myself these questions was because somebody I was extremely close to started getting involved, giving both their time and money to a charity that provided disabled individuals with access to support animals. They got involved because they had a family member who needed a support animal, and they were able to work with this charity to get the animal trained and delivered and help fund it. They realized that many people don't have access to this support. They decided that their role in giving was to create a bridge between the solution that existed and the need.

Seeing this, I took a step back and I answered the questions: What role do I want to play in charitable giving? Do I want to dedicate my time, my skills, my resources? Do I want to volunteer strategically for boards and help drive the direction of charity?

My answers will likely change over the course of my life, but I decided to get involved and donate my time, energy, and resources. Then I identified what types of charities matter the most to me. My friend Christian asked me while we were sitting on a rooftop in Chicago: "Jamie, what keeps you up at night?" He was really asking about my business. But I said, "You know what, Christian? Nothing in my business world keeps me up at night. I don't lose sleep over the business side of things I lose sleep because I know that there are people out there who don't have access to clean water, who can't eat, whose children are going to bed tonight hungry and thirsty."

We know what the solution is: clean water and food. There's enough food and water to make sure that nobody on this planet goes to bed hungry or thirsty, yet the resources and dedication to close the gap between the two are not there.

After that conversation I realized I wanted to give back by donating time to food banks and also donating my money to help with that supply chain and solution issue.

Tying giving to your values

I ended up working with a firm that Carson has supported tremendously, called Charity Water. Charity Water puts every dollar of your donation towards clean water for those who don't have it today. This tied what I wanted to do with what I cared about and my core values. I didn't want to donate to a charity that I felt was inefficient with their resources. I didn't want to donate to a charity where I couldn't see the impact that they were having. I wanted to understand the impact my money and time were making.

What I was able to create by being thoughtful about how I give, what I want to give, and the impact I want to have was a sense of control and connection to the charitable work being done, which has inspired me to give more each year.

I often say that charitable giving is like a yawn—it's contagious. You see one person yawn and another yawns. This is also true with charitable giving. Once you start giving in a meaningful way, the giving grows. Once you see somebody else's life impacted by the charitable decisions you make, you want to give more.

Not everybody can give resources today. It can be hard for some people, early in their careers when they're in the fundamental planning stage, to give lots of time or money. But if you take care of yourself and start building quality financial behaviors, you can start building charitable giving into your plan. Once you get a little bit further down the line and you're becoming more stable, you can start giving back to your college, your church, and some of the local organizations that are uplifting your communities more easily.

Eventually, you can get strategic about giving and start to add in the tax benefits. You can go from inefficient giving to efficient giving. Many people just give when they're asked, which is not efficient. In some cases this will actually eliminate your ability to give more. When you can get strategic and improve the efficiency of your giving through tax-efficient and planned giving strategies, you can save money in taxes and also increase the amount that you give over time.

Once we get past that, we can work on leaving a legacy. We can start thinking about transformational gifts that uplift communities and have a lasting impact for generations. Our legacy can be part of fundamentally changing the direction of an organization, an area, research on cures for diseases, or a group of people. That's really what we mean when we talk about legacy—how we're giving our dollars, time, and energy to create the impact we want to see.

Building the emotional connection

Another question you have to ask before you start charitable giving is: are you a charitably inclined person? It's not for everybody. You have to create that connection. If you feel no connection to what you're doing in the charitable organization that you're donating time and resources to, you won't end up having the impact that you want.

We see it time and time again in different surveys: people feel disconnected from the charities that they give to. When people get more, they give more. When I talk about giving, it's not just money—though money is often important for charities—it's also your time, your thoughts, your energy, and your connection. But again, you have to be able to find that connection. Examine why you give. Decide who you want to give to and how you want to give to them, and then you can plan and become more efficient with your giving.

It's important to test out different charities. Try some charities you might like, to see if you have a connection. Ask them how many of your dollars are going to the charitable initiatives that you want. Ask to hear stories and see impact numbers. Ask them how they measure success.

Often people give to charities and don't ask those questions to really see if their money, time, and energy are having an impact. I'm going to push and question you right here, right now: have you done this? If not, why haven't you done this? If you haven't, you're being less efficient and limiting your impact because you didn't put in the work on the front end of giving.

Start crafting the plan

After you test it out and you find a charity that you feel good about, and you know the impact that's having, you can start to get a plan in place. Your plan can address how often you want to give, how much you want to give, and whether you want to increase giving over time. You can explore whether there are other types of assets and strategies to pull in. Once we have built the emotional and cerebral foundation of charitable giving, we can get to the financial planning, tax, investment, and tactical parts.

Here's where the rubber meets the road of your personal goals, beliefs and desire to have an impact, and the financial planning tactics that can best help you accomplish those outcomes. When we start looking at those tactics, we can think about cash giving, non-cash gifts, appreciated asset giving, charitable remainder and charitable lead trusts, and beneficiaries of accounts (so more at death or through our estate transfers to charities). We can consider bunching strategies to become more efficient with our giving, and also things like qualified charitable distributions, or even a charitable gift annuity. We start running through all of these different strategies and tactics. There's no one strategy or tactic that is best for us, but they can all play important roles.

Let's run through that list of strategies here really quickly. Note that this is by no means an exhaustive list of all the approaches we could use in our financial plan to increase the effectiveness of our giving.

Cash

This is the easiest way to give to charity, but it's often the least efficient from a tax and financial planning standpoint. The majority of gifts to charities come in the form of cash, however, the majority of assets in the United States exist in non-cash assets. We have a fundamental problem because most people think that they need to give cash to charities when other assets tend to be more efficient.

If you go to charitable websites, you'll see many charities accept non-cash assets. They will accept land, cryptocurrencies, paintings, stocks, bonds, and any other assets you can think of.

One of the reasons that charities like to accept non-cash gifts is because there's a tax benefit attached to gifting appreciated assets.

Appreciated assets

Let's quickly talk about the value of gifting appreciated assets. This is one that should challenge the way you think about giving today. If you take one thing from a tactical standpoint from this chapter, it's to think differently about the way you give in the future. Let's say you have a stock that you bought for $1,000 but is now worth $20,000. You decide you want to give your favorite charity $20,000. You have two choices: cash out that stock, pay taxes on the $19,000 (because you had $19,000 of growth and a $1,000 basis), gift the remainder to charity, then get a deduction for the amount you gifted. Or you could give the charity the appreciated stock worth $20,000 and get a deduction for the $20,000. The charity can then sell the stock. Because they're a charity they don't pay income taxes, and you still get a deduction for the full amount of the $20,000. This second option is the more efficient way to give. You gave away the same asset, you paid less in taxes, and you gave more to the charity.

But so often, people take the first option. If we're not engaging in financial planning, we don't know about these tactics. And if all we're doing is being reactive when we're asked for cash gifts, we'll likely continue to just give cash gifts and not get tactical about it.

Deeper into the tactics

There are many different giving tactics, like different types of trusts, that can also be efficient ways to give. Some that have become very popular in recent years are charitable remainder trusts (CRTs) and charitable lead trusts.

Charitable remainder trusts

CRTs are in essence an irrevocable trust in which you put assets to provide income to you or another beneficiary for a set period of time, with the remaining assets going to a charity. I often call this a "gifting for income" strategy—you give away assets, but you keep income out of it.

If you were to set up a CRT today, you'd be able to generate a deduction of the present value of the remainder interest expected to go to the charity. This can be a dynamic way to create a large charitable deduction (and a charitable impact), but keep the income off of the assets placed into the trust for the remainder of your or your spouse's life, so that you can maintain your quality of living. You'll create a charitable impact today, while you're alive, and the charity will be excited because they'll know assets have been set aside in this trust for them. It creates a connection between you and the charity today, versus waiting until you pass away.

Charitable lead trusts

A charitable lead trust is the flip of the CRT—the charity gets the income stream now and the remainder goes back to your heirs. This could be a good option for somebody who has income-producing property and wants to leave a legacy while maintaining their generational wealth and supporting a charity today.

Qualified charitable distributions

Another strategy that I like is marrying our retirement savings and charitable giving together with QCDs. These can be used after you reach age 70½ and you can send up to $100,000 directly from your IRA to a qualified charity—that distribution will not be treated as taxable income. It's a very efficient way to give. For instance, if you're just giving $1,000 a year to charity and you're over age 70½, you have an IRA, and you're a standard filer, you're not getting a tax benefit for that donation. But if you sent that money directly from your IRA to the charity, that wouldn't show up as taxable income and you can use that amount to offset RMDs that are owed that year. So you can reduce the RMD amount you have to take as taxable income, still give to charity, and not have any of it show up as taxable income, which is actually better in most situations.

Bunching

Like we've talked about before, spreading charitable gifts out over time isn't always the best way to give. If we bunch those gifts together in a particular year, we could give more and reduce our taxes by being strategic about getting that charitable tax deduction. This strategy can be used in years when we want to itemize instead of taking the standard deduction.

Donor-advised funds

Donor-advised funds (DAFs) allow you to put money into an investment fund, spread out your charitable distributions from the donor-advised fund over numerous years, but receive the full value of the charitable contribution in the year you put it into the DAF.

For example, you could put $50,000 into a DAF today, deduct that against your taxable income this year, but still have that money sent to your favorite charity in $10,000 checks over the next five years. You'll be invested over the next five years, and the charity also gets that investment return.

DAFs have seen huge growth in recent years and continue to be a very powerful planning tool for efficient and effective giving.

This is not an exhaustive list of charitable giving strategies or tactics, but hopefully it has opened your eyes to how a couple of small tweaks to your giving strategy can enhance the tax benefits, create more connection to your charity, and increase the impact of your charitable giving over time.

Giving isn't just about taxes, but we know that if we get a bigger tax benefit, we're more likely to give. We also know that the more connected we are to the charity, the more likely we are to give. And the more clearly we can see the impact of our giving, the more likely we are to give. So let's incorporate all those into our planning.

Giving: a family affair

I want to close with one last bit of advice when it comes to charitable giving: get the family involved. A strategy that my wife and I have adopted with our children is to get them involved with charitable giving and its impact at a very early age. Instead of giving gifts to our cousins come the holidays, we sit our children down and let them pick charities that they want to give to based on things that they care about. They've picked children's hospitals, a church, and a wildlife foundation. We're able to show them the impact—people getting food and animals being saved. They know that they're picking something meaningful. Then we send information about the charities' impact to the cousins who we've donated on behalf of.

You can start to develop the giving mentality within your young children. You can teach them to give back to the world that we benefit from, that they can have a positive charitable impact on things that matter to them in the world. This has been a transformative experience for my family.

It's important that your children and grandchildren know about the charities and causes that you care about so if they end up managing or inheriting your money, they will give back in a way that respects your legacy and wishes, even if you're not there anymore.

I've never met anyone who's said they didn't want their family to know about the causes they care about. People want those around them to care about the things that they're involved with and want their loved ones to become charitably inclined themselves.

Connect with charitable giving, plan to do it in an efficient way, get your loved ones involved, and build charitable giving into your legacy.

Five key takeaways

1 Charitable giving can be a meaningful way to make an impact.

2 Charitable giving can either be efficient or inefficient.

3 You have to determine why you give and what impact you want to have.

4 Charitable giving is contagious.

5 If you take care of yourself and build quality financial behaviors, you can start building charitable giving into your plan.

Five reflection questions

1 What causes are you passionate about that you'd like to give back to?

2 Are you reactive with your charitable giving, meaning you only give when asked?

3 Is your charitable giving strategy efficient or inefficient? In what ways can you improve?

4 What are some social issues that keep you up at night?

5 What is the charitable legacy and impact you'd ideally like to leave?

Notes

22

More Time for Fun

GG We don't stop playing because we grow old, we grow old because we stop playing. *DD*

—*George Bernard Shaw*

Financial Freedom Framework

Making time to have fun, take vacations, and do the things that make us happier can actually improve our memory and alleviate stress. In addition to your personal and professional goals, you should also have goals for the type of fun that you want to have in your life and be sure to incorporate those into your planning.

THE QUOTE ABOVE, from George Bernard Shaw, is one of my absolute favorites.

Fun should be something we strive for. If you look up some of the definitions of *fun*, it's about amusement, life, and being playful. I love these definitions. Think about how good we were at playing when we were children and living in a mindset of fun and activity. Interestingly enough, research shows that when we have more fun we decrease stress and live happier and healthier lives.[24] Yet as we move through life, and start to think about financial plans and work, we lose sight of fun. We see it happen to people all throughout the workplace, all throughout financial planning—they don't focus on fun.

When we lose sight of fun and play, it can harm our relationships, our connections, and our communities. It can harm our relationship with our spouse or our kids. Couples that know how to have fun together tend to be happier and show more affection toward each other. Having fun actually makes us smarter and improves our memory and concentration. If you look at students who take more breaks and schedule in time to have fun, they end up retaining more information. We can't just go, go, go and work, work, work all the time. We have to build fun into our lives to relieve stress, and to improve our brain activity, overall energy, and youthfulness.

I also think it's important to figure out ways to incorporate fun into our regular lives. How can we have more fun at work, in our relationships, and doing chores around the house? Simple things, like putting on music that you love while you do chores or while you cook or clean, listening to music when you work out, or listening to music at work. Taking breaks to do work in places that you love, like going to work at a coffee shop or outside in the sunshine. Change things up and incorporate fun things you enjoy into your life.

That actually requires us to define and envision what fun is for us. It might seem a little bit weird, but we should actually list out the things that we enjoy doing. Not just the things we want to do in the future, but the things we enjoy doing today. So what do you like to do? Do you like cooking? Do you like exercise? Watching TV? Reading? Spending time with family? Define what you enjoy and what's fun to you.

It's also helpful to draw out those things you would like to do and that you expect to be fun for you. Where do you want to travel? What do you want to do there? What vacations do you want to take? What experiences do you want to have? What food would you like to try? What restaurants would you like to visit? How would you like to spend time with your family? What things would you like to celebrate?

Often people talk about these items as forming a "bucket list"—things you want to do for fun before you pass away. But this list doesn't have to consist only of big items. They can be small things, like making sure you have dinners together on Sunday night at the table, because you enjoy that and have fun doing it.

So we can define what fun means for us. We can write out and envision how we currently have fun and how we could have more fun in the future. We can set goals for how much we want to play. We can measure whether we're meeting these goals, to understand if we're having enough fun in our lives. If we're not, we can start scheduling more fun. Understandably, fun can't be scheduled for everybody all the time, but if we start to notice the daily grind of work and life taking joy away, we can push back and schedule more fun.

For some people, fun needs to be spontaneous. If you're one of them, you can explore ways to encourage spontaneity, including not packing your schedule and balancing time to be free and to enjoy your life. Remember that finances are a means to an end, they're not the end goal. This is not a high-score game where you want to accumulate as much wealth as humanly possible and die with the highest possible dollar amount in your bank account. Finances provide us the means to do the things that we enjoy doing. We shouldn't let saving for retirement, for college education expenses, and investing for the future control our lives to the point that we lose sight of having fun. We have to find balance between the two. Balance isn't always the same thing for everyone. To take this a little bit into the work-life setting, I don't personally believe in work-life balance; I believe in work-life synergy. I think keeping the two separate is very hard. We have one life, one self, one being, and to act as if we're two separate beings—one in the realm of work and another in life outside of work—is very hard. If we try to put up walls between the two sides of ourselves, and then they end up mixing anyway, it starts creating conflict. Instead I believe in finding work that you love to do and incorporating that into your lifestyle to create a workplace synergy where work and life build and feed off of each other.

That doesn't mean that work needs to control your life, or your life needs to control your work. You have one life, so make all elements of it connected together and wonderful. That way when you're at "work," you don't feel like you're working. You feel like you're living and making the impact that you want to make in the world.

We talked about getting clear on your "why" earlier. What do you want in life? If you get clear on your "why" and then you build your life around it, you're going to have more fun than you've ever had before. This also goes back to the type of planning philosophy that we at Carson try to use with people, which is looking at needs, wants, and wishes. Our needs are the basics we have to take care of. If we don't take care of those foundational needs in our financial plans, we won't be able to focus on the wants and wishes—the things that actually bring us enjoyment and happiness in life.

When we focus on, and take care of, our needs and build a financial plan with those foundational pieces in place, we can start taking care of our wants. Then, if we get really deep into the bucketing plan, we can get to those wishes. We can bring back that enjoyment and fun in our vacations, spending time with family, breaking out of our routines, and having the lifestyle that we really want. That's financial freedom—to be able to have the fun and enjoy life like we want.

In the book *Paychecks and Playchecks: Retirement Solutions for Life*, the author states after we set aside money for basic needs in retirement, we can take our other paychecks, income sources, and money, and put those towards fun. This goes right back to needs, wants, and wishes and how we can set up our planning to encourage our spending for fun. I've seen this time and time again. I have retirees and people who have accumulated lots of wealth, but they don't have a financial plan in place, they don't have a spending plan, and they haven't figured out how much money they can spend. They're self-insuring against the risk of running out of money. But because they haven't done the planning, run the numbers, looked at their expenses and their income, or looked at their investment returns, they haven't actually figured out what they can spend over the rest of their life and they don't spend enough money. They actually end up underspending and they cut back on the things they enjoy because they're hyper-focused on taking care of their needs—they don't end up spending on their wants and wishes. Then they end up having a less enjoyable and satisfying life, even though they had the finances to live a more financially free and enjoyable one. They limited themselves by failing to do financial planning. That limitation seeped throughout their entire lives because they were living in fear of running out of money. When you're driven by fear and a scarcity mindset, you can't live in abundance. You won't spend and enjoy your life to the extent that you could.

So write out the things you like to do and want to do to have fun. Be crystal clear. Then incorporate more of them into your life. Put together a bucket list of the fun things you want to accomplish. Those can become your wants and wishes. Then you can build your financial plan to meet those wants and wishes over time and can set assets and income sources aside to make sure that you can accomplish those things on our path to financial freedom.

Five key takeaways

1 Fun should be something we strive for in life.
2 Research shows that when we have more fun in life, we decrease stress and we live a happier and healthier life.
3 When we lose sight of fun and play, it can harm our relationships, our connections, and our communities.
4 It's important to figure out ways to incorporate fun into our regular lives.
5 If we're not having fun in our lives, we need to start scheduling time to do so.

Five reflection questions

1 What are your favorite ways to unwind and relax? Do you do enough of them now?

2 How has focusing too much on work impacted your relationships?
   Your partner? Kids? Friends?

3 What does "fun" mean to you?

4 If you could take your dream vacation, what would that look like?
   Where are you going? With whom? How long are you staying?

5 What are the top five items on your bucket list?

Notes

23

Celebrate Your Accomplishments for Continued Success

“ You have to remember that the hard days are what make you stronger. The bad days make you realize what a good day is. If you never had any bad days, you would never have that sense of accomplishment! ”

—Aly Raisman, Olympian

Financial Freedom Framework

Acknowledging our accomplishments is a way of celebrating ourselves. It's also a way to gain confidence to continue to have success in the future. Celebrate how far you've come so you can get the confidence to achieve your ultimate aspirations.

" **S**TOP AND SMELL the roses." You've likely heard this saying before. Honestly, until I had kids, I don't know that I ever did stop and smell the roses. But my daughter loves roses and every time she sees them she wants to stop and smell them and ask if she can have one. She loves flowers and grew up helping her mom plant rose bushes around our house. Those are special moments for her and she feels connected to her mom and the flowers.

But many people aren't like my daughter. They don't stop and smell the roses throughout their lives and financial journeys. What do I mean by that? We need to stop to reflect on our accomplishments so far in the planning process that we use—all the positive momentum, accomplishments, and goals that we have reached.

We're on this journey to our ultimate aspiration. While we might never get all the way to the peak of that mountain—to that fully financially free moment in our life—we're on that journey. And along that journey, we're going to run into challenges and hurdles and we're going to achieve things that we never thought were possible. But we often don't stop and look back at them. We hit the goal, we say we're done, and we charge forward on our path.

Take the time to reflect

True reflection on our accomplishments is actually a form of self-care. Many of us focus on the to-do list, but when we're constantly focusing on the things that are ahead of us, we constantly feel empty inside because those things aren't checked off. So we're constantly looking at the things we haven't done and lose sight of how much progress we've made.

Perhaps you started saving, you got a job, you increased your pay, you started putting money in your 401(k) to invest, you paid down credit card and student loan debt, you bought a house, you bought a car, you refinanced, you reallocated, you filed your taxes each year on time, and you go back and you look and you think, "Wow, I've accomplished so much."

When you were standing at the bottom of the mountain, you couldn't see the top. And while the top is still above you, you're halfway up. You might not be able to see the top until you get there, but you're closer to the top than you were. Often we don't look behind us to see how far we've actually come and that the journey for many of us is the important part.

It's important for us to take periodic breaks from the busy day-to-day—the goal setting, the drive, the determination of moving forward—and take time to see how far we've come. Pat yourself on the back. Exhale. Write down all those accomplishments.

One thing I love to tell people to do is to write a thank-you letter to yourself for all the things that you've accomplished. You deserve it. You've done so many good things. Often we lose sight of this if we don't take the time to reflect.

When we take time to acknowledge what we're good at and what we've accomplished, we're essentially giving ourselves a compliment. We're saying, "Self, look, we went on a journey and we did a lot of good things." This compliment and recognition of what we're good at, and the ability to stop and praise the things that we have accomplished, let us increase our confidence as we move forward.

We recognize our strengths and we continue to build upon them to set new goals. Acknowledging our accomplishments is a way of celebrating ourselves. How else are we going to move forward and continue to have success if we don't have confidence in what we've already done? Taking the time to reflect helps us move forward.

Celebrate, for real

To recognize our accomplishments, sometimes we need to take more time to celebrate—have dinner with our family and friends and publicly acknowledge our accomplishments. This can actually inspire others. This might sound cheesy or corny, but these can be powerful and motivating factors in the communities around us. For instance, if you make a charitable gift that's going to change the course of a community or a group of people, you're often going to get a celebration, or at the very least a thank-you. People will take the time to reflect on the positive impact this has had.

But you can do this on smaller scales. You can have family over to celebrate saving more for college, paying off your mortgage, paying off your student loan debt. This also helps inspire others to act and to follow the more positive momentum.

When we take time to reflect on our accomplishments, we can learn from them. We get to look back and see what worked and what didn't. We get to figure out how to avoid mistakes we otherwise might make in the future, or to build upon the positive by identifying something that worked so we can repeat it. Not everything has to be focused on the negative in the past.

By building up our confidence through focusing on our strengths, we can increase our motivation for moving forward. We now know that by acknowledging our successes, we can fuel the motivation to keep going. It creates the mindset of success.

Start with gratitude

If you struggle to focus on your accomplishments because you don't want to get stuck in the past, consider journaling. Write these things down. Start with a gratitude journal. Writing down one thing that you are grateful for each day for seven days is such a powerful thing to do, because every day you should be grateful for something. There's always something to be grateful for in this world. Those small pieces of gratitude will build on each other and become massive mountains. With those mountains, we can do anything.

Often in life I see people reflect back on getting married and having kids, but we often don't take the time to specifically focus on the financial decisions and improvements that we've accomplished. This could involve looking at milestones—all the good behavior, decisions, and actions we took—so when we're trying to set goals in the future, we can know that we've done it before, which can help motivate us further and further along in our journey. Here at Carson, we show this in our planning process in something we call "Life's Moments." In essence it serves as a timeline of all the great moments, money successes, and financial planning accomplishments that you have achieved so far.

A reflection exercise

Let's do a task to help us with reflection. Let's write down one peak experience that's occurred in the last 12 months as it relates to your financial future. Write down that one accomplishment. Then write down why it's meaningful for you. Then write down what you learned from this accomplishment that you want to take forward with you in life. And finally, write down what you wish you'd have known before this accomplishment. In other words, what would you go back and tell your past self about this accomplishment?

Write down those four things about a financial accomplishment you've had in the last 12 months. If you can't think of one in the last 12 months, you could expand it out, but try your best to limit it to the last 12 months—even if it's a small thing, like you paid off a credit card or you did something on time. Remember that small accomplishments are still important.

In fact, all accomplishments are important. They help set a framework for what we've done so we can find a framework to move forward. If you start feeling hopeless, which happens to people at all stages of planning, you can change that mindset by focusing on the things you're good at and the things you can develop. I often tell people not to focus on their weaknesses. Often, we get this misconception that if we focus on our weaknesses, we could make improvements in our life. But we're often better off focusing on our strengths. We talked earlier about how the world's greatest athletes focus on what they're good at. They don't focus on aspects of the sport that they're not good at. In Chapter 5, I mentioned Tom Brady and how he doesn't focus on tackling in the off season. He focuses on his strengths, which include throwing the football and studying defenses and learning how to be a better quarterback. Of course he could focus on other aspects of football and improve those, but that won't make as meaningful an impact on his game as he will focusing on what he's good at.

I'm going to be honest, taking time to focus on achievements isn't an easy task for me. I struggle with this. I always want more. I want to keep adding new goals, keep building things, and keep moving forward. I often just pass over major accomplishments and projects in my life. Sometimes that's harmful to my team and people around me because they need time to stop and reflect, but I want to keep moving forward. So I've had to change my mindset around the importance of reflection on accomplishments. I've had to stop and ensure everybody who was involved with that accomplishment feels that positivity. You should do that, too. So if you bought a house, did you thank your family and those who helped you? If you paid off student loan debt, did you stop and thank your spouse or somebody else who helped you create a plan to pay it off? If you went on a vacation, did you stop and say thanks to somebody along the way who helped make that vacation better and more enjoyable for you?

That's part of looking back on accomplishments—recognizing those who helped us along the path and showing gratitude to them. When we show gratitude to others, it comes back to us tenfold, because the next time we need help along our path, somebody will be there for us. We'll have other people to raise us up in this interwoven web in which we live in our communities.

So stop along your way to financial freedom, smell the roses, and realize all of the amazing things that you and those walking this path with you have already accomplished.

Five key takeaways

1 Take time to reflect on your accomplishments.
2 True reflection on and celebration of our accomplishments is actually a form of self-care.
3 It's important for us to take periodic breaks from the busy day-to-day—the goal setting, the drive, the determination of moving forward—and take time to look back.
4 Take time to recognize people who've helped you achieve your goals.
5 Acknowledging how far you've come can give you the motivation to continue going.

Five reflection questions

1 When was the last time you achieved something you were proud of? Did you celebrate? How did you celebrate?

2 What are two to three accomplishments you've had in the last five years that you're proud of?

3 How do you usually celebrate things in your life?

4 What are you grateful for today?

5 When you achieve something, how do you thank the people who helped you get there?

Notes

24

The Estate and Emotional Sides of Legacy

> ❝ That is your legacy on this Earth when you leave this Earth: how many hearts you touched. ❞
>
> —*Patti Davis, author and actress*

Financial Freedom Framework

Planning for a good end of life and the legacy you want to leave is just as important as all the other aspects of financial planning. Legacy has two different aspects in end-of-life planning: the emotional aspect and the estate planning aspect.

LEGACY ISN'T JUST something from the past. We're not talking just about something you learned or saw looking backwards. Legacy is about looking forward to our end of life and the impact that we have after it.

Often people say, "I want to live a good life. I want to live a happy life." And I often question them: "Why don't you also want to plan for a good end of life?" We just don't think about it in those terms. We think about living well, but we don't think about dying well. Part of this is we live in a death-denying and death-defying society. We keep trying to live longer and longer. We improve wellness, but we don't like talking about death. We don't like discussing it with our families and we don't like planning around it. But guess what? Breaking research: 100% of people die. A study from Massachusetts Institute of Technology showed that over 40% of Americans will die with less than $10,000.[25]

Planning for a good end of life is not so much about the dollars and cents as it is about the impact and legacy that we leave behind. The legacy can be two different things as it relates to end-of-life planning. First, legacy can be the emotional and value-based aspects that we leave behind. Second, it also involves the financial planning side of an end of life, which we call our estate plan. Everybody, in my view, needs an estate plan.

Estate side of legacy

I've always used a ten-step process to plan for a good end of life and estate plan:

- Prioritize and understand your goals.
- Involve the family.
- Make a financial assessment.
- Review housing and care alternatives.
- Review the current plan.
- Establish advanced directives.
- Implement the plan.
- Communicate the plan.
- Distribute documents.
- Review and update.

This might seem simple and straightforward, but so many people fail to follow this repeatable, scalable, and impactful process. Now, let's go through each one of these steps.

Step 1: prioritize and understand your goals

A good estate plan starts with understanding and prioritizing goals that you might have. For instance, if your estate planning goal is to pay off the debt of your surviving spouse, that will take different tactics than if your estate plan is to transfer all of your wealth to a charity.

You need to start with your goals. Otherwise you'll walk aimlessly around in circles talking about the best solutions, best tax planning, and best vehicles for transferring wealth, when those are all really determined by the ultimate outcome that you want to achieve.

Step 2: involve the family

The reason to prioritize involving your family, friends, or loved ones so early in the planning process is that the vast majority of your estate and legacy plan has nothing to do with you and nothing to do with the money. It has to do with the impact you want to leave behind once you're gone. Do you want to leave your family in turmoil and suffering, or do you want to leave people in a better place?

This can be the basis of your estate plan—to give people guidance you need to tell them how you want to be taken care of, how you want your burial to occur, the values you want to instill in them, how you want money separated. Nothing will tear a family apart faster than fights over money after somebody has passed away.

Step 3: make a financial assessment

Your financial assessment is exactly that— you need to review where your finances are. This will start to determine some of the estate planning tactics that you'll use. If you're like many Americans and are not going to leave millions of dollars behind to a charity or family, you might not need certain tactics. You might not need trusts, life insurance, estate freeze techniques, qualified property trusts. You might not need to transfer as much money while alive to avoid estate taxes.

The financial assessment is also important for gathering every-thing and finding assets that might be difficult to value and transfer, like digital assets. During this step, you can determine what you're going to do with your digital footprint and all those photos that are online. And are you following the rules that were set forth in the Revised Uniform Fiduciary Access to Digital Asset Act, which many people don't even know is in place? In this step, you can update your documents to adhere to it. This review can help you figure out if you have digital assets and help you incorporate the required language in your will, trusts, and powers of attorney.

Step 4: review housing and health care alternatives

We've talked about both of these in this book, but where we live is such a crucial part of our happiness, especially as we near the end of our life. We want to live in a place where we're going to be happy. We want to figure out what's going to happen to our house after we pass away, because most often our kids don't want the house itself, they want to sell it. So are we just maintaining a house that nobody else really wants and limiting the quality of our own end of life?

In this step, discuss how you want long-term care with your family, where you want to get care, and how you're going to fund it. Then discuss what you would want to happen if you end up in a coma, need resuscitation, and whether you want a *do not resuscitate* order in place.

Lay out your care alternatives—what you want, where you want to live, how you want care, how you're going to fund it—and provide that direction to your family and loved ones.

Step 5: review the current plan

Everybody has a current end of life and legacy plan—it might not be written down, you might have not thought about the process or included it in your financial picture—but you have a plan. It's just probably not a good one if you haven't done any proactive planning.

Remember, if you don't do any planning around your estate, the government and state laws will determine where those assets go. Do we want to leave our end of life and legacy up to chance, or do we want to do the planning and have the will and legacy plan in place?

That's the difference between allowing a current plan to take hold and actually driving the plan forward.

Step 6: establish advanced directives

Next, you have to establish the advanced directives that you're going to need from your trust, whether it's revocable or irrevocable, whether it's going to be a trust you set up during life or one that gets set up at death. Whether you're going to have a power of attorney in place and whether you're going to limit that power of attorney to specific things. There are times when you might want to limit your power of attorney for one person to handle finances and another person to handle the health care.

Are you putting the right documents in place, so people can make those decisions?

Step 7: implement the plan

This is putting it all into place, making sure that you've drafted the right trusts and wills. You need to make sure that you fund the trust, that you've moved property into it. And if you want to leave a legacy to your loved ones through life insurance, you need to determine the amount you need, then go and set up the appropriate policy.

If there's tax planning that you need to do—maybe it's a Roth conversion—you need to start doing that. If you want to sell your house and move into a care facility, you need to get started on that process.

Step 8: communicate the plan

If you have a great plan and it's buried in your backyard, no one else can execute it if you're unable to. If you become incapacitated or die, do people know what they're supposed to be doing? Do your doctors know the orders that you want? Your family members? Your executor? The trustee of your trust? Your children?

If you need a guardian to watch out for your kids, do they know about it? Has that been set up correctly in your will? Have you funded for the future of your children and your surviving spouses and loved ones?

It also means communicating to people in your trusted circle of advisors and professionals—your attorney, CPA, doctors, and financial advisors.

Step 9: distribute the documents

Now you need to go and distribute these documents to the world. If your attorney is going to need to execute on something, you need to make sure they have the right document. If your kids need to follow a will, they need to know where the will is. If you want the hospital to know that you have a *do not resuscitate* order in place, they need to have it. If you have a health care power of appointment, you need to give that to the correct people and put them on file. You need your health care power of attorney to know where your insurance card is. Distributing the documents in the correct fashion allows you to execute on your plan, both during your life and when you're unable to execute on it.

Step 10: review and update the plan

You need to review and update this plan because things are going to change. Laws are going to change. You might move to another state. Family members might be born or pass away.

You might have to change your group of trusted advisors—your financial advisor, insurance professional, or trustee. The markets could shift and all of a sudden, you could have a lot more money than you thought you were going to have because you were doing great planning. Now you might need to engage in additional levels of planning to mitigate the tax impact of rising tax rates or additional assets that could then be subject to estate tax.

We have to plan for the future with the certainty of today, but with the flexibility of the unknown of tomorrow. That is what great end-of-life and estate planning does.

The emotional side of true legacy

Now, while the technical and tactical estate planning process is important, we also have to reflect on true legacy. True legacy is a little bit different.

Often when I bring this up with people, the first thing that I like to ask is, what are people saying about you at your funeral? When they get up to talk about your life, are they saying the things about you that you want them to say? Or are they describing you differently than how you want to be remembered?

Will they get up there and say, "Janet was a great business woman"? Or will they get up and say, "Janet was a caring, loving, kind soul, who took care of her family and friends—and by the way, she was very successful"? Are you the person you want to be, and making the impact you want to have first, and then doing the other things second?

Nobody wants to look back on their life and say, "I wish I had done more." Instead, you want to get to the end and say, "I'm proud of what I have done, I'm having the impact I want to have, and the things that I did were meaningful."

Define the values you want to pass on

Now, how do we get to that impact? We have to know what our values are, define them, and then align our lifetime actions and planning to those values. A lot of people think that they know their values but they've never really defined them. They don't have a family mission statement or family values indoctrinated. They haven't sat down with their children and said, "Here are values that I found very important in my life, and here's how we're going to pass them over to you." People used to spend more time doing this. They used to have family crests and coats of arms that visually identified the values that were important to that family.

One exercise I love to define the values I want to pass on to my kids is to write down the two most important values that represent who you are. These are the values that, if you're gone, your children, your loved ones, your friends would say were *your values*. For me, those values are resilience and community.

Draw your values as a coat of arms

What are the images that come to mind when you think of those values? For me, I drew an anvil to represent resilience and a pineapple to represent community. I want to be resilient and also welcoming to people in my communities, and that's what I want to pass on. I want my children to feel that they're resilient—they can overcome things, they've got grit—they can keep moving forward when they need to. And they're already welcoming to others and are finding their place in the community.

It wasn't until I wrote those values down and drew them that I felt connected to them. And I started figuring out how I'm acting in accordance with those values in my life.

Narrow down your impact

Many people fear overcommitment. They want to have an impact, but feel they can't say yes to everything. If you're one of these people, pick an area that you care about that aligns with your values, then find a good partner to help you. So if you want to have an impact on the community and you believe you can do that via education, find a great education partner that you can give back to, whether it's at the elementary, high school, or college level. Donate your time, energy, and resources to that one particular entity. Get involved. Get connected. If you try to do that with every category that you care about, you might overcommit and not do any of them well. So pick a particular category and start there.

Some people can have an impact through impact investing—aligning your values to your investments. This doesn't just mean ESG, or not investing in companies that are harmful to the environment, it can also be about investing in things that you feel make an impact, regardless of the investment returns. Maybe you decide that you want to contribute and invest in veteran-housing organizations and veteran-owned companies that hire veterans. Or maybe you really believe in education and you want to invest in education companies, for profit or otherwise. Maybe you really believe in farming and its importance in sustainability and you want to invest in sustainable farming and great farms. You can align your values to your investing and have a huge impact on the world.

When you leave this world, are you going to leave those you love in discord and chaos, or are you going to leave true generational wealth? True generational wealth goes beyond money—it goes to values, beliefs, and impact. If you can't answer that question with 100% certainty, without second-guessing yourself, you're likely leaving the former. Having a positive impact on the world that you can drive and be purposeful about is the pinnacle of true financial freedom.

Where are you on the journey we've described—foundational, stability, strategic, impact—and how are you and your trusted guide going to create that alignment between where you are today and your aspirational legacy?

Five key takeaways

1　We improve wellness, but we don't like talking about death.
2　Planning for a good end of life is not so much about the dollars and cents as it is about the impact and legacy that we leave behind.
3　Many people fail to follow a repeatable, scalable, and impactful process when it comes to estate and legacy planning.
4　A good estate plan starts with understanding and prioritizing goals that you might have.
5　If you don't do any planning around your estate, the government and state laws will determine where your assets go.

Five reflection questions

1 How do you envision the end of your life? Do you want to be in a hospital? At home?

2 Does your family have the means and the instructions for your funeral and burial? Do they know what you would want?

3 How do you want to leave your loved ones? In a better place financially?

4 Do you have digital assets? If so, have you planned for them?

5 What are the values you want to pass on to the next generation?

Notes

25

Not all Advisors Are Created Equal

❝ Hiring a financial advisor is equivalent to hiring a chief financial officer for you or your family. You want to use a disciplined process to find someone with whom you can work for many years. ❞

—*Dana Anspach, CFP®**

Financial Freedom Framework

Finding a trusted guide to help you on your journey isn't always easy. Making it harder is that many financial advisors lack transparency and a dedication to professional standards.

I'VE GONE ON record saying that I would only hire roughly 5% of the financial advisors out there. And even after 15 years working

---

* Dana is not affiliated with Cetera Advisor Networks.

with financial advisors, I feel the same.

This isn't to put down financial advisors, but rather to stress the need to find one that suits you. For comparison, I'm an attorney by trade and for all the funny jokes and bad connotations that come along with being an attorney, I would hire over half of the attorneys that I know. I think that they do great work.

Part of the difference between financial advisors and attorneys is the growing need to professionalize the financial services industry. Many financial advisors are still operating under an industry mentality and not a profession mentality. Some of this comes from a lack of transparency, lack of commitment to ethics, lack of commitment to education, and a lack of commitment to always putting clients first.

The reality is that not all advisors are created equal. There are some financial advisors I just wouldn't work with, and neither should you. It's challenging to find a good advisor to come along on that journey and be your trusted guide as you explore your aspirations and work towards your goals on the path to financial freedom.

Doing due diligence

The onus of finding an advisor who's a guide and trusted partner falls on you. There isn't a clear enough standard of care in the financial services industry to identify who is a good advisor for you and who is not.

You have to dive in and ask questions. You have to learn about the person—their philosophies and fees. Get referrals and shop around. Talk to more people before you make your decision. Too often I see people go with the first advisor or financial services professional that they talk to, and they're not 100% bought into that relationship and that person. Maybe they felt it wasn't the right person for them from the start. But it was hard for them to figure out all of the different steps and the right questions to ask.

Another thing to remember is that the financial advisor or advice that you need across your journey through the planning stages—fundamental, stability, strategic, and impact—will likely change.

You might need different advice and different professionals early in your journey than you do when you've accumulated wealth. The advice you need when you don't own anything won't be the same as when you have property in different states, have tax questions, are in need of legal advice, estate planning, and guidance on charitable giving. Your needs will change across your life, as will the level of difficulty of your planning. And the needs of your advisor and the team around them might change throughout their life.

A young person just getting started might not need an advisor relationship as deep as someone who's five years before retirement. Someone who has limited savings and income might not need the same level of financial advice as somebody who owns a business making multiple millions of dollars a year and is getting ready to sell it. Our need for advice evolves.

Not all advice is good advice. We have to figure out what type of advice, relationship and interaction works for us.

To a large extent, a financial advisor is a coach, and if you don't relate and feel comfortable with that coach, you have the wrong partner for your journey.

The trust factor

This relationship isn't all about the tactics, it's about connection and trust. Trust is a key factor in your relationship with a financial advisor.

Financial advice often deals with topics around death, our estate, our children and our grandchildren, and situations in which we may not be here anymore. Much of the work that's done from an investment, planning, and contract standpoint is being done outside of our view. So we need to trust in the relationship that we have with our financial advisor, and trust that they're going to do the right thing. We have to know they're going to do what they say they'll do. Trust is fundamental to the advisor relationship. If you can't trust that advisor, you need to find a new one. I'll say that repeatedly in this conversation: if you don't have what you're looking for, go find a new advisor.

Trust ties directly to transparency. I believe one of the reasons that the financial services industry remains an industry and not a profession is because of lack of transparency around what occurs within it. Things like the Bernie Madoff scandal are beyond upsetting. I told you at the beginning of the book that I actually got to work on one of the cases involving his fraud and abuse of client trust. It set me on this path to be here today, working to find trusted advisors, to build in transparency, and to always put clients' interests first. People trusted Bernie Madoff and he took advantage of that trust. But in those situations, there was a lack of transparency around what was actually happening with the client investments, returns, and access to their accounts.

Technology has enabled more transparency than ever before. Advisors that are incorporating technology to improve their practices and deliver better services to clients are becoming more trusted because they're more transparent than ever before. Know how transparent the advice of an advisor you're working with is. If you don't know what's happening with your advisor, there's a lack of transparency and an abuse of trust is more likely to occur.

Look for an advisor who leads with transparency. I've been a professor for years. I've got the alphabet soup of designations and graduate degrees. People often make fun of me because I just keep going to school because I love it so much. I do love education. Education is one of the most powerful tools that we have in existence to move humanity forward. Being a lifelong learner is an incredible goal to aspire to.

I also look for professionals in any area of the world who I want to work with to be committed to their profession. I want to see that they're committed to continued learning and education. I want to see that not only do they want to be educated, but they want to educate others. One of the best ways to learn a topic is to teach it to somebody else.

When you look across other professions, would you hire a doctor who didn't go to medical school to perform surgery on you? Would you hire an attorney who didn't have a law degree to represent you in court? Of course you wouldn't. You wouldn't hire most other professionals if they didn't educate themselves in the professional arena in which they practice. So why would you hire an advisor who hasn't dedicated themselves to education in the profession that they say they love and practice?

I want to see somebody who has a Certified Financial Planner (CFP®) designation or a Chartered Financial Consultant (ChFC®) designation. If a financial advisor specializes in divorce, I want to see that they have education in divorce planning. If they specialize in insurance, I want to see that they have insurance education. If they specialize in retirement income planning, I want to see retirement income planning certifications behind their name. I want to see a commitment to continued education and excellence in the area in which this person says that they're committed to practice.

It's a simple question: if you say that you care deeply about financial planning, why haven't you continued your commitment to the highest levels of financial planning education? Look for advisors that have committed themselves to this type of education.

The fiduciary commitment

To go one step further, ask whether the advisor is committed to you. More specifically, ask if they are a fiduciary. That means that they put their clients' interests before their own. It means that they mitigate and avoid conflicts of interest as much as possible. It means that they only charge reasonable fees for the services they provide, and that they provide advice to the best of their ability as a reasonable and prudent person would in those situations.

A fiduciary encompasses a lot. But in the financial advice profession, being a fiduciary is the highest standard of care that professionals can have. This has gotten muddier over the years as people who aren't acting as true fiduciaries try to disguise themselves as fiduciaries. They do this by using terminology that sounds better than the fiduciary language when you hear it. People will say, "I put your interest first. I work in my clients' best interests." But you have to ask specifically: "Are you acting as a fiduciary?"

I'd also ask them to put it in writing, even if they verbalized it. Because if they're unwilling to put into writing that they're a fiduciary, that should immediately raise a red flag. That typically means they're not acting as a fiduciary to you, but that they're able to wordsmith around it by using terms like "best interests" and "putting your needs first." They don't actually adhere to the legal requirement of being a fiduciary.

You don't need a fiduciary in every financial situation, but you do need a fiduciary if you want a financial advisor to do comprehensive planning and help you along your path to financial freedom.

Times you might not need a fiduciary include when you just need a life insurance policy, so you go to an agent or broker and they provide you that product and a service to solve your need. That person might not be acting under a fiduciary standard, but you know that. It's important to know what standard all your professionals are working under, which goes back to trust and transparency.

I'm not saying everybody who's not a fiduciary is bad and all fiduciaries are good, but I am saying that you have to understand the standard of care and the level of treatment and service that you're going to get when you engage with them.

Fiduciaries aren't always cheaper options. In many cases, fiduciaries are more expensive because they're delivering a higher level of service and standard of care than a non-fiduciary. It's important to ask the question and know who you're working with.

I've worked with lots of non-fiduciaries providing financial services that I would hire again for that particular need or service. But when I get to the comprehensive financial advice to get me to financial freedom, I want a fiduciary advisor.

The question of pay

When you're hiring an advisor, you need to know what you're actually going to pay. I hate the term "fees." I don't want to think about paying fees for advice, fees for investments, fees for my equities, fees for my products. These are *costs* associated with the value I'm getting. But I need to know what the total cost is for that value.

That means I need to know how and what a financial advisor is charging to deliver services. I want to know how they get paid and what my all-in costs are. This goes back to transparency. So many financial advice relationships start off with smoke and mirrors about the true cost of the relationship. Some advisors say there's no cost for the advice—that it's free with the product. In that case, there is a cost, they're just not being transparent about it.

Advisors often operate under a couple different fee structures.

Assets under management

There are advisors that charge by assets under management (often 1% or less of the assets under management). This has been an appealing cost structure because if a client does well, the advisor does well. It aligns advisor compensation with the growth of your assets.

Hourly or project-based fees

You might gravitate toward this if you want a financial plan and you engage with an advisor to deliver a one-time plan for a set fee.

Ongoing fee structure

These can include a retainer-style model or a monthly subscription-based model.

Commission

There are those advisors and financial service professionals who are compensated through commissions by way of selling investment or insurance products.

Again, there's not one ideal way to pay for services. I've bought commission-based products in the past, I've worked with hourly and project-based advisors, and I've worked with AUM-based investment and financial advisors. Advisors charge in a myriad of ways, but what's important for you to take away is you should know how they're compensated and understand the true cost and impact of those fees on their holistic plan.

Fee structures and conflicts

Certain types of fee structures will lead to certain types of conflicts. One challenge with the commission-based model is that professionals are encouraged to sell more products, which might not always be in the best interests of the client. Hourly advisors might not have the sale-based conflict, but they're encouraged to create projects and drive up time.

There's always going to be some type of conflict that arises with most compensation models. When we look for an advisor, it's not that we can remove all conflicts. We want people to get paid for the services they provide, but we need to know whether the cost is equal to the value we gain and that any conflicts that do arise won't put us on the wrong path. We need to know that our advisor is a fiduciary who's legally required to put our interests first and mitigate and disclose conflicts when they do occur.

It's all about knowledge and transparency.

Know their investment and planning strategies

You want to make sure that your advisor's success is aligned with your success. You want your financial freedom to be encouraged by your trusted advisor's journey with you. Don't walk a path where the advisor's financial freedom is separate from your own.

I also think it's important to ask your advisor about their own planning. Ask them how they invest, what they've done to set up their financial plan, and whether they work with their own financial advisor. Ask them what insurance products they have in place.

I've heard advisors recommend their clients put money into certain investments that they themselves don't put money into. That should also raise a red flag. While not every advisor should invest exactly like you, you should still ask. Some advisors might be willing to take more investment risk than you or are at a different age or life stage. But when they're recommending things they're not invested in, you should ask why.

Ask what their investment philosophy is and how it will apply to you. Ask how they view the markets. Ask what will happen if you invest with them. What type of allocation will they pick? How do they gauge your risk tolerance levels? What type of tax hits might occur if you move investments? Many people don't think about that, but sometimes when you move non-qualified investments from one advisor to another, you could get hit with a huge tax bill.

You should also ask the advisor about what types of funds they use—ETFs or mutual funds. Ask about the distributions from those and whether those will create ongoing tax problems for you.

It's important to know with whom they custody their investments. Are they doing so with a company that has transparency, low fees, and good service?

Does the advisor try to time the market? Are they an active investor or a passive investor? Do they strive to keep costs low for you and put your interests first when they invest?

There's not one right way to choose investments for everyone. You need to ensure that the advisor's investment philosophy matches up with your own view and that you feel comfortable with the way that they're going to approach investments.

You also need to look up their work and compliance history. You need to see if there are any black marks on the record. Have they sold a bunch of bad products to people over time? Have they abused their clients? You can look up what disclosures the advisor has with the Financial Industry Regulatory Authority or the Securities and Exchange Commission. Ask what fee structure they have, what conflicts they might have, and what other companies they've invested in.

Teamwork makes your dream work

Find out about the advisor's team and their years of experience. A talented team of advisors can serve you in the best way possible.

Even if you took Michael Jordan, perhaps the best basketball player of all time, and put him against five average Division One college players for a full court game of basketball, it would be as close to a shutout as possible in favor of the five average players. Team approaches are more powerful than setting one person on a task.

Obviously there's a level beyond which putting too many people into one spot creates inefficiencies, but overall teams become greater than the sum of their parts. No matter how good one person is, how smart one person is, how hard one person works, they can't outwork an effective team.

No one can be an expert in all things related to financial planning, so a team approach to your finances is important. Does your advisor have CPAs and attorneys as part of the team? Do they have investment specialists and planners? Can they pull a team together to deliver a holistic and comprehensive planning experience to you as you move throughout the different planning stages? Can they travel that full journey of financial freedom with you?

This is why it's crucial to understand who's part of their team, to meet them, and to understand the full level of skills that their team brings to the table to help you make your dreams come true.

Get it in writing

It's critical to understand how the relationship will work and get it in writing. Understand the full range of services you're getting for your investment with them and whether it matches up with what you want and need in your planning.

Ask how often they will communicate, how often you'll meet and in what form. Are you okay with a virtual advisor or do you want to know that somebody is on Main Street near you, so you can go in to meet with them when you have a problem?

Know what technology, reporting, and analytics resources you get when working with them.

Ask them what other types of clients they work with. Where do they get most of their clients? How long have they been working with many of their clients? What types of planning issues and topics do their clients bring to them? How do they specialize in these areas? Ask when the last time a client left them and why. Ask for a referral to talk to an existing client. If they're unwilling to give you that referral, that's a red flag.

You want to know that they work with people who experience things that you do so you know the advisor is learning from those relationships and planning. Then you know they can apply those learning experiences to your situation.

Ask them to explain a financial concept to you. At some point during your relationship this person is going to have to communicate effectively and explain something that is important to your financial future. If you ask them to explain a financial concept and they can't, you've just found out they're not going to effectively communicate to you when it's important, like when you need to make a decision that could impact your financial future.

Lastly, ask the advisor what they love most about their job. You want to work with people who are passionate and engaged in the profession. You want to work with people who have a compelling "why" that they can go to and pull from when they're tired. You want to know that they're committed and that they're going to be with you on this journey to financial freedom. You don't want somebody who's just in it for the money. You don't want somebody who's just here because this was the job that they got.

You want somebody who loves the profession that they're in because it's a noble profession. It's a profession where you can help other people's dreams come true. It's a profession that can help create financial stability for people who otherwise wouldn't have been able to pursue it if they didn't have quality advice. You want people who want to help people like my mom after my dad passed away. You want people who help young widows maintain greater financial confidience, knowing where their finances are and that they can take care of their family and work towards their goals. If somebody can't answer why they're in this profession, they're the wrong person to work with.

It can be a tall order to find a financial advisor with a fiduciary duty, transparent fees, great planning, and a clearly documented process that's focused around you.

At the end of the day, not all financial advisors are created equal. But if you ask the right questions and you know where you're going on your path to financial freedom, you can find somebody that will walk alongside you, be that guide and trusted advisor and help you work towards your goals, dreams, and aspirations.

Five key takeaways

1 Many financial advisors are still operating under an industry mentality and not a profession mentality.

2 The onus of finding an advisor who's a guide and trusted partner falls on you.

3 There isn't a clear enough standard of care in the financial services industry to identify who's a good advisor for you and who is not.

4 You have to learn about your potential advisor and ask them a myriad of questions to weed out the bad apples.

5 The financial advisor or advice that you need across your journey through the planning stages will change.

Final reflection questions

1 What was your first money memory?

2 What was the first big purchase you ever made?

3 How would you describe your current relationship with money?

4 What are your long-term aspirations for your life?

5 What are the two main values you want people to associate with you?

6 Would your family and friends associate these values with you today?

7 What is the single biggest positive money memory or accomplishment you have?

8 What is the biggest money failure or regret that you have?

9 What is one aspect of your relationship with money that you wish you could change?

10 What is one money lesson you wish you could pass along to your heirs or loved ones?

11 Think about one positive financial memory. Why was it positive? Have you tried to repeat this or systemize it in any way in your

life? If you haven't, why not? If you have, can the lesson you learned be applied more broadly? Have you ever told this positive story to anyone else in your family? If not, why?

12 Do most of the people you associate with (work, hobbies, religious/social organizations) think the way you think about money? How do your attitudes, beliefs, and behaviors align with those of the people in your community? How are they different?

13 Describe your current process for managing your finances. Do you feel confident that this process will help you to achieve your goals? How has it been successful so far? Where has it failed?

14 If you could sum up your life aspirations in a few words, what would those words be?

15 Do you work with a financial professional? If so, why? If not, why not?

26

Financial Freedom

> ❝ Life is meant to be fun, and joyous and fulfilling. May each of yours be that. ❞
>
> —*Jim Henson, puppeteer and creator*

Financial Freedom Framework

You must define your own path if you want freedom. No guide, no expert, no one besides yourself can create a path that will be as fun, joyous and fulfilling as the one you can create.

JIM HENSON WAS a lot of things—an animator, cartoonist, actor, inventor, creator, investor, and screenwriter. But to me, he was a dreamer. He dreamed big and imagined things we've never seen, experienced, or thought of before. His company helped create some of the most innovative shows and movies of all time, changing cinema forever. He also changed the hearts and minds of young people. He dared them to dream too—to become creators and innovators—and to define their own paths.

While this book was written to show you a path to get to your financial freedom, I know it will not be enough. It's just one way forward. Ultimately, much of the work and progress will come from you. But I do hope that his book inspires you to take that next step.

The next step is sometimes the hardest, but you can do it. But you need to start with your vision or your dream of what financial freedom means to you.

It might be helpful to show you a few examples of what financial freedom means to others. So I asked a few of my friends and colleagues to share what financial freedom means to them:

I believe that the journey to financial freedom is the ability to do what you want, when you want, where you want, how you want, and most importantly with those you love, enjoy and want to spend precious time with.

Having the foundation of a financial plan has helped me set the appropriate strategy to achieve my goals and dreams. By planning forward, I get the unique opportunity to paint the story I want to see for my future. Planning has also allowed me to adopt an investment discipline, so I don't risk trying to time the market, but to consistently put time in the market, and maintain a long-term investment perspective that's focused on legacy and generational wealth.

In short, proper planning can help prevent procrastination, by providing a clear pathway that helps to achieve the "prize" of defining and finding financial freedom.

—*Jaqueline "JaQ" Campbell, president and CEO, senior wealth advisor of Alexander Legacy Private Wealth Management.*

Financial freedom is control over my time and attention with money being no object. There's more than enough money to do or buy what I want (within reason), when I want. A key component is that my money works for me versus me working for my money; shifting more income from active to passive creates more available time and attention, thus freedom. I'm making money, not earning money.

—*Emily Binder, founder of WealthVoice**

---

* Emily is not affiliated with Cetera Advisor Networks.

As the daughter of a Chinese father and American-born mother, I have been exposed to many different stereotypes in the US, Europe, and Asia. I also grew up taking in mixed messages about what it means to be a successful, professional woman.

Indeed, juggling my responsibilities as a daughter, wife, mother, caregiver, professional, and professional financial planner has taught me to strive for balance—not perfection.

I can't promise the sun, moon and the stars to the people I serve and love. But I do promise them, and those they hold dear to their hearts, the "4 Cs": Clarity, Confidence, Control and Courage. This is what I seek out too. I have found the place where I can have the opportunity to transform lives and have a positive impact on my community. Financial planning is intellectually stimulating, emotionally gratifying, and financially rewarding to me.

—Marguerita Cheng, CFP®*

Financial independence and freedom is important to me because I am two generations removed from someone who grew up on a plantation and struggled her entire life.

I've known poverty for half of my life and I refuse for my kids to ever understand that pain.

Financial independence matters to me because achieving it can change the future for my family. It is also about leaving generational wealth and transforming the communities around me.

—Dr David Rhoiney, DO

The financial planning journey by design requires sharing goals, organizing financial information, and getting comfortable with how your assets support your life now and in the future. My family and I challenge ourselves to practice what I preach to my financial planning clients in a no-shame, no-fear zone! We view financial freedom as the ability to apply our human capital in gratifying ways, to earn equitable income to build wealth, and to create opportunities to spend our time as we desire.

—Lazetta Rainey Braxton, MBA, CFP, founder and CEO of
Lazetta & Associates

---

* Marguerita is not affiliated with Cetera Advisor Networks.

I had a moment sitting in the Santa Maria Abbey at Montserrat on a study abroad program in Spain, my mind occupied with thoughts of how my parents would have loved this place. I pictured my mom and my late dad both kneeling in the Abbey praying their rosaries and I was overwhelmed with a mixture of gratitude and sorrow. Grateful for the opportunities they provided throughout my life to put me in a position to be able to do this, and sorrow that they were never able to. I wish my parents had had the type of financial freedom to do things like this, but they sacrificed so that one day we could. To me, financial freedom is planning for and living the life my parents dreamed possible, while ensuring the next generation gets to do the same without sacrificing our own quality of life.

—*Ana Trujillo Limon, director of coaching and advisor content,*
Carson Group

These stories say a lot about financial freedom. When I think about it, I get emotional about my own financial freedom. It is about having control for me. To wake up and determine my day. I don't want to wake up and *have to* work to make money or pay bills, but I *can* work if I want to. Ultimately, it's about taking back my time to spend with my family and friends. Spending money to save time is how I get there. For instance, if I hire a local high-school student with a lawn business to cut my lawn, I don't just get the service, I get the freedom to spend more time with my family. This is how I am learning to live my own financial freedom daily.

This whole book is about defining what it means to be financially free, executing on the steps to get there, and then actually living that freedom. While you might not reach a full level of financial freedom today, you can start finding ways to live it in your life.

Remember, life is meant to be fun, and joyous, and fulfilling. While finances are important, they are just a means to an end. Use today to take the next step toward the rest of your life on your journey to that end. Your end? Well, you get to define it. What does it mean to you to find financial freedom?

Conclusion

by Ron Carson, CFP®, ChFC®

Improving the quality of financial advice

By now, you've no doubt been exposed to a mental framework that can forever change the way you think about money. I hope the stories Jamie told, the studies cited, and tools provided throughout the book give you a formula to light a fire for change. A fire that compels you to take charge of your freedom. A fire that inspires you to look deeper into your life and those around you. A fire that sets you on the path for living the life you always dreamed.

The unfortunate reality is you are among the fortunate few. You sit among those who educate themselves and use the knowledge they gain to improve their lives. This very moment is a crucial one for you. It's the moment that sits between the knowing and the doing. You now know what you must do; it's time to do it.

We collectively have a lot of meaningful work to do, when I think about just how many people need to know about the fundamentals covered in this book. The masses need a new way to approach their financial life. People of every age, creed, and culture are starving for trust. This is especially apparent in financial services, as the past two to three decades have obliterated any goodwill that was earned before it. From corrupt executives like Bernie Madoff to breakdowns in entire systems like the Wells Fargo account fraud scandal and the financial crisis of 2008, we've had plenty of reasons to lose faith in the industry.

But the industry is changing. In fact, that very word—industry—doesn't fully capture the transformational work happening among the top echelon of advisors across the country. We believe in treating the work we do as a legitimate profession.

The advisors out there who operate as true fiduciaries in this new era hold themselves to a higher standard, just as any doctor or attorney or licensed professional would. They don't let emotion get in the way of their decisions—or their clients'. They take all information into account to provide a holistic plan that addresses every aspect of your life, not just your financials. They care about your dreams, they communicate regularly to clarify the decisions they're making, and they are one of the first calls you make when something life-changing happens. In other words, they operate within the third level of trust.

Meeting your needs and answering your questions while providing sound financial advice for a reasonable fee is table stakes. Those operating at the third level of trust are anticipating your needs before you know you have them—and delivering on those needs. That's what it means to work in a profession.

Part of the responsibility of a profession means leading the charge in education, and in our case this equates to improving financial literacy. The Council for Economic Education found that Washington, D.C. and 26 U.S. states do not require high schools to offer a personal finance class. Think of the ripple effect this has—and will have—on the next generation of our workforce. We must teach every generation, not just the next generation, how the decisions they make and behaviors they act on influence their financial lives and connect to every other decision outside of it.

This lack of education leads to much more than a lack of business acumen. According to a FINRA study in 2021, 60% of adult respondents in the United States indicated feeling anxious when thinking about their personal finances, while 50% of respondents reported feeling stressed when discussing their finances.[26]

In 2016, the American Association of Individual Investors (AAII) conducted a poll and found that 65% of investors voiced some degree of mistrust in the financial services industry.[27]

Couple this internal anxiety, mistrust, and confusion with the external, cataclysmic events of the pandemic, war, mass shootings, climate change, social injustice, and the never-ending uncertainty of the markets, and you quickly see the role this profession can play in improving the human experience. It's no wonder Americans are out there demanding more from trusted financial professionals and looking for competent, empathetic advisors.

At the beginning of the book, we talked about the deep-seeded feelings we associate with money, and how they are often buried in our subconscious mind, steering us in ways we do not even recognize on the surface. Think about the feelings or memories you associate with the gain or loss of your assets.

Have you shared these feelings with your advisor?

What made you feel comfortable to do so if you have, and what obstacles can you name that stand between you and your advisor if you haven't? These are the important conversations that must happen, both for the benefit of your advisor and for you.

Our profession has traditionally over-charged and under-delivered. And I say this not as an indictment of the people in our profession but of the way our industry has been set up. It was an industry people could enter needing only a minimal formal education. The only thing that stood between a person and their ability to provide advice was essentially an exam. If you could pass the test, you could attain your registration and be on your way to advising clients. This brought a number of really bright people into the industry, but often encouraged those who were not meant to manage a business to be small business owners. It wasn't long before these individuals realized they couldn't wear all the hats and still serve their clients at the highest level.

With all this complexity built into the business, some advisors drifted towards a focus on investment management, placing their value on outperforming the market, while others leaned into client relationship building and goals-based planning. One style strictly focused on returns in the short term, the other focused on helping their clients in the long term. This created an awakening—the realization that both a sound investment strategy and a proactive, human-centric plan were necessary to meet the needs of the modern-day client.

Today, the industry finds itself in the middle of an evolution. Advisors who are rising above the fray have found a formula for building sustainable businesses. They are attracting the right people, creating innovative cultures, developing ground-breaking technology, and offering tangible value beyond a doubt. These are the advisors who have their heart in the business.

I've always believed that a core need still exists for those seeking sound financial advice. Our clients want someone who thinks about the things they don't think about, someone who has an integrated proactive service model designed to update them on what they need to know before they need to know it. Without the robust infrastructure of systems, data, and insight to support this model, advisors can only guess, and guessing isn't good enough.

Ultimately, these are all the things your advisor should be considering when thinking about what it takes to help you find your freedom.

Hope on the horizon

We live in a time of accelerating change, inside and outside financial services. This change can be paralyzing for some and exhilarating for others. Advisors around the country, much like our team at Carson Wealth, sit at the frontlines of this positive transformation. We believe that time will either expose you or promote you, so why not use this as an opportunity to create something better.

Advisors who believe in reinvesting in their businesses, who put the interests of their clients first, and who provide value beyond a doubt will redefine the nature of financial advice. One study conducted by Vanguard found that these planning-centric advisors can add as much as 3% to net returns when weaving in aspects of behavioral planning and financial planning. This is a testament to the benefits of embracing the whole human when examining someone's balance sheet.

A good financial strategy is more about how you treat the money you have than how much you have. In my family, my wife Jeanie and I have already decided that we're leaving most of our wealth to charity. Warren Buffett said it best when he said, "Leave the children enough so that they can do anything, but not enough that they can do nothing."

I've always connected with this piece of wisdom, but it wasn't until recently that I truly understood the impact we could have and the fulfillment we could experience by serving others. This is something Jamie touched on earlier in the book. When we move our way up Maslow's Hierarchy of Needs, we aim for self-actualization. In terms of our finances, this means reaching a place where we can focus on giving back and expanding our impact. Much of our time and effort now goes into a non-profit Jeanie and I started a decade ago called the Dreamweaver Foundation. We saw a need to support terminally ill seniors by granting them end-of-life wishes. Fulfilling these life-long dreams for those who have given so much throughout their lives is one of the most awe-inspiring endeavors we've ever had the honor of starting.

My advice for those of you who are contemplating that next leap on the planning pyramid is this: there's no better time than now. I've crossed too many individuals in my life who plan to reach this level of financial security but delay their legacy planning because they feel like they have time before that decision needs to be made. A desire of mine is to influence others who sit at the top of this pyramid. I want to drive urgency with those who have the resources to give back and make a monumental impact for the sake of the greater good rather than themselves. Our society needs that leadership more than ever.

Right about now you may be wanting to ask, "Ron, what about the rest of us? What about those of us who are fighting for a base level of financial security? Where do we begin?"

My wish for you in reading this book is that I want you to remove the "Am I going to have enough?" question. Most of our inability to move up the pyramid comes from our own behaviors and habits, but it also comes from finding the right advisor. Your advisor should be able to relieve some of the uncertainty related to the question "Will I have enough?"

The only way to get there is to do your due diligence. Ask your current advisor about the process they follow when developing your financial plan. Are they proactive in anticipating your needs based on how well they know you? Are they currently helping you build greater confidence that you are going to have enough to live the life you dreamed of by taking very clear steps?

If they can do this, you are with the right advisor. So much of what it takes to align our financial lives is rooted in answering this question.

Part of finding your freedom is finding your mind and not allowing other people to do your thinking for you. Go through the Blueprinting process we mentioned earlier in the book. Define where you spend your time and what you value most in life. We live in a society where everyone has an opinion of how we should think, how we should feel, and how we should act. Step away from this gravitational force. Think hard about what you want and what you need to do to progress forward.

Consider creating a goal that improves your current financial situation. A consumer survey at the end of 2021 explored the top ten financial resolutions that Americans made for 2022. Some of those goals included:

- Getting out of debt (student loans, credit card payments).
- Removing unnecessary bills.
- Reallocating a monthly budget.
- Applying for a credit card and improving credit score.
- Investing money or opening an investment account.

Identify the biggest lever you can pull in your financial life that can be easily tracked. Notice how none of the five resolutions listed were massive undertakings. Each one was a singular action that could lead to larger, life-improving changes down the line. No matter the decision or choice you make, share this with your advisor and have them weave your goal into your ongoing reviews.

These smaller, actionable commitments seem to be working. 2021 was a banner year for many American households. Financial wellbeing reached an all-time high, as did the share of households that said they could cover a $400 emergency with their savings, according to the Federal Reserve. Around 78% of adults reported either doing okay or living comfortably financially, according to the Fed's annual Economic Well-Being of U.S. Households report.[28] The report also outlined that financial wellbeing increased among all the racial and ethnic groups measured in the survey. Parents, in particular, saw large gains in financial well-being. 75% said they were doing at least okay financially, up eight percentage points from 2020.

One nuance I feel is important to highlight: there was a significant discrepancy in well-being by education level. 91% of adults with at least a bachelor's degree reported being at least okay financially, compared to only 49% of those with less than a high school degree.[29] This is more evidence for why financial literacy in our formative years is crucial to the tide lifting all boats in the future.

There's no time like the present

One thing is for certain. The ebbs and flows of life will always influence the path we take to achieve our dreams and find our freedom. There will be ups and downs, moments of momentum and stages of setback. Many of the gains we feel one year could be affected by losses in the next. Over the last couple of years alone we have been lifted by our collective resilience in pushing through a global pandemic, only to be cut down by the enduring effects of rising inflation, the likes of which we haven't seen in 40 years.

The last time I remember navigating rising interest rates like this was when I was a teenager, watching my parents go through the most heart-breaking financial experience of their lives, because they were leveraging and over-extending their own finances, which eventually led to their financial demise. My life has taught me that there will always be no time like the present to make positive changes for my future.

Live your life by design, not by default. You define what freedom means for you. The framework in this book simply gives you the path to help get you there.

As the Chinese proverb says, "The best time to plant a tree was 20 years ago. The second-best time is now."

Look at how you are currently spending your time. Reflect on where you expend your energy, and then chart a way to realign your time and energy with where you want to go. There is another level of fulfillment waiting for you on the other side of this process. There will always be another level of feeling free.

I believe in living a life that is in flow, not in force. This isn't so much about work/life balance as it is about attaining life harmony. Yes, we all have responsibilities and commitments, and things we need to get done in our daily lives, but we also need to create space for removing unhealthy habits, poor financial decisions, and toxic people. Chances are, a few of those aspects in your own life just popped into your mind.

Make decisions that will not only benefit you but will set positive change in motion for generations to come. It's a totally different way of thinking, but I promise you it will lead to a more fulfilling life.

Eliminate the elements that don't feed your freedom. Embrace the habits and actions that do. Your journey will never see a finish line, and that is what should inspire you to keep going.

This process, this adventure, is the art of finding your infinite potential—and the road to finding your freedom.

Acknowledgments

Jamie: I want to acknowledge a few beautiful and amazing people who have guided me, loved me, and cared for me over the years.

My parents, who gave me opportunities to succeed in life, my sisters that encouraged me through the years, and my wife and children who make me smile and laugh every day.

I want to thank Ana Maria Trujillo Limon, who helped me write and edit this book. Ana has been an amazing partner for me in this process.

Lastly, I want to thank all of those at Carson and in the broader financial services industry that have helped me become a smarter, better, and freer person.

Ron: I am a big believer in the fact that I am the sum of those who surround me in life. Throughout my journey, I've been fortunate to have my incredible wife, Jeanie, by my side through every chapter. We've lived so many chapters together throughout the past 40 years. I look forward to the unwritten pages ahead and what they hold for us.

To my children—Chelsie, Maddie, and Gracie—you have taught me so much about what it means to live on another plane of existence as a father and grandpa.

And to my extended family of stakeholders at Carson Group, without your endless dedication to helping people find their freedom, we couldn't have made it to where we are today, changing the world for the better. It's endlessly inspiring to live out my personal mission of helping each one of you find your freedom as you help others find theirs. I would not be where I am or who I am today, as a leader or as a human, without the bright, caring people who surround me. This book is a powerful reminder of what we're creating together, and how we can expand our impact in the lives of millions of people for generations to come.

Notes

1 Matthews, Gail. 2007. "The Impact of Commitment, Accountability, and Written Goals on Goal Achievement." *Psychology | Faculty Presentations*, 3. scholar.dominican.edu/psychology-faculty-conference-presentations/3

2 Seligman, Martin. 2018. "PERMA and the building blocks of well-being." *The Journal of Positive Psychology*, 13 (4), 333–335.

3 Seligman, Martin EP, Peter Railton, Roy F. Baumeister, and Chandra Sripada. 2013. "Navigating into the Future or Driven by the Past." *Perspectives on Psychological Science,* 8 (2), 119–141.

4 Schwab, Charles. "2021 Modern Wealth Survey." Retrieved from www.aboutschwab.com/modern-wealth-survey-2021

5 Norcross, John C., and Dominic J. Vangarelli. 1988. "The Resolution Solution: Longitudinal Examination of New Year's Change Attempts."*Journal of Substance Abuse*, 1(2), 127–134.

6 Stangor, Charles, Rajiv Jhangiani, and Hammond Tarry. 2022. "Understanding Altruism: Self and Other Concerns." *Principles of Social Psychology-1st International H5P Edition.*

7 Harkin, Benjamin, Thomas L. Webb, Betty P.I. Chang, Andrew Prestwich, Mark Conner, Ian Kellar, Yael Benn, and Paschal Sheeran. 2016. "Does Monitoring Goal Progress Promote Goal Attainment? A Meta-analysis of the Experimental Evidence." *Psychological Bulletin* 142 (2), 198.

8 Westbrook, Andrew, R. Van Den Bosch, J. I. Määttä, L. Hofmans, D. Papadopetraki, Roshan Cools, and M. J. Frank. 2020. "Dopamine Promotes Cognitive Effort by Biasing the

Benefits Versus Costs of Cognitive Work." *Science,* 367 (6484), 1,362–1,366.

9 Patrinos, Harry A., and George Psacharopoulos. 2018. "Strong Link Between Education and Earnings." World Bank Blogs.

10 Kattan, Raja Bentaouet, Claudio E. Montenegro, and Harry A. Patrinos. 2021. "Realizing the Returns to Schooling: How COVID-19 and School Closures are Threatening Women's Economic Future." World Bank Blogs

11 Arman, Jesse, and Joshua Shackman. 2012. "The Impact of Financial Planning Designations on Financial Planner Income." The Services Industries Journal 32 (8): 1,393–1,409. Blay, Joyce. 2020. "Advisors Who Earn Designations See Increased Income, Study Says."

12 Hopkins, Jamie P., and David A. Littell. 2015. "Retirement Income Planning Literacy in America: A Method for Determining Retirement Knowledgeable Clients." *Journal of Financial Planning,* 28 (10), 22–28.

13 Hopkins, Jamie P., and John A. Pearce II. 2019. "Retirement Income Literacy: A Key to Sustainable Retirement Planning." *Journal of Financial Planning,* 32 (1), 36–44

14 Zhang, Jia Wei, Ryan T. Howell, Peter A. Caprariello, and Darwin A. Guevarra. 2014. "Damned if They Do, Damned if They Don't: Material Buyers are Not Happier from Material or Experiential Consumption." *Journal of Research in Personality,* 50, 71–83.

15 Corley, Tom. 2016. *Change Your Habits, Change Your Life.* Minneapolis, MN: North Loop Books.

16 Fischer, Marcel, and Natalia Khorunzhina. 2014. "Family Composition and the Optimal Demand for Housing Over the Life Cycle." *Copenhagen Business School,*1–9.

17 Ibid.

18 Hershfield, Hal E., and Daniel M. Bartels. 2018. "The Future Self." *The Psychology of Thinking About the Future,* 89–109.

19 Kaheneman, Daniel and Angus Deaton. 2010. "Does Money Buy Happiness?" *PNAS Early Edition.* Retrieved from spia. princeton.edu/sites/default/files/content/docs/news/Happiness_ Money_Summary.pdf.

20 Whilliams, Ashley V., and Michael I. Norton. 2017. "Buyng

Time Promotes Happiness." PNAS. Retrieved from www.pnas. org/doi/full/10.1073/pnas.1706541114.

21 Kahneman, Daniel, and Angus Deaton. 2010. "High Income Improves Evaluation of Life but Not Emotional Well-being." *Proceedings of the National Academy of Sciences*, 107 (38), 16,489–16,493.

22 Fahey, Mark. 2015. "Money Can Buy Happiness, But Only to a Point." CNBC. Retrieved from www.cnbc.com/2015/12/14/ money-can-buy-happiness-but-only-to-a-point.html.

23 Bengen, William P. 1994. "Determining Withdrawal Rates Using Historical Data." *Journal of Financial Planning*, 171–180.

24 Pressman, Sarah D., Karen A. Matthews, Sheldon Cohen, Lynn M. Martire, Michael Scheier, Andrew Baum, and Richard Schulz. 2009. "Association of Enjoyable Leisure Activities with Psychological and Physical Well-Being." *Psychosomatic Medicine*, 71 (7), 725.

25 Dizikes, Peter. 2012. "Study: Many Americans Die with 'Virtually No Financial Assets.'" MIT News. Retrieved from news.mit. edu/2012/end-of-life-financial-study-0803.

26 "Weekly Poll from American Association of Individual Investors." Weekly AAII Digest/Blog. Backman, Maurie. 2017. "Most Americans Don't Trust Their Financial Advisors. Should They?"

27 Pierce, Timothy, and Angelita Williams. 2021. "Large Number of Americans Reported Financial Anxiety and Stress Even Before the Pandemic." FINRA Investor Education and GFLEC News Release. Pierce, Timothy. 2021.

28 Consumer and Community Research Section of the Federal Reserve Board's Division of Consumer and Community Affairs (DCCA). 2022. The Federal Reserve System: 7–8. "Economic Well-Being of U.S. Households in 2021." Federal Reserve Board Publication. May, 2022.

29 Sherter, Alain. 2019. "Nearly 40% of Americans Can't Cover a Surprise $400 Expense." CBS News, Moneywatch. Consumer and Community Research Section of the Federal Reserve Board's Division of Consumer and Community Affairs (DCCA). 2022. The Federal Reserve System: 7–8. "Economic Well-Being of U.S. Households in 2021." Federal Reserve Board Publication—May 2022.

About the Authors

Jamie P. Hopkins

Jamie P. Hopkins, Esq., MBA, LLM, CFP®, CLU®, ChFC®, RICP®, is a planning advocate, professor, coach, and retirement planning nerd. Named one of the top 40 financial services professionals under 40 by *Investment News*, and one of the top 40 young attorneys by the American Bar Association, he brings a unique skillset to his passion for educating consumers and advisors on retirement planning best practices.

Currently, he serves as the managing partner of wealth solutions at Carson Group and is also the co-host of the Framework podcast.

Ron Carson

Ron Carson, CFP®, ChFC®, is founder and CEO of Inc. 5000 firm Carson Group, a Barron's Hall-of-Fame wealth advisor,* *Forbes* contributor, and *New York Times* bestselling author. Ron is regularly featured on national broadcast television to share how individuals can attain their version of true wealth and help others find their freedom.

Throughout 40 years as a financial advisor and entrepreneur, Ron has always believed in fulfilling a deep-seeded purpose to be the most trusted for financial advice—to provide families and individuals with straightforward guidance, extensive expertise, and full transparency when it comes to planning their financial future. From the humble beginnings of starting his business out of his college dorm room in the early 1980s, Ron has grown to become an industry innovator, an influencer, and visionary for one of the top wealth management firms in the country, also recognized as a Best Places to Work for Financial Advisors and a Best Places to Work in Fintech.

---

* Barron's Magazine Hall of Fame Inductee—Ron Carson, October 20, 2014 issue. Advisors inducted into the Hall of Fame include those who were recipients of the Barron's Top 100 Independent Advisors ranking since the list's inception. The Barrons rankings are based on data provided by over 4,000 of the nation's most productive advisors. Factors included in the rankings: assets under management, revenue produced for the firm, regulatory record, quality of practice and philanthropic work. Investment performance isn't an explicit component because not all advisors have audited results and because performance figures often are influenced more by clients' risk tolerance than by an advisor's investment-picking abilities. No fees are paid for participation. Listing in this publication is not a guarantee of future investment success. This recognition should not be construed as an endorsement of the advisor by any client.

Finding your freedom takes a TEAM.

Get matched with a financial advisor who ticks all the boxes.

☑ Fiduciary who's duty-bound to put your interests first

☑ Focused on planning, not products

☑ Sees the whole financial picture, beyond just investment management

☑ Is the right fit for your goals and situation

Visit our Advisor Match Questionnaire now to find the advisor that's right for you.

Visit CarsonAdvisorMatch.com to learn more.

CARSON WEALTH

CPSIA information can be obtained
at www.ICGtesting.com
Printed in the USA
JSHW042309061022
31128JS00014B/18